Children as Teachers
THEORY AND RESEARCH ON TUTORING

EDUCATIONAL PSYCHOLOGY

Allen J. Edwards, Series Editor
Department of Psychology
Southwest Missouri State University
Springfield, Missouri

Phillip S. Strain, Thomas P. Cooke, and Tony Apolloni. Teaching Exceptional Children: Assessing and Modifying Social Behavior

Donald E. P. Smith and others. A Technology of Reading and Writing (in four volumes).
> *Vol. 1. Learning to Read and Write: A Task Analysis (by Donald E. P. Smith)*

Joel R. Levin and Vernon L. Allen (eds.). Cognitive Learning in Children: Theories and Strategies

Vernon L. Allen (ed.). Children as Teachers: Theory and Research on Tutoring

In preparation:

Gilbert R. Austin. Early Childhood Education: An International Perspective

António Simões (ed.). The Bilingual Child: Research and Analysis of Existing Educational Themes

Erness Bright Brody and Nathan Brody. Intelligence: Nature, Determinants, and Consequences

Donald E. P. Smith and others. A Technology of Reading and Writing (in four volumes).
> *Vol. 2. Criterion-Referenced Tests for Reading and Writing (by Judith M. Smith, Donald E. P. Smith, and James R. Brink)*
> *Vol. 3. The Adaptive Classroom (by Donald E. P. Smith)*
> *Vol. 4. Preparing Instructional Tasks (by Judith M. Smith)*

Herbert J. Klausmeier, Richard A. Rossmiller, and Mary Saily (eds.). Individually Guided Elementary Education: Concepts and Practices

Samuel Ball (ed.). Motivation in Education

Children as Teachers
THEORY AND RESEARCH ON TUTORING

Edited by

Vernon L. Allen
Department of Psychology
University of Wisconsin
Madison, Wisconsin

ACADEMIC PRESS

NEW YORK   SAN FRANCISCO   LONDON   1976

A Subsidiary of Harcourt Brace Jovanovich, Publishers

ACADEMIC PRESS, INC.
111 Fifth Avenue, New York, New York 10003

United Kingdom Edition published by
ACADEMIC PRESS, INC. (LONDON) LTD.
24/28 Oval Road, London NW1

Library of Congress Cataloging in Publication Data

Main entry under title.

Children as teachers.

    (Educational psychology series)
    Includes bibliographies.
    1.   Peer group tutoring of students.   I.   Allen,
Vernon L., (date)
LC41.C46   371.39'4   76-2940
ISBN 0–12–052640–9

PRINTED IN THE UNITED STATES OF AMERICA

Contents

List of Contributors

Numbers in parentheses indicate the pages on which the authors' contributions begin.

Vernon L. Allen (9, 113, 235, 253), Department of Psychology, University of Wisconsin, Madison, Wisconsin

Michael Argyle (57), Department of Experimental Psychology, Oxford, England

Victor G. Cicirelli (99), Department of Psychology, Purdue University, Lafayette, Indiana

Robert D. Cloward (219), Department of Psychology, Rhode Island College, Providence, Rhode Island

Emory L. Cowen (131), Department of Psychology, University of Rochester, Rochester, New York

Linda Devin-Sheehan* (235, 253), Wisconsin Research and Development Center for Cognitive Learning, University of Wisconsin, Madison, Wisconsin

Robert S. Feldman† (113, 235), Department of Psychology, University of Wisconsin, Madison, Wisconsin

Norma Deitch Feshbach (81), Department of Education, University of California, Los Angeles, California

Stephen Hansell (199), Social Psychology Laboratory, The University of Chicago, Chicago, Illinois

*Present address: Suffolk County Youth Bureau, New York.
†Present address: Department of Psychology, Virginia Commonwealth University, Richmond, Virginia.

xi

Willard W. Hartup (41), Institute of Child Development, University of Minnesota, Minneapolis, Minnesota

Peggy Lippitt (157), Human Research Development Associates of Ann Arbor, Ann Arbor, Michigan

Ralph J. Melaragno (189), System Development Corporation, Pacoima, California

Fred C. Niedermeyer (179), Southwest Regional Laboratory, Educational Research and Development, Los Alamitos, California

Donald Ronchi (199), Center for Human Resource Research, College of Administrative Science, The Ohio State University, Columbus, Ohio

Theodore R. Sarbin (27), Adlai E. Stevenson College, University of California, Santa Cruz, California

Fred L. Strodtbeck (199), Social Psychology Laboratory, The University of Chicago, Chicago, Illinois

Grant Von Harrison (169), Department of Instructional Research, Development, and Evaluation, Brigham Young University, Provo, Utah

Preface

Though I realize that it may be an unusual occurrence in the world of publishing, the title of the present book—*Children as Teachers: Theory and Research on Tutoring*—does reflect quite accurately its contents. The use of children to tutor other children in school is the central theme of this volume; secondary themes of the book are helping relationships in general, and cross-age interaction by children. These closely interrelated topics have been the object of widespread interest expressed by social scientists, educators, and policy makers within the past several years.

This volume brings together original work of persons who are intimately knowledgeable about recent advances in theory, research, and applications in this field. The book is addressed primarily to professionals who have a scholarly interest in these areas, but at the same time the interests and problems of practitioners are not slighted. The problem areas examined in the book should be of particular interest to social scientists and educators.

Several important features of the present book are worth mentioning at this point. This book brings together for the first time a multidisciplinary group of scientists who focus their attention on the specific problem of tutoring by children in the schools and on the more general problem of cross-age interaction among children. The first two parts of the book establish the basic theoretical and empirical foundations for practical programs discussed in later chapters. A wide range of theoretical perspectives is offered in Part I. Following Allen's discussion of the relevant historical background, original theoretical contributions are proposed from the perspectives of role theory (Sarbin), ethological and cross-cultural research (Hartup), and social skills theory (Argyle).

Several chapters in Part II discuss original empirical research relevant to cross-age interaction and the impact of tutoring on both the tutor and the tutee. These chapters report interesting new scientific information on topics having obvious practical implications: social class and ethnic differences in tutoring by young children (Feshbach), teaching by siblings (Cicirelli), nonverbal skills and consequences of tutoring for the tutor (Allen and Feldman), and the use of a variety of nonprofessionals as helpers (Cowen).

A central feature of the present volume is the discussion of a wide range of tutoring programs that operate in the schools (Part III). The authors of these chapters (Lippitt, Harrison, Niedermeyer, and Melaragno), who have all been responsible for initiating a variety of cross-age tutoring programs in the schools, give us the benefit of their extensive observation, practical experience, and research. Evaluation of large tutoring programs in the schools is dealt with in the chapter by Strodtbeck, Ronchi, and Hansell, and that by Cloward.

Finally, two useful chapters in Part IV of the book summarize and integrate an extensive amount of previous work. One chapter critically reviews existing research on tutoring by children. In another chapter, research and experience are utilized in suggesting the advantages and disadvantages of several alternative decisions when establishing a tutoring program in the school.

Material in most of the chapters in this volume was presented earlier (in somewhat different form) at a research conference held at the Wisconsin Center for Research and Development in Cognitive Learning, University of Wisconsin, Madison. Appreciation is expressed to the National Institute of Education for providing funds, through the Wisconsin Research and Development Center, that made the conference possible. I am grateful to Professor Richard A. Rossmiller, director of the Center; Dr. William R. Bush, deputy director; and Professor Herbert J. Klausmeier, former director, for their constant support and encouragement throughout the stages of planning, organizing, and conducting the conference.

My research assistants during the time of the conference, Dr. Robert S. Feldman and Ms. Linda Devin-Sheehan, richly deserve my thanks for the indispensable and cheerful help that they gave on so many occasions. Thanks are also due to Dr. Patricia S. Allen for advice and suggestions during the preparation of this manuscript. Finally, my thanks to Derek and Craig Allen: By playing "school" so often with their friends they drew my attention vividly to questions concerned with teaching and helping by children.

Children as Teachers
THEORY AND RESEARCH ON TUTORING

I

Theoretical Considerations

The basic theme of the present book is captured aptly and succinctly in the title of an article by Jerome Bruner (1972): "The Uses of Immaturity." In that article Bruner discusses the enormous difficulties created for the young by the necessity of delaying their vocational identity; for a lengthy period of time it is possible to enact only one legitimate role, that of student. Not until fairly late in the life cycle can a young person make serious job decisions and start to clarify his identity as an adult.

As one means for dealing with the psychological problems associated with prolonged schooling in a technological society, Bruner proposes giving students more responsibility for the education of their fellow students. In his words, "I would strongly urge . . . that we use the system of student-assisted learning from the start in our schools" (Bruner, 1972, p. 63). In contrast to the traditional competitive structure in the school, Bruner urges that education should be a "communal undertaking." By giving older children some responsibility for helping others—especially younger children—the "intermediate generation" of youth could gain a sense of purpose and useful participation all too often lacking in their lives.

1

The tocsin sounded by Bruner was echoed in a recent important and provocative book (Coleman, 1974). In this book, which is the report of the Panel of Youth of the President's Science Advisory Committee, several social scientists take a critical look at the environments available for young persons while making the transition to adulthood. At present one of the most pervasive contexts in which youth are socialized into adulthood is, of course, the institution of the school.

In one section of the book, members of the Coleman panel attempt to formulate alternative environments for the socialization of youth. The panel asserts that two broad categories of objectives must be met if any environment is to qualify as being satisfactory for youth. The first objective is a self-centered one, consisting of the traditional goal of the schools: the acquisition of cognitive and noncognitive skills necessary for an individual to function adequately as a contributing member of society. The second class of objectives proposed by the authors is more unusual, and centers on others rather than self: that youth should have an opportunity for responsibilities that affect the lives of other persons. In the panel's words: "Only with the experience of such responsibilities can youth move toward the mutually responsible and mutually rewarding involvement with others that constitute social maturity" (Coleman, 1974, p. 3).

To help reach the second objective (social maturity) the panel offered several recommendations, one of which was establishing programs of part-time teaching for older children in the schools. Having the responsibility for teaching younger children—or for caring for younger persons, the elderly, the sick, or persons otherwise dependent—ensures that a youngster will engage in behavior that is important because of its consequences for other people. Through such experiences a child learns the kind of behavior required of a socially responsible adult; unfortunately, the opportunity for such relationships traditionally has not been recognized as an important component of the school curriculum.

Immaturity does, then, have its uses, to return to Bruner's words. Furthermore, by helping other persons a child is being helped himself as well—whether or not he realizes it. The social analysis and related proposals in the Bruner (1972) article and the Coleman (1974) report are finding concrete expression in some schools. The spirit of these recommendations is reflected in the many tutoring programs in which older students help younger children. A large number of tutorial programs using children to teach other children are currently in operation throughout the United States, and are beginning to appear in Britain (Goodlad, 1975). A recent report has stressed that peer tutoring techniques are especially appropriate and useful for the understaffed schools in developing countries (Klaus, 1973).

Preliminary results reported from tutoring programs have indicated strongly that when a child helps teach (tutor) another child in school, both the older and the younger child may profit in terms of better academic achievement and improved personal–social behavior (Gartner, Kohler, & Riessman, 1971). Unfortunately, children do not have many opportunities either in or out of school to interact in a responsible and helpful way with children older or younger than themselves; a tutoring program does provide a structured setting for cross-age interaction.

The present book constitutes a forum for the exploration of structured helping relationships among children in school (i.e., tutoring). The research and theory discussed by the authors will deal with both the cognitive and social consequences of tutoring for the helper and for the child receiving help. In a more general sense, then, it is clear that the broader theme of this book is cross-age interaction and its consequences for children.

The book contains chapters on recent theory, empirical research, and practical work being conducted by experts in this problem area. Since tutoring and interaction among children of different ages can be analyzed from several different points of view, a multidisciplinary effort is essential. The diverse issues related to teaching by children are examined by authors who represent several different disciplinary perspectives. The instructional material used in tutoring sessions in school is the domain of educators and curriculum specialists; the optimal conditions for learning in children and the assessment of effectiveness are types of problems dealt with by educational psychologists; the potential impact of tutoring on socialization of children would interest developmental psychologists; social psychologists are concerned with social interaction and with the psychological processes that mediate the effects of tutoring; sociologists might pose questions about the impact of this innovation on the social structure of the school and the relationship of the school to the community. Thus, the problem of children teaching children in the school represents a nexus in which several areas of social science meet, each discipline asking different kinds of questions and bringing different perspectives to the analysis of a single phenomenon.

A brief overview of the structure and organization of the present book may be helpful. Included are four major sections: Theoretical Considerations, Helping Relationships With Children, Tutoring Programs in Schools, and Problems and Possibilities. The presentation of broad theoretical and historical perspectives in the first major section establishes a foundation for later chapters in which research and applied programs are described. Theoretical concepts introduced in these four chapters will often find application in research and applied programs discussed in later sections.

The second major section of the book (Helping Relationships With Children) consists of chapters that report research on the tutoring relationship, and discusses helping in a more general sense. Most of the studies were designed as short-term experiments to test specific hypotheses. Complete tutoring programs in the schools are not the primary concern of this research, but in the last chapter in this section, longer-term field studies using children and other nonprofessionals as helpers are summarized.

Specific tutoring programs in the schools—including their development, management, and evaluation—constitute the topic of the third major section of the book. The tutoring programs described in this section range from highly structured to unstructured, and a wide array of variations on the basic program designs are described. The central purpose of chapters in this section is to describe viable tutoring programs that are now operating in the schools. Evaluation of the programs is touched upon in passing in all chapters, but the last two chapters in this section concentrate on the analysis of data collected in connection with research evaluating nationally prominent tutoring programs.

The fourth major section (Problems and Possibilities) is an attempt to add breadth and balance to the book by covering issues not receiving sufficient attention in earlier chapters. It contains two chapters. In one chapter the existing empirical literature on tutoring is critically reviewed. The advantages and disadvantages of available alternatives when implementing tutoring programs and the problems of conducting field research are discussed in the second chapter.

Now we turn to the first major section of the book, which presents several theoretical approaches that are relevant to tutoring and interaction between same-age and different-age children. It is hoped that a discussion of theoretical issues will help clarify empirical studies and tutoring programs reported throughout the remainder of the book. The application of a broad conceptual context to a specific behavioral result can enhance greatly our understanding. In the following introductory comments, the content of the four chapters appearing in the first section will be described briefly.

The first chapter by Allen attempts to place tutoring by children in a broader historical and psychological context. Segregating children in school into different classrooms according to their age is so commonplace that it may seem only natural; nevertheless, such an arrangement is actually a development of recent history. According to one historical study, the easy mixing of children across a wide range of ages was characteristic of life in school and out until the late Middle Ages. The gradual increase in homogeneous-age classrooms probably contributed to the decreasing amount of social contact between older and younger children.

To provide a better understanding of the historical origins of teaching by children, Allen reviews the Bell–Lancaster instructional system. In the early nineteenth century, schools in which children functioned as teachers for other children became very popular in Britain, and the idea even spread to other countries. Thus, tutoring by children is certainly not a recent discovery. Children also were used to teach younger students in the old one-teacher schools, where tutoring by older students was more a matter of necessity than of educational philosophy.

In his chapter Allen maintains that tutoring can make important contributions to the socialization of children. In particular, when an older child tutors a younger child both of them may benefit in a number of respects. Tutoring offers a way for older and younger children to engage in constructive social interaction; useful psychological consequences can result from such cross-age relationships. Hence, tutoring can play an important role in the socialization process, in addition to any academic or cognitive benefits that may be realized.

The second chapter in this section offers a theoretical analysis of the tutoring relationship from the role theory point of view. Sarbin poses the following question: Why does the tutee acquire skills as a result of being tutored by another child when he fails to learn from a professional teacher? To answer this question Sarbin utilizes a three-dimensional model of social identity based on role theory constructs. A crucial distinction is drawn between ascribed (granted) and achieved (attained) statuses or positions. According to the social identity model, qualitatively different reactions derive from the proper role performance of ascribed roles (e.g., mother) and achieved roles (e.g., teacher). Positive reinforcement or esteem (e.g., gold stars) is given for the proper performance of achieved roles, whereas affective responses or respect (e.g., a hug) is given for proper performance of an ascribed role. Ascribed and achieved roles also differ in that ascribed roles are more involving.

Applying the social identity model to tutoring, Sarbin posits that children are likely to construe the tutoring situation as an ascribed role relationship. The tutor and tutee will be concerned primarily with affect or friendship in an ascribed role relationship. (Importance of the affective relationship between tutor and tutee is also stressed by Lippitt in Chapter 9.) The teacher role is primarily an achieved position, but the child views the teacher–student roles as being an ascribed relationship. Role confusion results from the conflict between the child's expectation of affective evaluation from the teacher and the teacher's actual behavior. Though initially patterned after the achieved roles of classroom teacher and pupil, the tutor–tutee relationship gradually becomes transformed into an ascribed and highly involving role relationship.

Sarbin's analysis has several very interesting and testable implications. For example, prediction of individual differences in outcomes of tutoring might be improved by measuring the tutor–tutee dyad as a unit. The analysis also has obvious implications for the training of tutors and teachers, and the hypothesis that a confusion of role expectations exists between the classroom teacher and the young child is easily amenable to empirical test.

The chapter by Hartup discusses the issue of cross-age versus same-age peer interaction from ethological and cross-cultural perspectives. Most research on children's social behavior has been conducted with same-age peer groups, therefore controlled empirical data are not available for making any definitive conclusion about the consequences of cross-age versus same-age interaction in human children. To examine this problem from a very broad point of view, Hartup reviews relevant socialization literature from four nonhuman primate species and from cross-cultural studies with humans.

Most of the heterogeneous-age contacts in primates seem to occur in species living in very small groups; homogeneous-age play groups are more characteristic of large primate societies. In the case of human children, cross-age contacts are observed in most societies, but are more prevalent in primitive cultures. Several studies have found high positive correlations between age similarity and friendship among children in industrialized societies.

From surveying the ethological and cross-cultural literature, Hartup draws an interesting conclusion about the adaptive significance of same-age versus cross-age relationships in the young. He suggests that same-age peer interaction seems to be more satisfying in large social groups and in complex societies. Mixed-age groups are therefore older, in the evolutionary sense, than same-age groups. As an explanation of the young's apparent preference for same-age peer groups in complex societies, Hartup suggests that same-age interaction offers the optimal ratio of positive to negative reinforcement for participants. If a child is socially immature as a result of poor socialization, however, then interaction with a younger child would afford optimal positive reinforcement. Thus, young children can help socialize older children. According to this theoretical analysis, the preeminence of same-age groupings is not due to age segregation in the classroom or to social-structural factors, but to the pattern of reinforcement.

Hartup's analysis cautions us about being too eager to implement cross-age programs, since the arrangement may conflict with children's natural same-age preferences. Nevertheless, many reasons for using different-age dyads in tutoring remain valid regardless of children's natural preferences (e.g., older children have more knowledge about the subject matter). A great deal of research must be conducted to determine the consequences of same-age versus different-age interaction. We do not know yet the answers to questions about children's preferred extent and type of social interaction with same-age versus different-age peers. By examining socialization in same-age versus different-age groups from the broad perspective of social evolution, Hartup has raised important questions that are directly relevant to the organization of tutorial programs in schools.

Social skills theory is described by Argyle in the last chapter in this section. Teaching is, of course, a social activity, and social skills take on even greater importance in two person, face-to-face teaching situations. The skills that comprise social competence include both verbal and nonverbal components. Nonverbal cues can effectively convey attitudes and emotions, and can influence ongoing verbal communication. Verbal and nonverbal cues emanating from another person must be monitored constantly in order to assess relevant information regarding an interaction.

Various verbal and nonverbal elements that contribute to social competence are interrelated in an exceedingly complex way. Nevertheless, it is possible to relate various aspects of social behavior to corresponding elements of the social skills model proposed by Argyle. The model suggests ways of determining the social skills necessary for certain kinds of social tasks—for example, interviewing, teaching, or helping others. The social skills model is also useful for analyzing failures in social behavior. It is possible to acquire or to improve needed social skills by a training regimen that includes role playing techniques and methods for increasing sensitivity to social cues.

Like any teaching endeavor, tutoring is a complex social process. The social skills model provides a valuable conceptual system for interpreting social interaction processes occurring in tutoring. The important role of nonverbal cues in tutoring is stressed in several later chapters (e.g., the chapters by Allen and Feldman, Circirelli, and Feshbach). Viewing tutoring as a task that requires a variety of verbal and nonverbal social skills will serve as a vivid reminder that children teaching children is a very complex social phenomenon.

REFERENCES

Bruner, J. Immaturity—its uses, nature and management. *The Times Educational Supplement.* London, October 27, 1972. Pp. 62–63.

Coleman, J. S. *Youth: Transition to adulthood.* Chicago: Univ. of Chicago Press, 1974.

Gartner, A., Kohler, M., & Riessman, F. *Children teach children: Learning by teaching.* New York: Harper, 1971.

Goodlad, J. S. R. (Ed.) *Education and social action: Community service and the curriculum in higher education.* London: Allen & Unwin, 1975.

Klaus, D. J. *Students as teaching resources.* Pittsburgh, Pennsylvania: American Institutes for Research, 1973. (Project no. 931-17-690-570)

1

The Helping Relationship and Socialization of Children: Some Perspectives on Tutoring

Vernon L. Allen
University of Wisconsin

By these means a few good boys, selected for the purpose, as teachers of the respective classes, form the whole school, teach their pupils to think rightly, and mixing in all the little amusements and diversions, secure them against the contagion of ill example, or the force of ill habits; and, by seeing that they treat one another kindly, render their condition contented and happy [Andrew Bell, 1797].

My school is attended by three hundred scholars. The *whole* system of tuition is almost entirely conducted by boys. . . . This system of tuition is mutually for the advantage of the lads who teach, and those who are taught; by it the path of learning is strewed with flowers. . . . [Joseph Lancaster, 1803].

"Qui docet discit." (He who teaches, learns) (An ancient dictum.)

As the quotations from Bell (1797) and Lancaster (1803) make clear, the use of children to teach other children in the schools is not by any means a recent innovation; the idea has had a long and lively past. The technique attained wide popularity, particularly in British schools, in the early nineteenth century. Nevertheless, the present revival of interest in tutoring by children should not be dismissed hastily as merely being old wine in new bottles. Happily, it is not uncommon to discover that, when examined in the light of contemporary knowledge, old ideas indeed contain a kernel of truth.

The remarkable appeal of the technique of children teaching other children is due to very promising reports about academic and social effects of tutoring programs (Gartner, Kohler, & Reissman, 1971). Results suggest that both the tutor and tutee not only gain in academic achievement, but sometimes improve in social behavior, attitudes, and self-esteem as well. Since classrooms are usually segregated into homogeneous groups on the basis of age, one special advantage of tutoring is that it provides a context in which children of different ages can interact in socially constructive ways. More generally, it seems that the amount of isolation and segregation on the basis of age roles is probably increasing. As Bronfenbrenner (1970) has said, "we are coming to live in a society that is segregated not only by race and class, but also by age" (p. 100). For a broader view of the basic theme that will be discussed throughout this book—social interaction and helping by children of different ages—historical and psychological contexts are provided in the present chapter.

HISTORICAL BACKGROUND

To gain a better understanding of the antecedents of present day age stratification in the schools and in society at large, it may be illuminating to take a brief excursion through social history. Three areas are worthy of our attention: first, the historical background of age gradation in the schools (the practice of assigning same-age students together in a class or grade); second, the nature of tutorial programs that existed in the British schools in the early nineteenth century; and, third, the one-room, one-teacher school of the recent past. To discuss the age gradation issue first, questions such as the following can be raised: What are the origins of the present day practice of segregating children in the schools on the basis of their biological age? How does our conception of the period of childhood differ from that of earlier historical periods? How does the conception of childhood affect the interaction between children and adults, and between younger and older children?

Origins of Age Differentiation

Light is thrown on these questions by a fascinating historical study by the French social philosopher, Philippe Ariès (1962). Ariès documents his contention that the idea of childhood as a separate category of life did not exist prior to the sixteenth or seventeenth century. In medieval society there was no conception of childhood as we know it today; after infancy the child was dressed like a miniature adult, and, indeed, was treated like an adult in most respects. As soon as the child could live without the constant care of his mother, he became a member of adult society, going directly into the great world of work and behaving as an adult. The modern conception of childhood as a special stage of life characterized by innocence and devoted to preparing for later adult life was foreign to the Middle Ages.

In Europe prior to the seventeenth century childhood was not a period of quarantine during which the child was sheltered and kept apart from the adult world. In work and in play children mixed freely with older companions and with adults. Once past the age of five to seven years, the child was absorbed into the world of adults, participating as an equal in all aspects of adult life, even, as Ariès notes, "in taverns of ill repute." Acquisition of work skills was transmitted from generation to generation by the apprenticeship system, so the art of work and the art of living were both acquired through direct contact with older children and adults.

Ariès contends that until modern times, that is, about the seventeenth century, there was extensive free and easy mingling among persons of all ages. The portrayal of the life of children in the late Middle Ages and up to the modern era represents a dramatic and remarkable contrast to the relative lack of contact across ages nowadays. How can such an evolution in social behavior be explained?

One of the basic sources of the origin of age differentiation stems from the institution of the school, according to Ariès. The school of the Middle Ages presents a sharp contrast to our current conception. A crucial difference was the absence of the concept of gradation of difficulty in material with a corresponding lack of differentiation among students according to their chronological age or intellectual development. Students simply memorized material from their textbooks; there was no distinction made between levels of difficulty in the subjects being studied. Thus, the school curriculum was not separated into different levels ranging from easiest to most difficult. Another difference was that all students were taught simultaneously, the older students being distinguished from younger ones only by virtue of having repeated the same material a greater number of times. Therefore, students of all ages—mostly boys and men of from 10 to 20 years of age—were mixed together in the same classroom. Robert of Salisbury describes a school he visited in the twelfth century as follows: "I saw the students in the schools. Their numbers were great. I saw there men of diverse ages: pueros, adolescentes, juvenes, senos." (That is, all ages of life were represented.) The mixing of diverse ages in the classroom apparently continued in out-of-school hours as well.

Toward the end of the Middle Ages changes began to appear that contributed strongly toward the eventual sharp differentiation among ages that is so characteristic of current society. It appears that some teachers began the practice of grouping together in one area of the large schoolroom those students studying the same lessons. This seems to have been the beginning of changes that eventually developed into the principle of separation of students by classes or grades on the basis of age. With the significant increase in the school population in the fifteenth century, the usefulness for disciplinary purposes of small classes—as compared to the normal 100 or 200 students—became readily apparent. The next natural step was the isolation of each small class in a separate room. Thus, by the seventeenth century, the classroom or grade as we know it was well established.

Although there were separate physical premises for each class, children still were not allocated to a classroom on the basis of their age. Only gradually did age come to be recognized as an important criterion for a child's membership in a classroom. Data presented by Ariès (1962) reveal the age composition of classrooms of two French schools, one in the early seventeenth century and a comparable school in the early nineteenth century. For illustrative purposes, I have calculated the data from these two schools in terms of the percentage of students of a particular age in each class. As shown in Figure 1, in the seventeenth century school there was a wide range of ages represented in each class or grade. For instance, in the third class there were children from 9 to 24 years of age; the age distribution for this class is almost rectangular. By contrast, as can be seen in Figure 1, data from the early nineteenth century shows a narrow range of ages at each class (and also a greater number of classes); the close correspondence between school class and age of students in this school begins to approximate the present day pattern of age homogeneity.

In summary, the analysis by Ariès (1962) suggests that the school contributed significantly to age consciousness and age segregation by evolving the system of school classes formed on the basis of age of students. Coinciding with this organizational development in the schools was the concomitant evolution of the conception of the nature of childhood. The modern characterization of childhood as a special stage of life, a period of innocence and a time for preparation for the later serious business of life was a conception of childhood that evolved slowly from the time of the Middle Ages. We see, then, that a sharp differentiation across age groups did not always exist in Western society; its historical roots can be located in the not-so-distant past.

The Bell–Lancaster System

Having taken one brief glance into social history, another relevant thread from the past—children helping children in the schools—should be picked up and woven into the texture of our discussion. In the early nineteenth century a system based upon the use of children as teachers of other children was the object of widespread public attention and acclaim and was adopted in many schools. A brief description of this movement—for movement it became, in the intensity of belief of its adherents—perhaps will place in perspective similar systems currently being introduced in many schools.

The Bell–Lancaster system (as it may be called) had a strong impact on education in Britain in the early nineteenth century. A Scotsman, Andrew Bell, became superintendent of a school ("asylum") in Madras, India, established for orphans, most of whom were sons of British soldiers and Indian mothers. Bell experienced a great deal of frustration in his efforts to teach these students; they showed a surprising resemblance to teachers' stereotypes of modern students, being, "in general, stubborn, perverse, and obstinate" (Bell, 1797, p. 19). Bell, who was not a professional educator, finally devised a system which had as its basic and most novel component the use of older children to teach other children. Not only did this system appear to be successful as a means of providing elementary instruction, but it also brought about a marked improvement in behavior of the students. Using this system transformed the school; in Bell's words: "The school is thus rendered a scene of amusement to the scholars, and a spectacle of delight to the beholder....For months together it has not been found necessary to inflict a single punishment" (p. 32).

Bell's description of his system is none too clear, but its basic feature seems to have been some one-to-one tutoring by the boys and, in addition, the teaching of the entire classes by one older boy with the aid of younger boys as assistants. The extent of involvement of the students in the teaching process is indicated by Bell's report that in 1791 a boy of 11 years of age was in charge of his school of 300 students. The children seemed to be quite successful in their teaching efforts, as exemplified by this passage from Bell's 1797 report of his Madras school: "Friskin, of twelve years and eight months, with his assistants of seven, eight, nine and eleven years of age, has taught boys of four, five and six years, to read *The Spectator* distinctly, and spell every word accurately as they go along, who were only initiated into the mysteries of their A, B, C, eight months before" (p. 21). After having learned to read *The Spectator*, there would seem to be few worlds left for these students to conquer!

Published in 1797, the report of Bell's system as practiced at the Madras school was enthusiastically accepted by a professional educator in England, Joseph Lancaster. Embellishing Bell's basic idea of using children as teachers, and adding new elements of his own, Lancaster (1803) vigorously publicized the system. In England and Wales alone around 100,000 children were being taught by the Bell–Lancaster system in 1816, according to Bell (1817). As his biographer puts it, the essence of Bell's "discovery" was not his "system," but taking into the classroom "... an old, old truth which we are all of us a little apt to forget. LEARNING IS A SOCIAL ACT: it is best carried on under social conditions" (Meiklejohn, 1882, p. 177, capitals in original).

Lancaster was perhaps the most avid public advocate of the "monitorial" system. He asserted that by using this system up to 1000 students could be taught by only one adult teacher. Such a remarkable feat required the maintenance of strict order and discipline, and entailed a table of organization that might be envied by many an army battalion. All the students were seated in neat

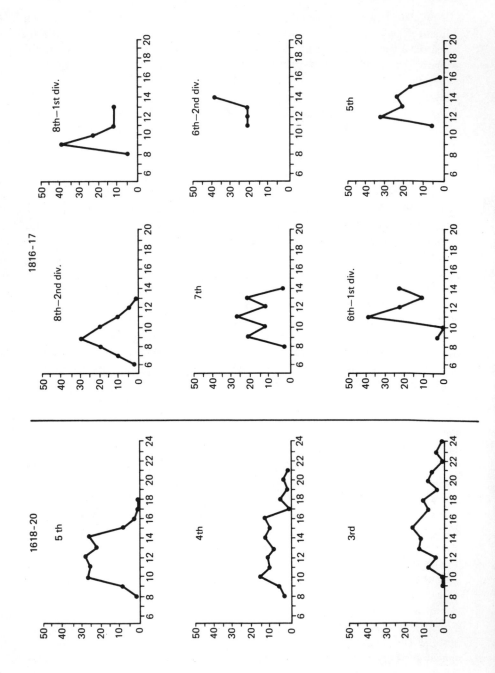

14

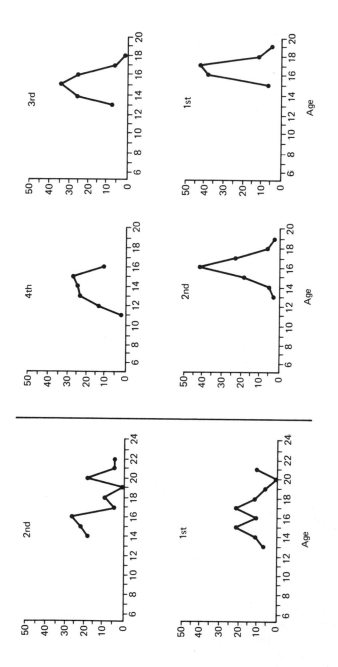

Figure 1 Age of children (%) in two schools in France in the seventeenth century (Jesuit college of Châlons, 1618–20) and in the nineteenth century (Sainte-Barbe, 1816–17). (The "first" class is the most advanced.) [Adapted from data provided by Ariès (1962).]

and symmetrical rows in a large classroom. Teaching was conducted mechanically and with great precision. First, the teacher drilled older children in the lesson; then these older children taught groups of younger children, who in turn might drill still other children younger than themselves. By this ripple or multiplicative effect the effort of a single "master" (teacher) could be increased manyfold.

Proponents of the system of using children as teachers were well aware that it had social as well as cognitive benefits for both the learner and the teacher. Both Bell and Lancaster commented explicitly on the improvement in behavior in school due to younger children's emulating the positive behaviors of older children who were placed in positions of trust and responsibility as teachers. A not insignificant social psychological feature of this system is that the individualized instruction afforded close surveillance of each child's behavior, a point mentioned by Lancaster (1803) and de Laborde (1815) as being important in reducing disciplinary problems.

The fame of the student-teaching-student system for inexpensively educating poor children spread beyond the borders of Britain and attracted attention in other countries. A Frenchman visiting England in the early nineteenth century wrote a book recording his impressions of the Bell–Lancaster schools and advocated establishing a similar system in France (de Laborde, 1815). As he noted, mothers who have children of different ages realize that they like to teach and help each other: "Toutes les mères de famille qui ont des enfans de differens ages, ont observé combien ils aiment á se reprendre l'un l'autre, à se corriger, et combien les grands jouissent avec une sorte de protection et de bonté des maladresses des petits" (p. 51). Expressing his amazement that such an obvious phenomenon has not been utilized in public education, de Laborde declared: "Il est extraordinaire qu'un spectacle que tout le monde a toujours sous les yeux, n'ait pas donné plus tot l'idée de l'appliquer à l'éducation publique" (p. 30).

Popularity of the Bell–Lancaster system gradually waned over the years, apparently for several reasons. It appears that the basic weakness of such schools was the generally low standard of teaching by the untrained children who were often only 8 or 9 years old (Dures, 1971). In addition, in the early nineteenth century facilities were not adequate for training professional teachers to use these techniques effectively. Interest in the Bell–Lancaster system also diminished as the state began to provide money for public education; the low cost of the tutorial schools as a means of educating the poor was a point frequently emphasized by its proponents. (Notice the title of Lancaster's 1803 pamphlet: *Improvements in Education as it respects the Industrious Classes of the Community, Containing, Among Other Important Particulars, an Account of the Institution for the Education of one Thousand Poor Children.*) Finally, it seems reasonable that the growth of professionalism among teachers also contributed to the decline of the tutorial schools. A self-conscious teaching profession is likely to look with disdain and derision upon the idea that untrained young children can perform the skilled functions of a teacher.

The Bell–Lancaster movement did, however, provide an important counter-force, for a time, to the prevailing movement in the schools toward ever greater differentiation and separation of students on the basis of age alone. Without a doubt the use of older students to teach younger children in school resulted in a great deal more interaction between children of different ages than would have occurred otherwise.

The One-Room School

If one were to search for a setting that offers maximal possibilities for interaction among children of diverse ages within a setting conducive to positive behavior, the one-room school of the recent past would seem to provide an ideal paradigm. Once very common, the one-teacher village school is now found only in sparsely populated rural areas. In these schools several children of a wide range of ages received instruction within the boundaries of a single room.

Being in the same room with several older and younger students enabled the child to overhear lessons the teacher gave to those more advanced and less advanced than himself. In addition to the advantages of review and preview of material made possible by this arrangement, there were other advantages as well. For example, the older children often would be assigned to help the younger students with their lessons. The burden of being the sole teacher for several levels of students often made it necessary for the teacher to turn to the older children for assistance in instructing the younger students. On the playground the lack of a large number of children of the same age forced children of all ages to play together to a greater extent than in a traditional school.

In order to explore students' behavior and attitudes in the one-room school setting, we administered questionnaires to teachers and students in 110 one-teacher schools still functioning in the state of Nebraska (Allen & Devin-Sheehan, 1974). Responses were obtained from 1405 students and 110 teachers. The focus of the study was primarily on the extent and nature of cross-age contacts in these schools. Data were obtained on the use of children as tutors and helpers for other children, interaction across ages in academic and social settings, and teachers' views of the academic and social advantages and disadvantages of one-teacher schools as compared to graded schools. In addition, the study also assessed the children's attitudes about school, themselves, and older and younger children.

According to teachers' reports, some form of tutoring took place on a fairly regular basis in 31% of the schools, and in another 25% there was some kind of informal tutoring program. Moreover, 77% of the students stated that they sometimes asked other students for help with schoolwork when they were at their desks, and 88% reported working together with other students. In these schools it is clear that other students are important learning resources for a child. Students from all grades were used as tutors. Teachers reported that in the lower grades (one through three) boys and girls were tutors equally often; but in the upper grades (four through eight) girls were much more likely than boys to be tutors. This seems to be at least partially due to the teachers' preferences, for in 82% of the schools having a formal program, the tutors were selected by the teacher.

Most of the formal tutoring was on a one-to-one basis, with some being on a one-to-two or one-to-three basis. Tutors had more than one tutee in 79% of the cases, and usually worked with their students each day or two to three times a week. There was an equal number of same-sex and opposite-sex tutoring pairs. Various age differences existed between tutor and tutee, ranging from same-age to as much as 5 years difference. The most frequent age difference between tutor and tutee was 2 years, followed by 3 and 4 years' difference. The students who were tutored felt positive about the experience, with the younger students expressing more enthusiasm than the older. Student responses to questions about school were also generally favorable; for example, 59–64% of the students in each grade stated that they would not want to be in a school where all the children in the room were the same age as the respondent.

One item in the student questionnaire stated: "When you are working at your seat and you can hear the teacher giving a lesson to *older* students, do you ever listen? How many new things do you learn when you listen?" Interestingly, a large proportion of the students (more than 90%) indicated that they did listen to older students' lessons, and felt that doing so was useful to them. Similar data were found for students' responses to a related question ("When you are working at your seat and you hear the teacher giving a lesson to *younger* students, do you ever listen? Does this help you with things you've already learned?"). Again, it is noteworthy that most students said they listened to and benefited from other (younger) students' lessons. Older students listened less than younger ones, as would be expected, but even among the oldest students (eighth graders) 80% of the boys and 92% of the girls reported that they listened to the lessons and were helped by doing so.

A large amount of social interaction occurred across different age levels in these one-room schools. In response to a question asking how much time was spent talking with various age groups, students reported that they talked about the same amount with other students who were older, younger, and the same age as themselves. Consistent with these data, 76% of the students stated that it was easy to be friends with children of all different ages. According to information obtained from both teachers and students, it is clear that the older children felt a strong sense of responsibility for the younger children. When the older students (grades four through eight) were asked if they felt they should help take care of the younger children at school, 94% of the girls and 87% of the boys replied affirmatively.

Some information was obtained concerning role models. Among the older students 45% of the boys and 37% of the girls reported that younger children tried to act like them; one-third of the older students thought that the younger children did not use them as role models. Furthermore, 23% of the older students indicated that they themselves tried to act like students older than they, as compared with 39% of the younger boys and 31% of the younger girls.

Teachers were asked to list the academic and social advantages and disadvantages of one-teacher schools. In order of descending frequency, the 103 teachers who responded mentioned the following as being academic advantages: A teacher can give more individualized attention (54); children learn from each other (37); younger children learn from older ones (36); students can progress at their own rate (34); and older children get review from younger children's lessons (27). As academic disadvantages teachers listed most frequently: not enough materials (30); not enough time for teacher to get around to everyone in every subject (17); and lack of competition from students' own age group (10). As for advantages for social and character development of students, the following were listed most often: Students learn to work and play with children of all ages (78); older children learn to take responsibility for and to understand younger ones (51); and a feeling of family-like closeness and togetherness (19). The two most frequent social disadvantages mentioned were: social shyness of students (9); and inadequate environment for seventh and eighth graders (9). The open-ended responses given by teachers revealed strong enthusiasm about their schools; they believed that the advantages greatly outweighed the disadvantages.

The limiting case of the one-room school closely approximates a large family. In fact, one teacher reported that a student had recently stated to her: "We are just like a big family and you are the mommy." (The teacher asked us, "Is this an advantage?") In a large family, as in a one-teacher school, adults cannot give a great deal of individual attention to each child; as a consequence, the children are forced to help each other. In particular, the older children substitute to some extent for parents by providing help, nurturance, and individual attention for younger children that the parents do not have the time to offer. In large families, where a wide age range is likely between the older and the younger children, the family setting affords an opportunity for extensive contact among children of quite different ages.

An interesting study of the large family was undertaken by Bossard and Boll (1956). Case history data were collected from adults who had grown up in a family of at least six children. Results of Bossard and Boll's study revealed several findings relevant to the interaction of children of different ages. A strong positive affective relationship among children in these large families—and in

particular between the oldest and youngest siblings separated by an age difference of several years—was manifested in numerous areas. Older siblings frequently gave advice and assisted the younger children in many ways, such as
helping with schoolwork. Moreover, in 91 of the 100 families, older siblings were
mentioned as being involved in attending to the children, usually in connection
with discipline. It is interesting to note that the younger children who were
disciplined by their older siblings accepted it, in general, with good grace.
Bossard and Boll (1956) remarked, that "siblings feel that they understand each
other and each other's problems, and that often they do so better than the
parents" (p. 184).

What was the impact on the older child of his performing almost as a parental
surrogate to the younger children? In analyzing their case history material
Bossard and Boll detected two themes: quicker maturity and greater responsibility on the part of the older child. Under conditions of severe economic
pressure or in the extreme event of death of a parent, the oldest children often
assumed very great responsibility for the other children. Several instances were
reported in which the eldest child sacrificed his own early adult life to care for
his younger brothers and sisters.

AGE STRATIFICATION, SOCIALIZATION, AND TUTORING

According to sociologists and anthropologists, social stratification based on age
is a characteristic of most societies (Radcliffe-Brown, 1929). It is all too easy to
fail to recognize in our own society the importance of the diffuse roles that are
associated with age. Though perhaps less so than in certain primitive societies,
nevertheless we do clearly allocate differential expectations concerning behavior
and character on the basis of a person's age. One has only to think of such terms
as "childish," "juvenile," "youth culture," "senior citizen," "adolescence," and
"the generation gap," to be aware of the potency of age in determining
expectations about behavior in our own society.

It appears evident that in present day social life, values and norms are
associated increasingly with membership in a broad age category; "youth culture" and the "adolescent subculture" even transcend national boundaries.
Common interests, values, and shared experiences bind together persons in one
stage of life to a greater extent than in the past, with resultant ingroup solidarity
often accompanied by hostility toward outgroups. Furthermore, little contact
occurs between persons fairly close in age, such as younger and older children.
The consequences of age differentiation at periods of life other than childhood is
even evident in geography. Apartments for a particular age group (e.g., singles)
and cities for certain age groups (e.g., retired people) are institutional manifesta-

tions of the psychological fact of the increasing segregation between persons of different ages.

Data have been collected recently by psychologists interested in comparing the extent of children's interaction with same-age peers relative to different-age peers and adults. Children spend by far the greater proportion of their time with same-age peers—not only during school but in out-of-school situations too. One study disclosed that sixth-grade children spent twice as much time with other children of the same age as they spent with their own parents (Condry, Siman, & Bronfenbrenner, 1968). The time that in former days would have been spent with parents or other adults is now spent with same-age peers or with that surrogate peer, the television set.

Socialization in childhood clearly is affected strongly by the extensive time spent with peers; in addition, children older and younger than oneself are important sources of socialization. Overall, the peer group and the school probably are exceeded only by parents as important agents of socialization. Since much of a child's time is spent in school, the nature of social interaction occurring there can play a major role in determining the direction of growth of social behavior and development of personality during childhood. It is from this perspective that the tutoring situation can be seen to offer an excellent mechanism for facilitating positive experiences conducive to personal and social growth, particularly when it involves an older child helping a younger child. The relationship between a tutor and tutee is, of course, a reciprocal influence process, so the role of the tutoring relationship in socialization should be examined for both the tutor and the tutee.

The Tutor

Abundant anecdotal evidence suggests that the tutor may profit in a variety of ways relevant to socialization; thus, academic motivation, sense of responsibility, and attitude toward school all appear to improve. Some objective data lend support to these subjective reports (Cloward, 1967; Gartner *et al.,* 1971). Accepting such claims for the moment, how can one explain these apparently beneficial effects of tutoring on the tutor?

First, it is clear that there are many very attractive elements that constitute the teacher role: responsibility, status in the eyes of other students, attention and reward from adults, and respect from younger children. Role enactment may increase self-esteem and produce positive attitudes towards school and teachers due to identification with the teacher role. It is almost as if when the child is placed in the tutor role he discovers that he must live up to its expectations.

Being a tutor should in addition enhance the child's role-taking skills—the ability to understand better another person's point of view by cognitively placing himself in the other's position. One study found that older children used simpler and shorter utterances when speaking with younger listeners, and made special efforts to maintain their interest and attention (Shatz & Gelman, 1973). Improvement in taking the role of the other should generalize to the classroom and to social interaction with other persons outside the teaching setting.

The social relationship between the tutor and the tutee is another source of potential benefit for the tutor. When tutoring a younger child, the older child can learn to be nurturant and to take responsibility for another person, which may foster more socially mature behavior in general. Being emulated and respected by a younger child enhances the tutor's self-esteem, and at the same time promotes positive social behavior. Thus, an older child should be less likely to engage in undesirable and antisocial behavior if he realizes that a young naive child may imitate his actions; being a role model for a younger child constrains one's behavior along socially desirable directions.

In more general terms, the most central and pervasive characteristic of the role of teacher is helping another person. It is interesting to note that the helping relationship often seems to be as beneficial to the helper as to the help-recipient. Across diverse areas of behavior, it has been observed repeatedly that an individual who helps others experiences positive dividends of a psychological nature himself. Evidence from several areas in addition to tutoring supports this conclusion. For instance, research has shown that young persons engaged in various types of volunteer service (e.g., community service or overseas service such as the Peace Corps) derive personal benefits from the experience of helping others (Gillette, 1968). In the mental health field, several programs have employed college students to visit and socialize with patients in mental hospitals. Research shows that the students are affected by the experience of being useful to the patients. One such program had an important psychological impact on the students: Results showed more self-acceptance and tolerance of others, and greater self-awareness and self-examination (Holzberg, Knapp, & Turner, 1966). Clarification of self-identity and feelings of increased personal competence seemed to be responsible for these effects.

It is clear that the process of helping another person results in beneficial psychological changes taking place in the person providing the help. Unfortunately, in our society children are typically the recipients of help from others, rather than the givers of help. Thus, a program such as tutoring, which allows children to help others, would contribute significantly to their feeling useful and needed. The feeling of being useful to others is particularly important for adolescents; being caught between childhood and adulthood, they realize that they are not yet useful and needed members of society. In summary, from interacting in a tutorial setting with a younger child the older child may derive a number of outcomes that contribute toward more positive social behavior both in and out of school.

The Tutee

Several factors can be mentioned that are likely to contribute to the impact that tutoring has on the tutee. First of all, tutoring is an eminent example of individualized instruction. By virtue of the one-to-one situation, the material to be learned—whether cognitive or social—can be matched closely to the learner's interests and ability, and immediate feedback can be provided.

It is interesting to point out that the tutor—tutee relationship possesses an important element that is lacking when an adult is the teacher. In the child-teaching-child situation, it is more likely that an affective relationship will develop; the emotional component may be an important factor contributing to the tutee's learning. Also, it is reasonable to believe that the communication occurring during teaching between children who are close in age could be more satisfying and acceptable to the tutee than the communication with an adult; as a result, the material would probably be learned more efficiently.

In terms of socialization, some of the possible beneficial consequences for the younger child in a different-age tutoring interaction are quite apparent. The natural respect and emulation that younger children display for older children can be utilized to convey cultural or social information in the tutoring situation. An older tutor is useful as a role model—as a source for the younger child's setting a level of aspiration for achievement. Older children also can play an important part in the social development of younger children in a more direct way, by influencing their prosocial behavior. Research shows that older age is positively valued by younger children (Lohman, 1970); hence, being a friend of a prestigeful older child can enhance a younger child's self-esteem. Age seems to be particularly salient at the younger stages of life because it is highly related to noticeable and valued characteristics such as size and strength. In one pertinent experiment, the age discrepancy of the model was varied in a standard play situation. Results showed that 6-year-old boys imitated most often the older model (Peifer, 1972). Interestingly, telling the child that the model was older was as effective as having a model who actually was older. So perceived age rather than physical size was the effective variable in this case. In sum, it can be maintained, then, that the younger child stands to gain in many ways from social interaction occurring in the context of a helping relationship such as the tutoring situation.

Finally, one always learns a great deal about the complementary role when interacting with another person. Therefore, when interacting with an older child, the younger child also learns about a future stage in the life cycle that he soon will be entering; that is, anticipatory socialization can take place.

Before leaving this section, we should consider the possibility that negative as well as positive psychological consequences will result from cross-age interaction.

Possessing greater strength and (possibly) cunning, an older child has the potential of bullying and exploiting a younger child. Neither should one minimize the capability of a younger child skillfully to provoke and torment an older child. Admittedly, the opportunity for mischief in cross-age interaction does exist; nevertheless, it can be maintained that interaction across ages has a great potential for contributing in a positive fashion toward the socialization—the "humanization"—of children. Provided that a context of benevolence or of a helping relationship exists, both the older and younger child stand to gain psychologically from the social interaction.

The School and Society

The school is important in any consideration of interaction across age levels simply because children spend such a great proportion of their time in school. Thus, any structural arrangement in the school that will affect the opportunity for contact between different age groups will have profound consequences for the nature of social behavior experienced by children.

Although most schools are presently still highly segregated according to age, signs of increasing flexibility are apparent. Tutoring or informal helping of some sort has been adopted by a large number of schools, as mentioned earlier. Another recent development is the multi-unit school, initiated by the Wisconsin Research and Development Center for Cognitive Learning (Klausmeier, Morrow, & Walter, 1968). The multi-unit school has as one of its central features the organization of students into groups on the basis of level of attainment in the subject matter rather than on the basis of age per se. Children of three or four adjacent ages are included together within a single instructional unit. The greatest amount of interaction still takes place between children of adjacent age levels, so the psychological advantages from this arrangement are not apt to be great. Nevertheless, the system does have the decided advantage of breaking the rigidity of the traditional age grade organization of the schools.

Interaction with persons other than one's own age mates is especially important for the socialization of younger children, as was emphasized earlier. The greater the extent to which younger children are segregated from older children and adults, the more likely the direction of peer influence will diverge from the norms and values of adult society. The emergence of a distinctive "youth culture" is a case in point.

It is instructive to take a brief look at a country in which cross-age interaction is strongly encouraged, in contrast to the situation in the United States. Bronfenbrenner (1970) reported that in the Soviet Union there is a great deal of involvement by adults and older children in the social life of younger children. Interaction between older and younger children, and between children and adults, is actively facilitated by a variety of techniques. Children in the USSR are explicitly taught in school to help each other, and especially to help younger children. It is common for an entire school or a class of older students to "adopt" a younger class; students take responsibility for the younger children in many ways, such as escorting them to school, helping with schoolwork, and reading stories. As an incentive for enacting the role of older "brothers and sisters" to the younger students, the older children's performance of these duties · are considered in evaluating their school performance. The "adoption" system also is extended to the adult world; a shop or factory or some other group of adults takes responsibility for a group of school children. During their spare time these adults engage in a variety of activities with the children. Using such procedures would be quite feasible in this country, and would contribute significantly toward breaking down existing barriers to social interaction between younger and older children and between children and adults.

REFERENCES

Allen, V. L., & Devin-Sheehan, L. D. Cross-age interaction in one-teacher schools. Unpublished manuscript, Wisconsin Research and Development Center for Cognitive Learning, Madison, Wisconsin, 1974.

Ariès, P. *Centuries of childhood.* New York: Knopf, 1962. (Translated from the French by R. Balkick.) Originally published under the title *L'enfant et la vie familiale sous l'ancien regime,* by Librairie Plon, Paris, 1960.

Bell, A. *An experiment in education made at the male asylum of Madras: Suggesting a system by which a school or family may teach itself under the superintendence of the master or parent.* London: Cadell and Davis, 1797.

Bell, A. *Instructions for conducting schools through the agency of the scholars themselves: Comprising the analysis of an experiment in education, made at the male asylum, Madras, 1789–1796.* London: 1917.

Bossard, J. H. S., & Boll, E. S. *The large family system.* Philadelphia: University of Philadelphia Press, 1956.

Bronfenbrenner, U. *Two worlds of childhood.* New York: Russell Sage Foundation, 1970.

Cloward, R. D. Studies in tutoring. *Journal of Experimental Education,* 1967, *36,* 14–25.

Condry, J. C., Jr., Siman, M. L., & Bronfenbrenner, U. Characteristics of peer and adult-oriented children. Unpublished manuscript, Department of Child Development, Cornell Univ., 1968.

Dures, A. *Schools.* London: Batsford, 1971.

Gartner, A., Kohler, M., & Riessman, F. *Children teach children.* New York: Harper, 1971.

Gillette, A. *One million volunteers: The story of volunteer youth service.* Middlesex, England: Penguin, 1968.

Holzberg, J. D., Knapp, R. H., & Turner, J. L. Companionship with the mentally ill: Effects on the personalities of college student volunteers. *Psychiatry,* 1966, *29,* 395–405.

Klausmeier, H. J., Morrow, R., & Walter, J. E. *Individually guided education in the multiunit school: Guidelines for implementation.* Madison: Wisconsin Research and Development Center for Cognitive Learning, 1968.

de Laborde, Le Comte Alexandre. *Plan d'education pour les enfans pauvres, d'apres les deux methodes combinees du docteur Bell et M. Lancaster.* Paris: H. Nicolle, 1815.

Lancaster, J. *Improvements in education as it respects the industrious classes of the community.* London: Darton and Harvey, 1803.

Lohman, J. E. Age, sex, socioeconomic status and youth's relationships with older and younger peers. *Dissertation Abstracts International,* 1970, *31*, (5-A), 2497.

Meiklejohn, J. M. D. *Dr. Andrew Bell: An old educational reformer.* London: Blackwood, 1882.

Peifer, M. R. The effects of varying age-grade status of models on the imitative behavior of six-year-old boys. *Dissertation Abstracts International,* 1972, *32*, (11-A), 6216.

Radcliffe-Brown, A. R. Age organization terminology. *Man,* 1929, *19*, 21.

Shatz, M., & Gelman, R. The development of communication skills: Modifications in the speech of young children as a function of listener. *Monographs of the Society of Research in Child Development,* 1973, *38*, No. 5.

Cross-Age Tutoring and
Social Identity

Theodore R. Sarbin

University of California, Santa Cruz

> Our [pedagogues] never stop bawling into our ears, as though they were pouring water into a funnel; and our task is only to repeat what has been told us. I should like the tutor to correct this practice, and right from the start, according to the capacity of the mind he has in hand, to begin putting it through its paces, making it taste things, choose them, and discern them by itself, sometimes clearing the way for him, sometimes letting him clear his own way. I don't want him to think and talk alone, I want him to listen to his pupil speaking in his turn. Socrates, and later Arcesilaus, first had their disciples speak, and then they spoke to them. [As Cicero has written] *The authority of those who teach is often an obstacle to those who want to learn* [Montaigne, 1588].

In preparing for this paper I examined some of the recent research reports on cross-age tutoring. One conclusion appeared over and over: Profound scholastic effects are produced when an older child engages in a tutoring relationship with a younger child. In some studies the tutor's own performances improve as much as, or more than, the tutee's. These findings might have been taken for granted save for a counter-expectational observation: In the tutoring setting the tutee acquires skills that he could not or would not acquire in the conventional classroom setting.

This observation raises a nagging question, a question that educators and psychologists should try to answer, namely, what are the conditions that make such an outcome likely? More concretely, what conditions allow a 12-year-old tutor—with little or no pedagogical training—to teach a 9-year-old tutee how to read, spell, or do arithmetic, whereas a classroom teacher is unable to influence the same child to acquire these skills?

Counter-expectational observations are the events that direct theorists and practitioners to seek explanations. Parenthetically, the statement of the counter-expectational observation reminds me of a finding that in part started me on my research career about 35 years ago. I discovered that a clerk armed with two psychometric scores and a regression equation could predict academic achievement in college as well as—and, in some cases, better than—college counselors with Ph.D. degrees armed with a vast assortment of test scores and interview data. This finding was contrary to concurrent expectations and led to efforts that would make sense of this perplexing state of affairs. The development of a theory of clinical inference helped to dissolve the perplexity (Sarbin, Taft, & Bailey, 1960).

After my preliminary review of the cross-age tutoring literature, I found myself asking the parallel question: how to account for observations that are contrary to expectations? For an attack on the problem of inter-age tutoring, I turned to role theory, a set of conceptions that has proven useful in illuminating some of the dark corners of social science. A number of questions emerge under the constraint of a search guided by role theoretical notions, the most obvious being, "What are the characteristics of the *role* of tutor?" A moment's reflection suggests that, for our purposes, we need to modify the question and ask, "What are the characteristics of the tutor–tutee *role relationship* that results in favorable outcomes?"

The recollection of my own role enactment as tutor provided some direction in exploring the problem. As an undergraduate, I tutored students who were having difficulty in learning introductory psychology. I recall that I puzzled over the fact that some tutees did well and some poorly, although my instructional methods were more or less uniform. At the time, I made a general observation that the students who profited most from my efforts were those with whom I had developed a relationship that differed from the formal student–teacher relationship. The relationship was attended by warmth, good humor, freedom to exchange information of a personal nature, and some good-natured joking. The tutee's acquisition of knowledge about introductory psychology appeared to be interwoven with the acquisition of a "friendship" role. The tutees who made no progress were those with whom a more conventional teacher–student relationship was apparent. In at least two of the unsuccessful cases, I recognized that the tutee appeared not to like me, and, I should add, the sentiment was mutual. At first I attributed the differential response to my tutoring efforts as a function of the attitude and motivation of the tutee. On more careful analysis, I formed the hypothesis that the success or failure of the tutoring was related to the kind of role relations that emerged.

The reporting of these recollections of my tutoring experiences anticipates the direction of my analysis. Clearly, the understanding of the counter-expectational findings mentioned before will depend upon a detailed comparison of the social roles of classroom teacher and inter-age tutor. To provide such an analysis, it is necessary to sketch some of the variables of role theory (Sarbin, 1954; Sarbin & Allen, 1968) and also to present an account of the social identity model, a spinoff of role theory (Sarbin & Scheibe, 1976).

A THEORETICAL FRAMEWORK

The master variable in role theory is role enactment. Most of the studies reviewed in Sarbin and Allen (1968) focus on the conditions that favor appropriate or inappropriate role enactment. In the present context, the target question is: What are the conditions that favor the appropriate or inappropriate enactment of the role of pupil?

We have identified six variables that influence the appropriateness, propriety, and convincingness of role enactment: *(1)* accuracy of the actor's role expectations; *(2)* validity of the actor's location of self in his various social systems; *(3)* sensitivity of the actor to subtle role demands; *(4)* congruence of self (values) and role requirements; *(5)* role taking skills; and *(6)* reinforcing and guiding properties of relevant audiences. All these variables are applicable to the role of pupil. In the present analysis, I shall concentrate on the second in the list of variables, a variable that takes us into the very center of the problem of social identity.

It is self-evident that role enactment is likely to be inappropriate, improper, or unconvincing if the actor fails to locate himself with reference to other actors who are participants in some form of social organization. The most common illustrations of failure in locating self are those that are reported as social embarrassments. On analysis, such embarrassments result from the recognition that one has engaged in conduct not appropriate to the situation and that such conduct followed from mistakes in establishing the identity of self or other.

It is helpful to discuss social identity—the identification or location of self *and* others in the social context—as the complex of answers to questions of the form *Who am I?* The form of the question constrains the form of the answer; "who" is a social term and its use in a question connotes a social system. No answer to the *Who am I?* question is possible without positing a social system—even a two-person system. Therefore, the *Who am I?* question implicitly contains an alternate question, namely, *Who are you?* Both questions are answered simultaneously: My identification of self as teacher (*Who am I?*) is correct only insofar as I correctly identify my audience as my students (*Who are you?*). This illustration, incidentally, is not an idle one. I once arrived late for the first meeting of an extension class and without preliminaries began my lecture by outlining the course content. After about 5 minutes, I noticed that some students were looking at me quizzically; others appeared to be amused; and still others were whispering to their neighbors. It turned out that I had blundered into the wrong room. I had answered the *Who am I?* question ("teacher of Abnormal Psychology 168") by assuming the answer to the *Who are you?* question: that members of the audience were students registered for the course in Abnormal Psychology 168. In fact, the room was filled with first-year dentistry students.

Needless to say, the concept of social identity is an important one. Alienation, deviant conduct, powerlessness, and similar conceptions have their roots in the social, economic, and political antecedents to seeking answers to questions of the form *Who am I?* The problem of cross-age tutoring may not have the cosmic significance of, let us say, alienated youth in industrialized nations, yet it may be approached with the same conceptual tools.

Briefly, I shall outline here a three-dimensional model of social identity. Then I shall use these dimensions to try to make sense of the counter-expectational observation that cross-age tutors succeed where adult classroom teachers fail.

I have already suggested that we begin from an analysis of the social system of which the teaching–learning enterprise is a part. Social systems such as government bureaucracies, military establishments, and religious orders provide illustrative material for more or less formal organizations. In such systems, the answer to the *Who am I?* question is ordinarily a routine one and is derived from the formal table of organization. In less formal organizations, the answers are not routine because the "table of organization" is not explicit. However, the dimensions from which answers are constructed for both explicit and implicit systems are the same.

The understanding of social relations was greatly facilitated by the social anthropologist Ralph Linton, who, in the 1930s, clarified the functioning of individuals in groups by an extension of the corollary concepts of status and role. The meaning of *status* is equivalent to *position* in a social structure, or *office*. *Role* is the set of actions that an individual performs to make good his occupancy of a status.

Linton (1942) found it useful to distinguish between ascribed and achieved statuses. Ascribed statuses are given or granted by birth, age, sex, kinship, and so forth. Examples are mother, son, male, infant, person. Achieved statuses are not granted, but attained through election, promotion, appointment, preparation, and so on. Occupational, recreational, and leisure-time statuses would exemplify the "achieved" category. The reader will recognize that the underlying conception is the lack of choice for ascribed statuses and the relative freedom to choose for achieved statuses.

For the analysis of esoteric ethnographic materials, the ascribed and achieved categories have been useful. When applied to analysis of social systems in which we are active participants, the categories are too gross. Many statuses and their correlative roles contain both ascribed and achieved components. For example, until recently in some American communities, the role "police officer" could be enacted only by individuals who could pass certain tests of knowledge and skill (achievement criteria) and who were male, Caucasian, native born, at least 21 years of age, and at least 70 inches in height (ascribed criteria). The status of "teacher," as I shall point out presently, may be understood better in terms of an analysis that includes ascribed elements as well as the more obvious achieved elements.

The observation that Linton's categories were too gross led to the rejection of the categorical definition of status and the positing of a dimension of status, a continuum, anchored at one end by ascription or granted criteria, at the other end by achievement or attained criteria.

The employment of the concept of status as a dimension is limited, however, to formal or sociological analysis, as in occupational sociology. To extend the usefulness of this conception, it is necessary to examine the actual conduct of individuals in their efforts to make good the occupancy of their various statuses, that is, the role enactments. One observation stands out: Roles are performed in the context of audiences. The audience may be a reciprocal other, as in a two-person situation, a small group, as in a family, or a large group, as in a theater. Further, audiences may be imaginary, that is, constructed by the actor.

A second dimension is posited, the dimension of value, or valuation. Audiences declare valuations on performances. My first efforts at coordinating the status dimension with the value dimension was simple: The relevant audience could declare a positive, neutral, or negative valuation on any performance; the expressed valuation would serve as positive, neutral, or negative feedback. A role performance that resulted in positive valuation, then, would increase the probability of the same role performance on subsequent occasions. This formula proved to be oversimplified. Observation of the conduct of persons as audiences for others' role performances led to the conclusion that the act of valuation is more complex, that the declaration of value for the enactment of roles in the ascribed region of the status dimension is qualitatively different from the valuations declared on role performances in the achieved region. Performances designed to make good the occupancy of achieved statuses, for example, school superintendent, violinist, congressman, quarterback, are assigned positive declarations of value if the actors do what they are supposed to do, if they perform according to job specifications. If the performances are unsuccessful or unconvincing, the valuation is neutral. The most felicitous label to attach to such valuations is *esteem* (derived from the same root as "estimate"). The appropriate enactment of the achieved components of a role, then, are betokened by declarations of esteem, such as prizes, compliments, money, gold stars, and so on. When the occupant of an attained status such as, for example, violin virtuoso, gives an uninspiring concert, the audience simply will not deliver tokens of esteem, but he will not be removed from his status as violinist, nor will his audience be outraged and demand sanctions that would degrade the person.

For the enactment of the ascribed or granted components of a role, a qualitatively different form of valuation occurs. As I mentioned before, roles that are loaded with ascription are taken for granted. Family and kinship roles are thrust upon actors, so to speak. They are expected to perform actions appropriate to the status assigned by birth or by unquestioned cultural arrangements. The role of mother, for example, when performed so as to meet community standards, produces no declarations of esteem. Being a proper mother, son, male, or American simply is expected. Valuations for proper performances, therefore, are neutral. But improper performances are met with negative valuations. The mother who wilfully abandons her child is likely to be the object of sanctions by the relevant community. The audience is outraged. The most descriptive term to denote such negative valuations is *disrespect*. It is as if the ascribed component of a status carries a grant of respect which may be withdrawn when role expectations are violated. Respect is betokened through communications that are qualitatively different from those employed to denote esteem. As I said before, esteem valuations are declared through the employment of prizes, awards, medals, and emoluments. Respect (meaning "to look again") is betokened through ritual expressions. For example, kissing the Pope's ring, genuflection before a queen, standing when one's mother enters the room are ceremonial responses of respect. Behind the responses are deep-seated, granted, affective dispositions. Respect responses clearly carry more emotional freight than esteem. They are tied, as I have already mentioned, to conduct initially generated in family and kinship roles. As a result, the sentiment of respect is intermingled with and probably arises from other sentiments that may be identified as caring-for, affection, loyalty and guardianship. Such associated and prior sentiments usually are not expressed in ritual form, but more directly through both verbal and nonverbal channels. (To anticipate somewhat: I shall discuss the role of cross-age tutor in the context of declaring valuations through the expressions of the sentiments of caring-for and respect.)

A third dimension is related to the already constrained model. Just as valuations are qualitatively different for performances at one or the other end of the status dimension, so is the degree of involvement in the role. Clearly, the individual whose roles are heavily loaded with ascribed characteristics has little freedom to become disengaged from the obligations of such roles. A woman who has acquired the status of mother must be "on" nearly all the time. The person in a primarily achieved status, for example, member of the Urban League, has the freedom to withdraw temporarily or permanently from the requirements of the role. The essential notion of this dimension is the freedom or lack of freedom to become disengaged from a role and its attendant relationships. The report of Peggy Lippitt (Chapter 9, this volume) makes use of the involvement concept in a similar way. (Again to anticipate a later argument: In the successful cross-age tutoring role relationship, if both participants perceive their roles as equivalent to granted roles, then there is little freedom for disinvolvement.)

To recapitulate: A three-dimensional model makes use of the sociological concept *status,* the psychological concept *valuation,* and the action concept *involvement.* Each dimension is constrained to a degree by the other dimensions. If represented graphically, the model would not be a rectangular solid but a modified wedge.

THE ROLE OF TEACHER

Employing the concepts sketched in the preceding pages, I offer a social psychological formulation to help account for the counter-expectational observation that pupils who fail to acquire skills in the classroom situation subsequently profit from the inter-age tutorial interaction.

"Teacher" in contemporary American society is a status that is primarily attained. That is to say, the person elects to follow the career of teacher, preparing himself or herself through the various steps to become certified. Like many statuses that appear to fit the criterion of achievement, some ascribed characteristics may be noted. The fact that "teacher" is primarily an achieved status is supported by the observation that it is one of a large number of roles from which a person may make choices. Further, the teacher may disengage himself from the role about four o'clock each day and enact other nonoverlapping roles, for example, parent, shopper, golfer, citizen. (As late as 1950 in many communities the "schoolmarm" was expected to stay "in role" even when not in the classroom. In the language of the present analysis, the role of teacher was heavily ascribed—nonenactment or improper enactment of the almost totalistic role was responded to with heavy sanctions: becoming a nonperson through public degradation and loss of job.)

The granted or ascribed portion of the teacher's role enactment varies with the age of the pupils. The nursery school and kindergarten teacher's role enactments in many ways are identical with those of the pupil's mother or father. A condition of complementarity exists: The status of the child in kindergarten is predominately ascribed—little choice in role enactment is allowed.

Although the kindergarten teacher may acquire esteem from his fellow teachers, principal, and so on, the nature of his duties are similar to those of parent, a role that carries no esteem if performed appropriately, but carries the potential for disrespect if performed contrary to the community's expectations. As we consider preschool teachers, primary teachers, secondary teachers, and college teachers, in turn, the attained component becomes more and more prominent and the granted component less prominent. A kindergarten teacher might reward a student by a hug or a caress—mutually experienced. On the other hand, the college teacher is constrained to assigning grades or writing evaluations, dealing primarily in the assignment of esteem. He usually is not involved in the declaration of value for role performance in affective, nonverbal actions, actions that are clearly indicators of caring and respect. As we move from the early years through high school and college, then, the nature of the teacher's valuations on the pupil's performance changes—from primarily affective, nonverbal, caring valuations to primarily rational, verbal, esteem valuations.

I am not unmindful of the fact that the teacher performs all kinds of instrumental acts in the conduct of his office, and that teacher-training institutions have in the past centered their efforts on the transmission of such instrumental acts. In employing these acts to carry out his role, the teacher is subject to declarations of esteem by significant others—principals, fellow teachers, parents of pupils, and, not unimportantly, pupils. As I pointed out before, instrumental acts—the antecedent condition for esteem—are but one feature of the human relations aspect of teaching and learning.

The pupil's perception of his role in school is at first undifferentiated from his other roles insofar as his placement on the status dimension is concerned. For the young child, all statuses are almost exclusively ascribed. As a result, valuations have meaning for him insofar as they are appropriate to the ascribed nature of his roles. It is patently absurd to use tokens of esteem, such as letter grades, to reward the role performance of a 3-year-old for dressing himself or a 5-year-old for saying "thank you." But a declaration that symbolizes positive feelings, such as a smile, a hug, a pat, eye contact, or an exclamation of delight is appropriate and has a reinforcing effect for the acquisition of a role repertory.

Most pupils and most teachers somehow manage to adjust to the apparent conflict in their perceptions of their role relations. If a person is to continue in the status of teacher of young pupils, he must accommodate to the fact that he is enacting an attained role, at the same time recognizing that he must engage in caretaking or parent-surrogate conduct that ordinarily is associated with the enactment of ascribed roles. The child, too, must accommodate to the fact that, as he matures, the pupil status becomes less and less ascribed; he learns that his teachers will declare valuations on successful role performance not through the nonverbal expression of positive feelings, but through marks, occasional prizes, awards, and letters of commendation.

The fact of individual differences in teachers' styles needs no elaboration here. Similarly, individual differences characterize the rate at which children learn that the form of valuation declared on one's role performance is a function of statuses becoming more and more attained. A 9-year-old child's failure to respond to the teacher's efforts to teach him simple arithmetic may be accounted for by the teacher's perception of her role as that of assigning tokens of esteem (such as gold stars) for good performance before he (the pupil) understands the meaning of such esteem valuations. It is as if the pupil perceives both his role and the complementary (teacher) role as ascribed. His unstated expectations, then, are that the teacher will assign affective valuations for proper role performance. His expectations are not fulfilled. The structural features of the classroom situation preclude the teacher's use of respect valuations through individualized, often nonverbal communications. The pupil fails to grasp the operations of arithmetic, then, not because he is stupid, nor because the teacher is incompetent, but because of the confusions that arise when two parties engage in role behavior that is nonreciprocal. Although in a formal sense their statuses are complementary, their role enactments are not—the child expects one kind of valuation and receives another. Such role confusions can be important background factors in a child's failure to learn in the traditional classroom situation.

The theory presented here places its emphasis on a different set of categories than used in traditional analyses. In the past, educators and psychologists have attributed slow learning in the classroom to lack of aptitude or intellectual, motivational, or even neurological deficit. In so doing, they have overlooked the fact that teaching and learning are activities carried on by persons in role relationships and that the roles constrain not only the instrumental acts of the participants but also the kinds of valuations (reinforcements) declared on the performance of such acts. Such ignoring of the social bases of classroom learning is witnessed by the stock treatment of "learning disabilities": the use of remedial classes. That remedial classes are notoriously unsuccessful needs no documentation here. It is my belief that the lack of success of remedial classes is due to the same set of conditions that causes failure in the regular classroom: The teacher—pupil role relation is noncomplementary. The pupil's positive performances are met with the teacher's *esteem* responses when esteem has not yet become a supplement to *respect* and *caring* as the valuational responses that reinforce conduct.

THE ROLE OF TUTOR

The content of Lippitt's paper supports my belief that the explanation for the relative success of cross-age tutoring over classroom teaching is to be found in the nature of the tutor—tutee role relationship. A clue to the role relationship is provided in an etymological analysis of the word "tutor." Derived from the Latin "tueri," originally it carried the meaning "to protect, to guard, to care for." The same root meaning is found in the concept of tutelage. Protecting, guarding, and caring for, of course, are actions supporting an ascribed type of role relation; the person denoted by the term "tutor" could act *in loco parentis*. The occupant of the status "tutor," then, in the context of education and socialization was obligated to look after and to care for and even to discipline the occupant of the complementary status. The concept of tutelage found its way into the English schools in the Middle Ages and endured until very recently. There were two classes of students, identified as "tutores" and "scholares." The "tutores" were older boys charged with the tutelage of "scholares," the younger boys. The requirements of tutelage were both academic and moral.

The etymology suggests a clue to the tutor–tutee relationship. It is clear that the concept of tutelage dealt with the enactment of granted roles. One might say that the tutor and the tutee are primarily ego-oriented and secondarily task-oriented. In a basically attained role, the orientation is primarily, if not exclusively, the accomplishment of instrumental acts. In a role that is heavily weighted with ascriptive elements, the maintenance of the relationship has priority, a relationship that deals with sentiments, affects, feelings. For this reason, much of the communication is necessarily nonverbal. The hypothesis is suggested that school age children acquire a syntax that is submerged as the child acquires more and more attained statuses, depends more on conventional verbal symbols, and focuses on more analyzable esteem valuations.

The research reported by Allen and Feldman (1975) is pertinent here. Videotape records were made of a child listening to a difficult and an easy lesson. Short segments of the films of several stimulus children were then shown to other children and adults, who were asked to estimate how much each child understood the lesson. The only cues available for the judges' estimate of understanding were the subtle nonverbal facial responses displayed by the children on the short film clips. Results showed that third graders and sixth graders were more accurate than adults in discriminating between instances of understanding and nonunderstanding on the basis of very minimal nonverbal cues. That children were superior to adults on this task involving making judgments about other children suggests a sensitivity to subtle cues that are part of a syntax of nonverbal operations.

When the older child is assigned the status of tutor, what are his initial perceptions of the role enactments necessary to make good the occupancy of that status? Obviously he does not classify roles with the language used here. Since his models of pedagogy have been classroom teachers, it is probable that his first location of self in the tutor–tutee role relationship is that of "teacher." He probably does not enter the role with a preplanned program that depends upon the use of the rhetoric and affective expressions that are natural to ascribed roles.

He is placed in a one-to-one situation. Although he has been exposed to the use of esteem rewards, he lacks experience in the scheduled use of such reinforcements. Recognizing the inappropriateness of esteem valuations in the peer setting, the potentially successful tutor quickly dispenses with the use of such an interpersonal tactic. I might add that esteem is basically an adult kind of valuation—it is acquired over time and, as I said before, is inappropriate to young children.

The one-to-one setting encourages an ascribed role relationship. The form of the relationship is at first circumscribed by the tutorial task, the acquisition of skill in reading, for example. From an adult's standpoint, a role relationship is constructed that differs little from other achieved relationships. From a child's standpoint, the mutual actions of the participants, unskilled in the use of conventional esteem valuations, lead to a ready dependence on affective communications. Here respect, or its antecedent or corollary sentiment, *caring*, becomes the *modus vivendi*.

The dimension of involvement comes into play to the degree that the tutor perceives his role as a granted one. To the degree that the older pupil locates his role at the ascribed end of the status dimension he is involved in his role enactments as tutor. Further, within institutional or neighborhood constraints, the involvement may spill over into activities that extend beyond the tutoring assignment.

I do not want to minimize the importance of the tutor's pedagogical skills. As Harrison (Chapter 10, this volume) has demonstrated, tutors who have been exposed to "methods" are better performers than those who enter the tutoring situation unprepared. That is to say, the variation in the quality of the outcomes of tutor–tutee relationships may be accounted for in part by the tutor's preparation for his role. But the stress on skill acquisition for the tutor, I believe, is a misplaced emphasis. Skill acquisition is secondary to the development of a role relationship that portrays the features of friendship and makes possible the activation of skills. If the relationship is characterized by high involvement—which would be the case if both actors located their identities as ascribed—then the tutor and tutee would actively expend more time and more effort on shared tasks. The involvement dimension is not an idle one. It has been employed fruitfully in other contexts: Janis and Mann (1965), for example, have demonstrated how attitudes and conduct are influenced by high involvement in role playing. Eagly (1967) experimentally manipulated ego-involvement in studies of self-esteem.

The degree of involvement of the actors, of course, is not determined by their mere assignment to tutor and tutee roles. As I said earlier, it is probable that the tutor's initial location of his role (answers to the identity question *Who am I?*) is patterned after his observation of classroom teachers. Under these conditions, he would in the beginning simulate the role of the classroom teacher in providing feedback of the *esteem* variety. But a subtle transformation may occur when such reinforcements fail. As a result of the one-to-one relationship, physical and psychological distance between tutor and tutee is reduced. Conditions develop for an ascribed type of relationship—the tutelage relationship where the older child takes on the obligation of caring for, looking after, the younger. That is to say, the structure of the social situation provides a *linkage* between the achievement components of tutor (patterned after classroom teacher) and the ascription components of tutor (patterned after guardian).

The concept of role linkage has wide application. Role linkage occurs when the assignment to a specific achieved role provides opportunities for the enactment of quasi-ascribed roles. Let me insert a parenthetical remark to illustrate further the concept of linkage. On the premise that self-esteem and suicide are contradictory, work roles have been prescribed as *the* prophylaxis for suicide, the assumption being that self-esteem follows from esteem valuations declared by others for job performance. On the present theory, work roles are effective as prophylaxis *only* if they provide opportunities for being respected and being cared for. The lonely 50-year-old widow is less likely to commit suicide if she has a job that makes possible the enactment of quasi-ascribed roles such as, for example, mother substitute for younger employees.

A word is in order about the observation that cross-age tutors frequently increase their own skills as a result of the tutoring program. The social identity model provides a tentative explanation. I have already suggested that skills are acquired as a result of the employment of affective reinforcements. The sentiments expressed in the ascribed relationship may be mutual: The tutor works hard to maintain his tutelage relationship. This is another way of saying that he is highly involved in his role. And, as I pointed out before, high involvement is a condition of learning. But the tutor has a second role relationship, a relationship with his supervisor, usually a school psychologist, a classroom teacher, a principal. In this relationship, particularly if he is supervised in a group with other tutors, he is a candidate for the receipt of esteem publicly declared by his adult supervisor. Thus, he is reinforced in two ways: by the expression of the respect—caring complex of sentiments in the tutelage situation, and by tokens of esteem in the group situation. If there is any validity at all to reinforcement theory, the successful tutor is in a setting that encourages improved performance in tasks related to the focus of the tutoring. He is in a setting in which his conduct is reinforced in two ways, through respect and through esteem. Incidentally, a by-product is the acquisition of self-respect and self-esteem, as Peggy Lippitt has so clearly demonstrated.

I recapitulate here the basic distinction between the role of the classroom teacher and the role of the cross-age tutor. In the context of reinforcement as a component of learning, the social organization of the classroom restricts the teacher to the exclusive employment of esteem as reinforcement. In the cross-age face to face tutoring relationship, the opportunity exists for affective expressions of the sentiments of respect and caring to serve as reinforcers. Such reinforcers are the currency for early childhood learning. Only gradually does the child add esteem to his repertory of behavior. The classroom teacher must function, then, in an attained role, sometimes with pupils who identify themselves as occupants of a noncomplementary ascribed status. A nonreciprocal condition exists, a condition of strain that inhibits the acquisition of skills, and, unless the teacher can supplement esteem valuations with affective valuations, the pupil fails to learn.

THE PROBLEM OF INDIVIDUAL DIFFERENCES

Before closing, I offer some hypotheses to help clarify the fact that there are large differences in the outcomes of cross-age tutoring. Cloward (Chapter 14, this volume) has provided us with a pessimistic report about "personality traits" as correlates of tutoring effectiveness. His review of the literature has uncovered no stable relations between psychometrically assessed traits and tutoring outcomes. This should not be surprising in view of the current challenges to the premises of trait psychology (Mischel, 1971). The psychometric approach to the study of individual differences need not be abandoned entirely. If we take into account the fact that tutoring occurs in the dyadic context, then assessment needs to incorporate "the situation." Assessments of tutor *and* tutee should be the object of our attention. In another context, Smelser (1961) demonstrated the predictability of dyadic performance when attention was directed to the "traits" of both participants. On a complex task, the most successful pairs were those where the leadership role was assigned to the subject with a high score on dominance and where the subordinate role was assigned to the subject with a low score on dominance. The least successful pairs were those where the role assignments were in the reverse direction.

Another approach to individual differences is suggested in earlier work stimulated by role theory. Considerable evidence has accumulated to support the proposition of a generalized role taking aptitude or skill. Given an initial impetus by George Herbert Mead (1934), the concept has been discussed as a cognitive taking-the-role-of-the-other. An individual who is a good role taker appears to have acquired the skill in imaginative rehearsal (Sarbin & Juhasz, 1970) and, as a result, can accommodate his performances to the role of another actor in a social drama. It might prove fruitful to compare effective tutors with ineffective tutors on tests of skill in imagining what it would be like, say, to be a nonreader.

CONCLUSION

The foregoing remarks are intended to demonstrate the potential utility of a social psychological theory in accounting for the perplexing counter-expectational finding that juvenile tutors are sometimes more effective than adult classroom teachers. In the foregoing pages, I have tried to show how cross-age tutoring can be analyzed in terms of identifiable features of a role relationship created when the older and the younger child interact. The model of social identity employed here focuses attention on the *role relationship* rather than the special characteristics of each participant.

ACKNOWLEDGMENT

I owe a debt of gratitude to Professor Joseph B. Juhasz for a critical discussion of the contents of this paper. I also want to thank Ron Allen from the bottom of my heart for his help in completing the final version.

REFERENCES

Allen, V. L., & Feldman, R. S. Decoding of children's nonverbal responses. Technical Report No. 365, Wisconsin Research and Development Center for Cognitive Learning, Madison, Wisconsin, 1975.

Eagly, A. H. Involvement as a determinant of response to favorable and unfavorable information. *Journal of Personality and Social Psychology Monograph*, 1967, *7*, (no. 3).

Janis, I. L., & Mann, L. Effectiveness of emotional role-playing in modifying smoking habits and attitudes. *Journal of Experimental Research in Personality*, 1965, *1*, 84–90.

Linton, R. Age and sex categories. *American Sociological Review*, 1942, *7*, 589–603.

Mead, G. H. *Mind, self, and society*. Chicago: Univ. of Chicago Press, 1934.

Mischel, W. *Introduction of personality*. New York: Holt, 1971.

Montaigne, M. E. *The complete works of Montaigne*. (D. M. Frame, Trans.). Stanford, California: Stanford Univ. Press, 1958.

Sarbin, T. R. Role theory. In G. Lindzey (Ed.), *Handbook of social psychology*. Vol. I. Reading, Massachusetts: Addision-Wesley, 1954. Pp. 223–258.

Sarbin, T. R., & Allen, V. L. Role theory. In G. Lindzey & E. Aronson (Eds.), *Handbook of social psychology*. Vol. I. Reading, Massachusetts: Addison-Wesley, 1968. Pp. 488–567.

Sarbin, T. R., & Juhasz, J. B. Toward a theory of imagining. *Journal of personality*, 1970, *38*, 52–76.

Sarbin, T. R., & Scheibe, K. E. The transvaluation of social identity. In C. Bellone (Ed.), *The normative dimension in public administration*. New York: Dekker, 1976.

Sarbin, T. R., Taft, R., & Bailey, D. E. *Clinical inference and cognitive theory*. New York: Holt, 1960.

Smelser, W. Dominance as a factor in achievement and perception in cooperative problem-solving interactions. *Journal of Abnormal Social Psychology*, 1961, *62*, 535–542.

3

Cross-Age versus Same-Age Peer Interaction: Ethological and Cross-Cultural Perspectives[1]

Willard W. Hartup
University of Minnesota

Hard data are lacking concerning the contributions of cross-age peer interaction to child development. Observational studies have focussed almost exclusively upon behavior in peer groups composed of agemates, and experiments on peer influences seldom include the age difference between subject and influence source as an independent variable. Moreover, studies of children's social attitudes, inferences about other people, and attitudes toward themselves almost never yield estimates of the variance associated with the age differential between "self" and "significant other." Thus, we know little about cross-age interaction—either the circumstances of its occurrence in naturalistic socialization or its functional significance. Intuition suggests that children should be influenced differently by peers who are younger or older than they are by peers who are roughly their own age. But this supposition has only the anecdotal reports of sharp-eyed group workers, teachers, and parents to support it.

In this paper it is contended that cross-age peer interaction should be examined from two vantage points: (1) evolutionary and comparative analysis, and

[1] This chapter was completed with the assistance of financial support from Grant No. 5-P01-05027, National Institute of Child Health and Human Development.

(2) cross-cultural studies, especially with reference to the relation between the social ecology and the composition of children's play groups. Such considerations are essential to the construction and evaluation of programs which would utilize the peer group as a constructive force in childhood socialization.

AN ETHOLOGICAL PERSPECTIVE ON PEER GROUP COMPOSITION

The immature members of many species live in close proximity with one another. Such proximity lasts for periods that vary greatly in length and that occur for different reasons. The composition of these peer groups varies enormously. In some species, the group consists of a cohort in which all individuals are born within days or hours of one another, but, in others, the group consists of individuals of many different developmental levels.

Peer groups occasionally form the entire "social" context for development. Reptiles and fish mature within peer clusters in which the young animals have relatively little contact with adults. In some of these species, bonding to other members of the group does not occur; individuals remain in proximity with one another as a consequence of species-specific behavior rather than particular attachments. In other species, however, group relations emerge within a context that proceeds from maternal bonding to bonding that involves various secondary objects including nonrelated age mates. Maternal bonding sometimes temporarily excludes contact between the immature individual and other immature members of the species, although it is rare for such exclusion to last beyond the animal's infancy.

Regardless of the mechanism underlying group formation, opportunity for cross-age or cross-cohort contacts among immature members of a species is relatively rare except among mammals. In some cases, the very attributes which act specifically to keep young animals of similar ages in close proximity with each other (e.g., gradations in body color or particular action patterns) act specifically to keep more mature members of the species at a distance. Distal contact with more mature animals may occur, although the amount of such contact is highly variable across species.

Actually, there is a paucity of naturalistic data concerning the ratio of cross-age contacts to age-specific contacts as these occur during the socialization of the various species (Crook, 1970). There has been tremendous variation among existing studies in conditions of data-gathering, and techniques of reporting have also varied widely. For these reasons, definitive statements cannot be made concerning the relation of various species' characteristics and social ecological conditions to the composition of juvenile peer groups. Nevertheless, a careful reading of the primate literature offers the possibility of considerable gain in hypothesizing about the qualitative features of human peer interaction.

Observational studies of four nonhuman primate species are particularly instructive and will be summarized briefly here. Three of these species—langurs, baboons, and vervet monkeys—have similar social developmental histories. Each baby experiences an early specific attachment to the mother; each is weaned by the time the mother begins to be sexually receptive; and, at that point, the focus of socialization in each species shifts to the peer group. Although the timing of these events in langurs and baboons is nearly parallel, the progression is speeded in the vervet; infant vervets are born more mature developmentally than infants of the other two species (Dolhinow, 1970). There are also marked differences among these species in the relation of the infant to other troop members, and these differences deserve specific comment.

The Langur

For the first month the langur is held constantly by the mother or some other adult female. Between 2 and 5 months, accompanied by changes in locomotor skill and physical appearance, the infant ventures from its mother's side and comes to spend several hours per day in contact with age mates. Through the remainder of the infant period (until 15 months) the infant spends increasing amounts of time in play groups. Such groups may include as many as 16 monkeys, but most contain from 2 to 4 individuals. There is very little contact with juvenile monkeys or sub-adults, and, until 10 months of age, there is no contact with adult males. (At that time, contact with the adult males is initiated for male infants but not for female infants.) Maternal contact decreases after 5 months of age. It is during this late infancy period, according to Dolhinow (1970), that basic patterns of social behavior, including dominance and sex, first appear. Note that it is an age-specific group that has singular importance at this stage in langur socialization. When the langur reaches the so-called juvenile stage, cross-age interaction becomes somewhat more frequent. Such interaction is observed always to be unisexual, however. For males, cross-age contacts with sub-adult males increase, but there is virtually no contact with younger individuals (i.e., infants). For females, social life consists of continued age-specific interaction (i.e., with other juvenile females); cross-age interaction involves only a preoccupation with very young infants. With the approach of sub-adulthood, the peer contacts of both sexes come increasingly to involve adult-like behavior rather than the rough-and-tumble activities of earlier childhood, but cross-age contacts change relatively little. Female interest in young infants intensifies further at the time of first oestrus.

Baboon

The infant baboon is heavily shielded from contact with other immature members of the species until at least 6 months after birth (this neonatal isolation is much more complete than in the case of the infant langur). By 10 months, play groups have been established, but these continue to be protected by adult males. These play groups are relatively small, containing 6 to 8 individuals, and they are separated into groups of similar developmental levels. As in infancy, cross-age interactions during the juvenile era are not extensive. Play groups are unisexual. With the approach of sub-adulthood, parental supervision decreases; play among males is characterized by dominance interactions, while maternal types of behavior, with infants, are primary features (along with grooming) of juvenile female play.

Vervet Monkeys

Although maternal interest and attention to the newborn vervet is substantial, immature females ranging from 6 months to 4 years of age are allowed to carry, handle, and groom the newborn infant. This handling is at first terribly awkward, but, in contrast to the langurs and baboons, the infant is exposed to cross-age peer interaction from birth onward. When the infant is assimilated into play groups, social contact is experienced with vervets of a variety of ages. The age range in such groups may be from 15 days to 4 years, thus encompassing infants, juveniles, and sub-adults. Unlike many other primate species, adult vervets also will play sometimes with the infants in these groups (Struhsaker, 1967). In this species, then, all of the socialization of aggression and sex takes place within the context of cross-age interaction.

Chimpanzees

According to Van Lawick-Goodall (1965), play is an important aspect of social life among juvenile chimpanzees. Of all the species mentioned, however, the period of infancy is longest for the chimpanzee, and maternal contact remains preeminent for an unusually long period of time after birth. Such contact remains important for the young chimpanzee through 3 to 4 years even though peer contacts increase. After that, mother–child contact continues for purposes of tutoring in tool-using and other skills. Juvenile chimpanzees play within their own loosely defined age groups, although they also may play with infants and sometimes with younger adolescents.

Explaining species variations in play group composition by reference to features of the social ecology is a hazardous undertaking. Nevertheless, it is interesting to note that the most rigidly age graded play groups are found among the langurs and baboons, species which live in large groups that include individuals of all ages and sexes. Langurs have been observed living in groups ranging in size from 5 to 120; groups average from 18 to 50 individuals depending on the region of India in which they were observed (Jay, 1968). Baboons, depending on the subspecies and ecological conditions, live in groups ranging from 40 to 130 individuals with the added socio-structural complication that small subgroups are formed around individual adult males. Chimpanzees, the species characterized by both age-specific and cross-age peer interaction, live in very loose social groupings. Van Lawick-Goodall believes, however, that the Gombe group constitutes a single group (in a loose sense) since subgroups are in constant flux. Note, in contrast, the social ecology of the vervet (Jay, 1968). Their groups range from only 6 to 21 individuals; groups split when they become larger than this, and modal groups consist of only 10 to 11 animals. Thus, it appears that the most sustained and intense cross-age peer interaction occurs within primate species which live in very small groups.

Could the relative maturity of the newborn be related to the evolution of the cross-age interactional life style of the vervet? Of the species mentioned, the vervet is the most mature animal at birth, thus making it possible for social contacts to be heterogeneous without endangering the infant. However, the species producing the least mature newborn—the chimpanzee—produces play groups of more variable composition than either the baboon or the langur. This suggests that some other factor, such as troop size or composition, may be more salient in the evolution of the primate play group than maturity at birth.

Does the cycling of reproduction within the various species account for variations in the composition of the peer group? Although time of birth obviously is related to whether individual A ever is found in the same location as individual B, there are no systematic variations between compositional characteristics of peer groups and degree of seasonal concentration of reproduction in the species. Vervet reproduction is no less concentrated seasonally than langur reproduction, and yet the composition of vervet and langur peer groups is quite different.

Does small troop size promote cross-age peer interaction simply because large numbers of same-age peers are not available? It may be the case that limitations on troop size produce limitations on peer group composition, but these constraints do not account for the fact that age-specific peer groups characterize species that live in large troops. To put the problem another way: If older and younger members of a species are both readily available, why do not primate peer groups always encompass individuals who vary widely in terms of developmental status?

The discussion to this point can be summarized as follows: (*1*) Contact with peers (loosely defined as all immature members of a troop) is a salient aspect of social ontogenesis in all primates. (*2*) Peer contacts are restricted for longer periods among those species in which maternal bonding is strong than among those in which such bonding is weak. (*3*) Play groups appear to have important functions in social development by contributing to the acquisition of effective coping mechanisms in such areas as aggression and sex. Contact between the peer group and adult members of the species extends the socialization of aggression and sex that occurs within the peer group itself. (*4*) Learning to modulate behavior in these two areas may be accomplished in groups that are either age-specific or heterogeneous with respect to age, although such learning always takes place in unisex groups. (*5*) Although the formation of peer groups is ubiquitous among the primate species, the social ecology of the population produces considerable variation in peer group composition with respect to the ages of its members. Large primate societies foster play groups that are homogeneous with respect to age; heterogeneous play groups are formed when the primary social group (i.e., the troop) is relatively small.

CROSS-CULTURAL STUDIES

The relative importance of sex and age in the formation of juvenile peer groups is the same in *homo sapiens* as among the nonhuman primates. Age sets limits on the composition of such groups; these limits operate within others established by gender.

Numerous studies reveal the various ways in which age functions in the formation of children's play groups. Almack (1922) found correlations within classrooms which ranged between .42 and .53 between the chronological age of chooser and chosen on sociometric tests. Considering the restricted age range found in most public school classrooms, these coefficients probably provide an attenuated assessment of the importance of age in friendship choice. Other, more differentiated, findings are available in a report by Challman (1932). He found that the closeness of friendship was correlated with similarity in age at the level of .56 for boy–boy pairs, .35 for girl–girl pairs, and .30 for boy–girl pairs of preschool children. Illustrating the cross-societal generality of this aspect of peer relations, Chevaleva-Janovskaja (1927) reported that 67% of some 888 spontaneous groups of Russian preschool children contained children who differed in chronological age by one year or less. Research also confirms that age is an important element in clique formation during adolescence after the sex variable has begun to lose some of its potency as an influence on the composition of the peer group. Hollingshead (1949) reported contingency coefficients of .86 for boys and .90 for girls between high school grade and membership in particular cliques.

Given this state of affairs, how much variation exists across cultures in the opportunity for children to experience cross-age peer contacts? What conditions, ecological or otherwise, account for such variation? To our knowledge, no intensive study utilizing the Human Relations Area Files has been focused upon these questions. It is clear, however, from the most cursory reading of the ethnographic literature that primary peer group organization varies widely across cultures. The volume *Six Cultures* (Whiting, 1963) contains the following information from Orchard Town, U.S.A. (a community of 5000): "We regularly observed children of this age playing with children as much as three or four years older or younger. The population of Orchard Town is dispersed enough so that a strict age segregation would leave many children without any nearby playmates of the same sex" (pp. 990–991). In Tarong (a small village in the Philippines): "Tarongan play groups at the primary school level typically cross grades easily and involve children of both sexes and various ages, all having *sitio*-residence in common" (pp. 847–848). (Play groups in this village do not commonly cross *sitio*, i.e., household, barriers.) In Juxtlahuaca (a poor village in Mexico) contact between nonrelated peers is severely limited, but "the children of early childhood age were part of a group formed by the siblings and cousins and other close relatives. The social context for the children was equivalent to an extended family in all cases" (p. 661). In Nyansongo (an isolated community in Kenya) the sibling group (with concomitant variation in age of its members) tends to be the most important nonparental socializing force for the children, since families live in relative isolation from one another. Sibling groups mix, however, in the pastures, and these mixes are quite heterogeneous. "In herding groups consisting of children from several homesteads, the oldest dominates the others, ordering them about, occasionally beating them, taking whatever articles they own" (p. 171). Oldest girls tend to dominate in sibling interactions in the home. In Taira (an Okinawan village) the kindergarten group (which meets as a group each day) "includes all children from weaning until the age of six. The younger ones are carried to the morning sessions, whereas the older ones go on their own. Kindergarten may thus be likened to a mass baby-sitting session" (p. 480). The composition of school-age groups is unclear. It is reported that "those of the same age watch and control each other, while older children remind younger ones who neglect a crying young sibling to attend to his needs" (p. 535). The Rajput (residents of an Indian city of 5000) also appear to foster either mixed or less-mixed groups: When they are mixed, the older children direct the play of the younger ones. Anyone who has seen Eibl-Eibesfeldt's recent films on social interaction among children of the !Kō Bushmen (Eibl-Eibesfeldt, 1972) knows that social contact, caretaking activities, and other aspects of socialization often occur within groups of children that are heterogeneous with respect to age.

The observations on the !Kō Bushmen, the observations in Orchard Town, and the observations in Okinawa could not be duplicated in most American metropolitan areas. The prevailing norm in large, Western, urban social structures fosters age-specific peer groups. This is true in Amsterdam, Jerusalem, and Munich, as well as in Minneapolis, even though there may be some variation in amount of cross-age peer contact between inner city ecologies and the middle-class suburbs. When congregated in cities, human children seem to behave much as do nonhuman primates who live in large enclaves: They participate in relatively more age-specific groups than they would in a culture composed of fewer individuals. Documentation of this state of affairs, however, is not extensive.

INTERPRETIVE COMMENT

Mixed-age peer groups would appear to be older than same-age peer groups in the evolutionary sense. All of the primate species, including man, evolved within the context of widely dispersed, small social groupings. The long periods of development characteristic of most of the primate species, and the vast needs of these species for "learning by tradition" probably came to necessitate the utilization of nonparents as well as parents in the socialization process. Lacking access to large numbers of age mates, however, the first nonparent socializing agents were probably siblings; and sibling groups vary widely in age. But extrafamilial socializing agents also became necessary during the course of evolution because of the necessity for some kinds of social experiences to take place outside the "bonded" relationships. The types of interaction necessary for the adequate socialization of aggression, for example, are incompatible with the behaviors involved in bonding. Yet the socialization of aggression must occur at a point in primate ontogenesis when fundamental social bonds, such as the tie to the mother, cannot be undone. The nonfamilial juveniles available for such interactive purposes in early primate groups, (including early man) tended to be small in number and widely varied in age. The heterogeneity of these peer groups was, of course, perpetuated by the facts that troops were small and primate pregnancies tend to result in single rather than multiple births.

The evolution of large and complex societies, however, has apparently produced adaptational demands upon primate children for which the mixed-age group is not as satisfactory as the same-age peer group. Both types of groups possess potential for contributing to socialization in such sensitive areas as sex and aggression. However, as pointed out above, when young primates can choose between these two types of groupings, they tend to form groups composed of individuals who resemble each other closely in size and developmental status. Only when ecological conditions prevail that resemble those of an earlier evolutionary era do children participate extensively in cross-age interaction.[2]

What factors account for the preeminence of the age-specific peer group in human socialization? It does not seem that pressures emanating from contemporary social institutions are entirely responsible. Although our educational system is rigidly age graded, it does not produce age-specific peer cultures in every instance. Note, for example, that the children of Orchard Town and the children of Tarong both participated in heterogeneous peer cultures in spite of the fact that they attended age graded schools. Is the tendency to form age-specific play

[2] Certain temporary shifts in the ecology seem to precipitate the formation of heterogeneous peer groups even within the context of complex, urban societies. When economic conditions or family values delegate child care responsibilities to older siblings, and when vast numbers of children of all ages move freely in and out of the house, heterogeneous peer societies are the result.

groups a consequence of parental pressure in large, complex societies? Only minimally so. United States parents frequently state that they believe their children should have opportunities to play with children of their own age, but sanctions against contacts with older or younger children are not uniformly strong.

A more persuasive explanation for the preeminence of the age-specific peer group is to be found by examining the social interaction occurring within these groups themselves. It seems clear, for example, that a more optimal ratio of positively reinforcing events to negatively reinforcing events is to be found in the interaction of age mates than in the interaction of non–age mates. How often, for example, does a 6-year old child achieve success in dominance interactions with a 10-year-old child? Rarely. How often are succorant overtures reinforced in the context of these same interactions? Seldom, at least by boys. How often are achievement efforts reinforced? Not very often. Some accomplishments, of course, receive relatively high rates of positive reinforcement in such contexts: for example, effective communication behaviors, facility in assuming reciprocal role relations, adherence to sex role norms, and so forth. But, overall, schedules of reinforcement in cross-age interaction will not be rich across the entire behavioral spectrum, and we know from the experimental work of the Lotts (Lott & Lott, 1972) that such events play a crucial role in the determination of peer bonding.

Cross-age interaction probably produces higher rates of aversive feedback than does interaction among age mates. The dependence of the 6-year-old is aversive to the 10-year-old: Such behavior arouses anxiety in one who is struggling with independence problems of his own. Besides, associating with younger children inhibits the 10-year-old's freedom of movement, and the social norms promulgated in the preadolescent peer group prohibit associating with "babies." Such interaction also may constitute an aversive experience for the younger child: The dominance and criticisms of the older child, the negative social comparisons, and the consequent lowering of self-esteem all militate against the maintenance of the younger child's sustained participation in cross-age interaction. Thus, it is hypothesized that the same-age peer group is maintained in complex societies by optimal ratios of positive to negative reinforcement. Through these processes, over time, the simple proximity to age mates also may become secondarily reinforcing or provide signals eliciting positive expectancies of one sort or another (Lambert & Taguchi, 1956).

There also may be some basis for age mate preferences in genetic preprogramming. Greenberg, Hillman, and Grice (1973), for example, have found that young babies react more positively to the approach of a strange 4-year-old child than to the approach of a strange adult female or a strange adult male. Where did the positive reactions to the 4-year-old come from? The subjects had had relatively little preexperimental contact with 4-year-old human beings.

One conclusion to be drawn from this analysis is that same-age groups have greater adaptational significance for children than cross-age groups. Cross-age interactions contain considerable adaptational potential, as evidenced by the contributions that such interactions make to socialization in smaller societies. But children who live in complex social worlds in which large numbers of age mates are available do not find cross-age interaction to be as functional as age-specific interaction; the incentives to engage in peer interaction on a sustained basis are not built into the cross-age social system. Thus, when socialization of an urban child appears to be satisfactory, one could question whether contrived programs of cross-age contacts engineered by teachers and social workers will contribute enough to the child's development to warrant the effort required to produce the programs. Furthermore, one must be cautious about "missionary" efforts that invade the natural world of children's peer relations just as one must be cautious about "missionary" efforts that invade the natural world of the Australian aborigine.

Cross-age contacts, however, may be particularly useful as a means of intervening in inadequate socialization (e.g., Suomi & Harlow, 1972). The data bearing on cross-age interaction in smaller societies, for example, suggest that such contacts have considerable potential for improving the socialization of children who are poorly adjusted socially. Even so, attention must be paid to the problem of how to induce children to participate in such social experiences. Cross-age tutoring for poorly adjusted children cannot be introduced and maintained in the city of Minneapolis in the same way it can be utilized in the village of Sleepy Eye.

SOME THOUGHTS FOR DESIGNERS OF CROSS-AGE PROGRAMS

To illustrate the complex and subtle ways in which cross-age peer influences differ from same-age influences, Ferguson's (1965) study can be cited. The investigation was based on 18 boys and 18 girls randomly chosen from 2 second grade classrooms in an urban public school and the same number of boys and girls chosen from 2 fifth grade classrooms. Each child served in 2 capacities—first he was a "subject," and then he was an "experimenter." The sample was divided into 4 groups of pairs, one member of the pair served as subject and one member served as experimenter: (1) second grade subjects paired with fifth grade experimenters; (2) fifth grade subjects paired with second grade experimenters; (3) second grade subjects paired with second grade experimenters; and (4) fifth grade subjects paired with fifth grade experimenters. (The design of the study was, of course, not really complete: No second graders were studied who were reinforced by preschool children and no fifth graders were observed when reinforced by eighth graders). The experimental paradigm was based on a procedure popularized by Stevenson and Fahel (1961). Subjects picked up marbles from a bin and dropped them through holes into a second bin. A 1-minute baseline period during which the experimenter silently watched the subject began the experimental session. Then the experimenter was surreptitiously signalled to say "Good" or "Fine" on a 20-second interval schedule for the remaining 6 minutes of the session.

Although the older children generally worked harder at this task than the younger children, the difference between baseline and reinforced performance for the subjects showed a most interesting interaction effect ($p < .001$). Subjects reinforced by non–age mates steadily increased their rate of marble dropping over the 6-minute experimental period in contrast to subjects who were paired with age mates. The performance of the latter children remained steady during this period only slightly above the baseline rate. This interaction is shown in Figure 1. These effects were clearest for boys; the slopes of the gradients looked somewhat different for the older girls. For them, performance evidenced only slight change when the reinforcing agent was a non–age mate, and it actually declined from the baseline level when the agent of reinforcement was an age mate.

Regardless of the fact that marble dropping is a very constrained social situation, this study presents clear evidence of the effects of a cross-age procedure. Even though dyadic effects were not measured (i.e., performance of the reinforcing agent was not measured simultaneously with performance of the subject), the differential power of cross-age and same-age situations is demonstrated unequivocally.

Cross-age interaction tends to differ from same-age interaction in both free play and problem-solving situations. Lougee, Grueneich, and Hartup (1976) examined activity in two-child groups comprised of preschool-aged children. One set of pairs consisted of children who differed in chronological age by less than a month; another set of pairs consisted of children who differed by 16 months. The children were observed during two play periods, each of which was videotaped. The analysis showed that the exchange of social rewards was greater among the younger children in the sample (3-year-olds) in the cross-age condition than in the same-age condition, while, at the same time, such interaction was less frequent among the older children (5-year-olds) in the cross-age situation than in the same-age condition. Attentional behavior also varied with the composition of the dyad, but mainly in the second session: (*1*) among younger children, attention to the task was greater in cross-age dyads than in same-age dyads, while the reverse was found among older children; (*2*) looking at one's partner was less frequent in the cross-age situation than in the same-age situation among younger children, but the opposite was found for the older

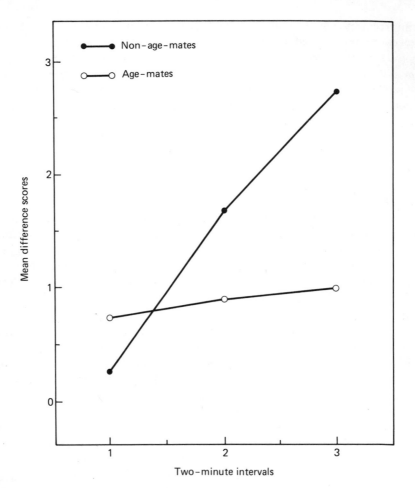

Figure 1 Interaction of age of subject, age of reinforcing agent, and minutes in session for subjects reinforced by peers who were either age-mates or non-age-mates. (From Ferguson, 1965.)

children; and (3) looking at the surroundings was less frequent in the cross-age situation for younger children, but more frequent in the cross-age situation for the older children.

Same- and cross-age interaction in problem-solving situations was studied by Graziano, French, Brownell, and Hartup (in press). Here task performance of elementary school children working in three-person groups was examined under two instructional conditions (group or individual reward). Four types of triads were studied: (1) all first graders; (2) two first graders and one third grader; (3) two third graders and one first grader; and (4) all third graders (the children in each triad were all from different classrooms). Overall, group productivity and the general strategies employed in problem solving did not vary as a function of group composition. Children in mixed-age groups talked with each other less than children in same-age groups, and performance was generally better in group reward than individual reward conditions, but the performance of the group as a whole was not related to composition. The performance of individual group members, however, was different in same- and cross-age triads with the difference occurring mainly among the third grade children. Those who were the only third graders in their triad had higher performance scores, showed more initiative, and assumed strategic roles more frequently than did children whose triads were composed entirely of third graders. Thus, differentiation of individual performance according to the composition of the triad seems to increase with age.

Designers of cross-age programs must thus consider that their programs may have complex effects on both social and cognitive behavior. To strengthen this argument, we can refer to provocative findings from the Primate Laboratory of the University of Wisconsin (Suomi & Harlow, 1972; Novak & Harlow, 1975). Reports from this laboratory suggest that the untoward effects of prolonged isolation on the social development of rhesus monkeys may be reversed by a carefully managed program of contact between the isolated monkey and other monkeys who are noticeably younger in age. The data indicate that such a program of social rehabilitation ameliorates the effects of social isolation more effectively than any other rehabilitation effort yet devised. As yet, the critical features of cross-age interaction that are responsible for the rehabilitation have not been isolated, and the early studies have been based on very small numbers of subjects without benefit of ordinary control groups. Nevertheless, the results are compelling. For primates who evidence low social involvement, poor social skills, and high anxiety in age mate situations, one particular cross-age peer group (i.e., one which is composed of younger individuals) appears to enhance the individual's chances of survival to a greater extent than age-specific interaction. Thus, the peer group that is maximally adaptive for the normal child (i.e., the age-specific group) may be the less adaptive for the socially inadequate child.

This state of affairs is not difficult to explain. For socially incompetent children the reinforcement balance inherent in age-mate interaction probably does not produce an optimal ratio of positive to negative reinforcements. On the contrary, a more optimal balance of reinforcements may be found for such children in interaction with younger peers. This is an assumption, of course, and requires empirical demonstration.

If it can be demonstrated that cross-age interaction contains a more favorable balance of reinforcements than age-specific interaction for a socially withdrawn child, a potential treatment regime then presents itself. One can simply arrange a program of unstructured social interaction between the target child and a small group of children who are younger than he is. Actually, such strategies have been employed by nursery school and kindergarten teachers for many years. In those "open" environments, two practices have been common: (1) socially unskillful children often are assigned to classes of younger rather than older children; (2) ad hoc subgroups are formed within classes in which less skilled youngsters are placed with younger (but not necessarily inept) peers. Both of these procedures maximize the withdrawn child's chances of securing positive reinforcement for selected social overtures and minimize chances of social punishment.

CONCLUSIONS

The following general conclusions can be suggested. Same-age peer contacts appear to possess special adaptational significance for children who live in large, complex societies. The significance of same-age contacts is thought to derive from the more optimal balance of positive and negative feedback that occurs when children interact with age mates than occurs during interaction among children of differing developmental levels. Nevertheless, deliberately designed cross-age interactions may facilitate socialization for children who have encountered certain kinds of developmental difficulties. Such interactions have dyadic properties, however, that should be considered in light of their consequences for the older members of the group as well as for the younger members. Unless cross-age programs provide mutual benefits, they may be difficult to maintain and not completely justified. In any event, consideration of the adaptational value of cross-age interaction is necessary before such programs are implemented.

ACKNOWLEDGMENT

The helpful comments of Everett Waters are gratefully acknowledged.

REFERENCES

Almack, J. C. The influence of intelligence on the selection of associates. *School and Society,* 1922, *16,* 529–530.

Challman, R. C. Factors influencing friendships among preschool children. *Child Development,* 1932, *3,* 146–158.

Chevaleva-Janovskaja, E. Les groupements spontanes d'enfants a l'age prescholaires. *Archives de Psychologie,* 1927, *20,* 219–223.

Crook, J. H. *Social behavior in birds and mammals.* New York: Academic Press, 1970.

Dolhinow, P. J. The development of motor skills and social relationships among primates through play. In J. P. Hill (Ed.), *Minnesota symposia on child psychology.* Vol. 4. Minneapolis: Univ. of Minnesota Press, 1970. Pp. 141–198.

Eibl-Eibesfeldt, I. Buschmannfilme des humanethologischen filmarchivs der Max-Planck-Gesellschaft. M.P.I. fur Verhaltens Physiologie, Humanethologie Abteilung, Percha/Starnberg, West Germany, 1972.

Ferguson, N. R. Age-mate and non-age-mate peers as reinforcing agents for children's performance. Unpublished master's thesis. Univ. of Minnesota, 1965.

Graziano, W., French, D., Brownell, C. A., & Hartup, W. W. Peer interaction in same- and mixed-age triads in relation to chronological age and incentive condition. *Child Development,* in press.

Greenberg, D. J., Hillman, D., & Grice, D. Infant and stranger variables related to stranger anxiety in the first year of life. *Developmental Psychology,* 1973, *9,* 207–212.

Hollingshead, A. B. *Elmtown's youth.* New York: Wiley, 1949.

Jay, P. (Ed.) *Primates: Studies in adaptation and variability.* New York: Holt, 1968.

Lambert, W. E., & Taguchi, Y. Ethnic cleavages among young children. *Journal of Abnormal and Social Psychology,* 1956, *53,* 380–382.

Lott, A. J., & Lott, B. E. The power of liking: Consequences of interpersonal attitudes derived from a liberalized view of secondary reinforcement. In L. Berkowitz (Ed.), *Advances in experimental social psychology.* Vol. 6. New York: Academic Press, 1972. Pp. 109–148.

Lougee, M. D., Grueneich, R., & Hartup, W. W. Social behavior in same-age and mixed-age dyads. In preparation, Univ. of Minnesota, Minneapolis, Minnesota, 1976.

Novak, M. A., & Harlow, H. F. Social recovery of monkeys isolated for the first year of life: Rehabilitation and therapy. *Developmental Psychology,* 1975, *11,* 453–465.

Stevenson, H. W., & Fahel, L. S. The effect of social reinforcement on the performance of institutionalized and noninstitutionalized normal and feebleminded children. *Journal of Personality,* 1961, *29,* 136–147.

Struhsaker, T. T. Social structure among vervet monkeys (*Cercopithecus aethiops*). *Behavior,* 1967, *29,* 83–121.

Suomi, S. J., & Harlow, H. F. Social rehabilitation of isolate-reared monkeys. *Developmental Psychology,* 1972, *6,* 487–496.

Van Lawick-Goodall, J. Chimpanzees of the Gombe Stream Reserve. In I. DeVore (Ed.), *Primate behavior: Field studies of monkeys and apes.* New York: Holt, 1965. Pp. 425–473.

Whiting, B. B. (Ed.) *Six cultures: Studies in child rearing.* New York: Wiley, 1963.

4

Social Skills Theory

Michael Argyle
Oxford University

In this chapter we will give an account of an approach to social behavior that is highly relevant to tutoring, helping, and similar activities. It provides a way of studying social behavior and social competence in terms of the detailed verbal and nonverbal signals of which social performance is composed. This approach pays particular attention to the sequence of interaction and to nonverbal signals and social acts, the meaning of which depends partly on the social context. The social skills approach is linked with two important spheres of application: (*1*) discovering social techniques that are most effective in teaching, interviewing, and the like; and (*2*) determining the best methods for training persons in the use of social skills.

. Social behavior consists of a complex two-way stream of verbal and nonverbal signals that are coordinated in a number of ways. For example, a speaker receives nonverbal feedback on what he is saying at the same time that he is sending verbal signals. Words, sentences, and larger units constitute verbal elements. From the point of view of social performance, these can be classified into different types (Robinson, 1972): (*1*) conveying information about objects, other people, or self; (*2*) asking questions; (*3*) giving instructions or orders of varying degrees of directiveness; (*4*) social routines such as greetings and thanks;

(5) performative utterances such as promising, appointing, giving a verdict, and so forth; (6) informal chat or gossip, making jokes, sustaining and establishing social relationships; (7) expressing emotional states or interpersonal attitudes; and (8) latent messages (e.g., hinting at the importance of the speaker). Every utterance is delivered with appropriate nonverbal accompaniments, so it is not possible to separate completely the two kinds of signals. Verbal behavior, though important, may be of less significance in everyday social interaction than nonverbal behavior. Therefore, more attention will be given to analyzing the nonverbal components of social interaction.

NONVERBAL ELEMENTS OF SOCIAL BEHAVIOR

In this section a brief description will be presented of the various types of nonverbal responses used in social interaction, followed by a discussion of their functions and the impact of nonverbal behavior on the meaning of speech.

Types of Responses

During social behavior every part of the body is active, but certain parts convey more information than others, and do so in distinctive ways. The human face is a specialized communication area that conveys seven main emotions (Ekman, Friesen, & Ellsworth, 1972). It also displays fast-moving accompaniments and commentary on speech (e.g., the raising and lowering of eyebrows). Both intermittent gaze and mutual gaze occur during social interaction. People look in order to collect information, but in doing so they also send information—for example, about their liking for others. Gaze is coordinated with speech, and is used to collect feedback and manage the synchronising of utterances.

Bodily contact is the earliest form of communication used by infants; probably for this reason it is a powerful signal in later life indicating sexual, affiliative, or aggressive attitudes. Bodily contact is controlled by elaborate social rules, and in Western "non-contact" cultures is permitted only in the family, at greetings and other ceremonies, by doctors and other professionals, and in anonymous crowd situations. Spatial behavior can be used to communicate liking for another person by, for example, sitting or standing nearer and in a side-by-side orientation. Status is signalled by the use of symbolic space, by, for example, taking the head of the table. Gestures by the hands can communicate by illustrating the object of discussion, pointing, and by sign language. A close linkage exists between hand movements and speech. The hands also indicate level of arousal, display truncated acts of touching, and "autistic" gestures of self-touching are thought to show attitudes towards the self.

Other parts of the body function in different ways. For example, head nods indicate agreement and willingness for the other to continue speaking. Bodily posture varies mainly along the tense—relaxed dimension. A relaxed posture is used by the higher-status person in an encounter and comes to signal status. The feet do not convey much information, though they can indicate level of arousal. Aspects of appearance such as clothes, hair, skin, and badges convey information about self (social status, occupation, and personality), and are basic forms of self-presentation.

Nonverbal aspects of speech are important in communication. The same words can be delivered in quite different ways by varying pitch, stress, and timing. Linguists distinguish between prosodic and "paralinguistic" sounds (Crystal, 1969). Prosodic signals are pitch and stress patterns and pauses and timing that affect the meaning of sentences. Paralinguistic signals include emotions ex pressed by tone of voice, personality characteristics expressed by voice quality, speech errors, and the like. The emotional state of the speaker reading a neutral passage can be recognized from a tape recording (Davitz, 1964). Thus, anxious people speak fast and in a breathy way (a high frequency distribution) and make speech errors. A dominant or angry person speaks loudly, slowly, and with a lower frequency distribution (Argyle, 1975). Accent indicates cultural and educational origins.

How finely do we need to subdivide nonverbal signals for research purposes? Although subjects can enact 40 distinct emotional states using the face, only 7 groups can be recognized by decoders (Osgood, 1966). On the other hand, a larger number of facial signals accompany speech—Birdwhistell (1971) lists 57 different categories. Evidence is not yet available concerning how many of these signals convey information successfully. Some small signals are certainly impor-tant—such as expansion of the pupils of the eyes and small shifts of gaze. Hand movements can be very intricate, but only the main movements may communi-cate effectively. As for discrimination of temporal units, elements down to one-fourth of a second can be perceived, though they usually form part of longer social acts. These nonverbal social signals are similar to signals used by animals, suggesting that they may have a partly innate origin. The seven facial expressions for emotion are found in all or most cultures (Ekman *et al.,* 1972), and laughing, smiling, and crying are found in blind infants (Eibl-Eibesfeldt, 1972). Expressive behavior that depends on the autonomic system is probably innate—pupil dilation, perspiring, bodily excitement, and tense posture, for example. On the other hand, meaning of gestures varies greatly from culture to culture, especially where arbitrary sign languages are used. Most social signals contain both innate and learned components. For example, greetings vary greatly across cultures, but they nearly always involve face-to-face approach, touching, mutual gaze, and some verbal formula. Speech itself is recognized now to have universal structures that enable specific languages to be acquired. Although partly innate and animal-like signals are used widely in human social behavior, they are used in a more complex way and reflect the operation of plans and rules.

Functions of Nonverbal Communication

Nonverbal communication in man is used to manage the immediate social situation, to support verbal communication, and to replace verbal communication. Animals conduct their entire social life by means of nonverbal communication, and it appears that human beings use rather similar signals to establish a similar set of relationships.

Managing the Social Situation

Nonverbal communication can be used to indicate a desired attitude, such as inferior–superior or like–dislike. Thus, a superior attitude can be conveyed by appropriate posture (body erect, head raised), facial expression (unsmiling, "haughty"), tone of voice (loud, "commanding"), appearance (clothes indicating high status), and eye contact (staring the other down). In one study the use of verbal and nonverbal signals for communicating interpersonal attitudes was investigated (Argyle, Salter, Nicholson, Williams, & Burgess, 1970). It was found that in judgments of inferior or superior status the variance due to nonverbal cues was about 12 times the variance due to verbal cues. Similar results were obtained in later experiments using friendly–hostile messages (Argyle, Alkema, & Gilmour, 1972).

Emotions are simply states of the individual, such as anger, depression, anxiety, or joy. A person may try to conceal his true emotional condition, but it is impossible to control autonomic cues. Emotional states can be conveyed by speech ("I am feeling very happy"), but statements probably will not be believed unless supported by appropriate nonverbal communication. By contrast, nonverbal communication can convey the message without speech. Information can also be employed about an interactor's status, group membership, occupation, personality, or sexual availability. Again, self-presentation by nonverbal communication is basically a matter of using signals that are understood to stand for the real thing (Goffman, 1956).

Sustaining Verbal Communication

Speech plays a central role in most human social behavior, but many linguists do not always appreciate the importance of the role played by nonverbal communication in conversation. Abercrombie (1968) has said, "we speak with our vocal organs, but we converse with our whole body" (p. 55). Moreover, a person would not be accepted as speaking a language properly (indeed he would scarcely be understood) if he did not deliver his sentences in the pitch pattern, stress pattern, and temporal pattern of grouping and pausing proper for that language. Kinesic signals can affect the meaning of a sentence by providing the punctuation, displaying the grouping of phrases and the grammatical structure, pointing to people or objects, providing emphasis, illustrating shapes or movements, and commenting on the utterance, for example, indicating whether it is supposed to be funny or serious (Ekman & Friesen, 1969). Graham and Argyle (1975) found that hand movements added to the efficiency with which two-dimensional designs and shapes could be communicated.

Scheflen (1965) postulated that nonverbal communication has a hierarchical, three-level structure corresponding to sentences, paragraphs, and longer sequences of speech. Bodily movements are coordinated with speech; a sentence may be accompanied by related hand or head positions. These movements have a hierarchical structure in which smaller verbal and bodily signals are organized into larger and coordinated groupings of both as shown in Table 1. Frame-by-frame analyses of small movements of hands, head, eyes, and so forth, in relation to speech have provided evidence of "interactional synchrony"—that is, coordination of bodily movements between speaker and listener over periods of time corresponding to sentences and even words (Kendon, 1971a, b). Kendon (1971b) suggests that in addition to displaying the structure of utterances these movements make the speaker more interesting, hold the listener's attention, and give advance warning of the kind of utterance that is to come.

When two or more people are conversing, they take turns speaking and usually manage to achieve a fairly smooth, "synchronizing" sequence of utterances without too many interruptions and silences. When people first meet, it is unlikely that their spontaneous styles of speaking will fit together; adjustments must be made—one person must speak less, another must speak faster, and so on. This is all managed by a simple system of nonverbal signalling, the main cues being nods, grunts, and shifts of gaze. For example, at a grammatical pause a speaker will look up to see if the others are willing for him to carry on speaking; if so, they will nod and grunt. Just before the end of an utterance, a speaker gives a rather more prolonged gaze at the others. If this system fails, interruptions will take place and there is a struggle for the floor (Kendon, 1967).

Table 1
Equivalent Verbal and Nonverbal Units

Verbal	Nonverbal
1. Paragraph, or long unit of speech	Postural position
2. Sentence	Head or arm position
3. Words, phrases	Hand movements, facial expressions, gaze shifts, etc.

Someone who is speaking needs intermittent but regular feedback about others' responses so he can modify his utterances accordingly. He needs to know whether the listeners understand, believe, disbelieve, are surprised or bored, agree or disagree, are pleased or annoyed. This information could be provided by *sotto voce* verbal muttering, but is in fact obtained by careful study of the other's face: Eyebrow movements signal surprise, puzzlement, and so on, and the mouth indicates pleasure and displeasure. When the other person is invisible, as in telephone conversation, visual signals are unavailable and more verbalized "listening behavior" is used: "I see," "really?", "how interesting" (Argyle, Lalljee, & Cook, 1968). For a conversation to be sustained, the persons involved must provide intermittent evidence that they are still attending to others. To signal attentiveness interactors use proximity, orientation, gaze, head nods, alert posture, and bodily movements (Argyle, 1972b).

SEQUENCES OF BEHAVIOR

The S–R Model

The simplest model for sequences of social behavior is the stimulus–response (S–R) model, in which each act by A is a response to the latest act by B, as shown in Figure 1. It is possible to find such sequences in social interaction. For example, Bales (1953) found that asking opinions led to giving opinions in 46% of the cases, which in turn led to agreement in 49% of the cases. One important sequence of this kind is response matching (a special form of imitation). One interactor tends to match the behavior of another in length of utterances, use of interruptions, silence, agreeing and disagreeing, posture and gestures adopted, and so on. This is a two-way influence, but it is likely that a person of lower status or self-esteem would follow another person. A second sequence involves reinforcement. If Person A smiles, nods, leans forward, or makes approving noises after Person B's response, B will emit this behavior more often. Thus, B can be induced to talk more, offer opinions, or talk about certain topics. The experimental literature suggests that this influence is rapid, reciprocal, and lies largely outside the conscious awareness of the senders or receivers of reinforcement (Argyle, 1969). It is possible to extend the S–R model to take account of the influence of stimuli other than the preceding stimulus (Clarke, 1975).

The S–R approach fails to deal with three features of interaction. First, the sequence of verbal and nonverbal events are complex and simultaneous—apart from verbal utterances, it is not possible to isolate distinct S's or R's. For example, while an utterance is being delivered, nonverbal feedback affects the content and manner of delivery of later parts of the same utterance. Second, interactors have plans and purposes; their successive acts are linked by common

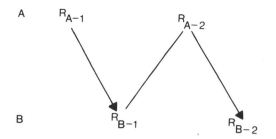

Figure 1 The stimulus–response model of social interaction.

motivation and modified by feedback. Third, social interaction has in some respects a "phrase structure" like language. That is, some sequences make complete wholes (e.g., a greetings sequence); others, though separated in time, are linked by embedded material.

Some researchers have tried to solve these problems by looking for a "generative grammar" of social behavior parallel to that for language. A number of interesting parallels between verbal behavior and social behavior have been found. The meaning of bodily acts varies with the situation and their position in a sequence of interaction—though some facial expressions and gestures do have fairly stable meanings (Birdwhistell, 1971). Goffman (1971) provided illustrations on the operation of phrase structure, embedded sequences, and transformations of familiar sequences of social behavior, as in the case of greetings and farewells. Evidently there are rules that limit which social responses may follow one another, as well as a number of standard sequences of four or five moves. On the other hand, there is no evidence yet of anything resembling a "grammar" of social behavior, or of units corresponding to parts of speech, and there is a very important difference between the generation of sentences and the generation of interaction sequences. A social sequence is the work of two people who may not share an initial plan but still manage to accommodate to one another and produce an acceptable sequence of events (Argyle, 1975).

The Social Skills Model

The social skills approach to social interaction was put forward by Argyle and Kendon (1967) and developed in Argyle (1969). We will not repeat the details here, but will show how it can be used as a conceptual model of social interaction. The model is represented in Figure 2. The social skills model is based on an analogy with serial motor skills (e.g., driving a car), except that quite different behavior is involved and more than one person is engaged at the same time.

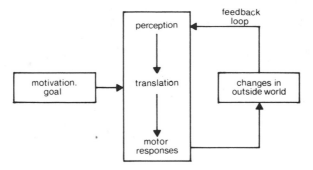

Figure 2 The social skills model of social interaction.

Components of the Social Skills Model

Priority is given in the model to motivation. It is postulated that each interactor has goals for a social encounter that can be restated in terms of the responses he wants others to produce. An interviewer wants candidates to produce accurate and relevant information, just as a motorist wants a car to follow a particular route at a certain speed.

A social interactor emits a stream of verbal and nonverbal motor (social) responses. As in the case of motor skills, these social responses have a hierarchical structure, large units (giving an interview) being composed of smaller units (individual questions, single smiles, head nods). The process is similar to sending Morse code—signals are delivered not as single letters but as words or phrases.

In motor skills there is continuous or intermittent monitoring of outcomes followed by corrective action. Such perception and feedback is also true of social behavior: The other's speech is listened to and his nonverbal signals are watched carefully. Research is described subsequently showing how the pattern of gaze is coordinated with speech so as to collect feedback when it is needed.

As shown in Figure 2, every skill involves a central cognitive store of information that is translated into appropriate corrective action for each kind of feedback. A person steering a rowboat has to learn which way to pull the oars to correct the boat's direction. Most people can deal with an individual who talks too little or talks too much and with other everyday problems of interaction. If someone cannot deal with such problems, he can be taught by use of techniques to be explained later.

The social skills model suggests that the monitoring of another's reactions is an essential part of social performance. The other's verbal signals are mainly heard, but his nonverbal signals mainly are seen—the exceptions being the nonverbal aspects of speech, and touch. It was this implication of the social skill model that directed us towards the study of gaze in social interaction. In dyadic interaction each person looks about 55% of the time; mutual gaze occupies about 25% of the time (Argyle & Ingham, 1972). Long glances are given by speakers at the ends of utterances; it is likely that one function of these is to collect feedback on reactions to the utterance (Kendon, 1967). Although people look in order to collect information, the act of looking also sends information to the other. Argyle, Ingham, Alkema, and McCallin (1973) separated the different functions of gaze in an experiment in which two persons conversed across a one-way screen. It was found that the person who could see looked 65% of the time while the person who could not see looked 23% of the time. We deduced that the person who could see is looking to collect information, while the person who could not is looking to send information. Kendon (1967) found that if a terminal gaze was not given by a speaker, there was a long pause before the other replied. Other information sent by gaze is of two main kinds: first, comments on and supplementation of the verbal message (e.g., adding emphasis at particular points, as is done also by tone of voice and gestures); second, communication of attitudes towards the other, as is done also by facial expression.

Gaze also acts as a signal for interpersonal attitudes. If A likes B, he looks more at B, and B correctly decodes this in terms of liking. But avoidance forces limit how much A can look at B without causing anxiety and discomfort. Argyle and Dean (1965) proposed that gaze acts as one signal for intimacy with others It was predicted that gaze would increase with the distance between two persons; this was found to be the case, and was confirmed in later experiments. In the Argyle and Ingham (1972) study, gaze reached an asymptote of about 65% at 10 feet. Gaze can signal other interpersonal attitudes such as dominance, threat, and love, but these depend on the use of other signals or on the timing of glances (Argyle & Cook, 1975).

Limitations and Extensions of the Social Skills Model

The social skills model has been useful in drawing attention to the feedback process and the importance of gaze, in suggesting ways in which people may be socially incompetent, and in devising methods of social skills training. As it stands, the model cannot explain all the phenomena of interaction; we shall now consider the model's inadequacies and possible extensions.

First, consider the importance of taking the role of the other. Drivers of cars don't worry about what their cars think of their driving, but social interactors are often concerned about the reactions of others. A person who is able to see another's point of view is more effective at certain social tasks (Feffer & Suchotliffe, 1966); those who have experienced some form of distress are more helpful to others in the same condition (Lenrow, 1965). Concern with meta-perception (perceiving the other's perceptions) occurs under certain conditions, for example, being assessed and being with an older person (Argyle & Williams, 1969). Although these kinds of behavior require extra cognitive processes, they can be seen as examples of social skills which have as their goal a change in the perceptions or feelings of another. Special cognitive ability is required in such cases—the ability to perceive another's inner state accurately.

Secondly, the independent activity of the other person affects social interaction. The social skills model works very nicely for primarily one-way skills like interviewing and teaching. What happens though, when two people have independent plans for an encounter? Unless persons synchronize their social moves very closely, there will be no social behavior. They must time their utterances properly, talk about the same subject, engage in the same activity, follow questions by answers, adopt appropriate spatial positions, and in a number of other ways accommodate to each other. Neither the social skills model nor any other model has succeeded so far in providing a complete analysis of the sequence of interaction, which would make it possible to predict the course of interaction. This may indeed be impossible, since, like language, each sequence of social behavior has never occurred before and is created afresh. It appears necessary to introduce additional concepts for the analysis of interaction sequences. Scheflen (1965) has suggested a hierarchy of units of individual performance. This could be extended to a hierarchical set of units of interaction. One such unit would be the "social episode." Examples are entertaining visitors for the evening, having a meal, having one course of the meal, asking another about his job, and so forth. Each social episode (of whatever size) is recognized as a bounded unit of interaction, and there are rules governing behavior within it.

A third limitation of the social skills model concerns the importance of rules governing particular situations. All social behavior takes place in specific social situations, and in every culture rules govern behavior in common situations. Barker and Wright (1954) found 800 standard "behavior settings" (e.g., church, drug store) in a small town in Kansas, each setting having its own rules. Unless all persons present agree on the definition of the situation and the rules to be followed, chaos usually ensues. As in the case of games, rules develop in the culture because they provide a satisfactory way of handling certain situations. We can discover which rules are essential by breaking them to see what happens (Garfinkel, 1963). We have found that there is a difference between rules and conventions. Certain rules seem basic to each situation. For example, at an interview it really does not matter if the candidate wears the wrong clothes, but it does matter if he does not tell the truth or refuses to speak at all. Similarly, if a guest at a meal uses the wrong implements it does not matter very much, but if he refuses to eat or is rude to the other guests, it does matter (Argyle, 1973).

THE EFFECTS OF SOCIAL SKILLS

The effects of different styles of social behavior can be studied quantitatively in the case of many professional social skills. Thus, selection interviewers vary in the validity of their ratings, and supervisors produce widely varying levels of absenteeism, labor turnover, and complaints (Fleishman & Harris, 1962). The social skills model suggests a number of ways in which social competence might fail, corresponding to the different elements of the model. Thus, there could be lack of perceptual sensitivity, inability to make the social responses, or failure to react appropriately to feedback. We shall illustrate some principles from research on skills relevant to the theme of our book (teaching, helping and making friends, and failures of social skills in neurotics).

Teaching

Two principles will be illustrated here: identifying the goals sought with the responses of others, and the need for sensitivity to their reactions. Teaching seems to have one primary goal and two subsidiary ones. The primary goal is to increase the knowledge, understanding, or skills of pupils. The subsidiary goals are to increase motivation and interest of pupils, and to maintain order and discipline. These goals are subsidiary in the sense that the primary goal cannot be attained without them. Further goals could be listed, for example, that pupils enjoy the classes and they they show development in mental health, self-control or other aspects of personality. The commonest source of failure in teaching is in problems of discipline. There is evidence that young teachers (especially females) find this the most difficult problem in teaching; it is probably the main reason for their abandoning the profession. The specific skills required for teaching can be ascertained by their contribution in reaching these three main goals.

Several studies have compared the general style of classroom behavior of effective and ineffective teachers. Pupils like their teachers better and learn more if the teachers are, for example, friendly, warm, fair, stimulating, imaginative, and expert in their subject (Ryans, 1962). A study of Canadian university students found that the teaching techniques that were most disliked were the following: ignoring, discouraging and restricting questions; reacting to students with ridicule, hostility, and arrogance; squelching students; interrupting contributions or failing to promote discussions or questions (Crawford & Signori, 1962). Teachers need to be sensitive to the reactions of their pupils. Jecker, Maccoby, and Breitrose (1965) found that many experienced teachers were very insensitive to the facial and gestural cues for understanding and not understanding; but the skill could be improved quite easily by training.

What are the implications of the social skills approach for cross-age tutoring (older children teaching younger)? At first it might be expected that children would be quite incompetent because of their limited subject knowledge and lack of relevant social skills. On the other hand, the brighter children probably do have sufficient knowledge to teach others. Some children will have acquired relevant social skills from having younger siblings or from being leaders of a peer group. In any case, the social skills involved in teaching one person are much less demanding than those involved in teaching an entire class. Children younger than 8 or 9 years of age have limited ability in taking the role of the other, a skill which is probably very important in teaching. On the other hand, the cognitive structure of older children is more similar to that of the pupil than is the cognitive structure of adult teachers. Experiments have found that similarity in cognitive constructs makes communication much easier (Bonarius, 1965). There are many reasons for expecting that tutoring would help the tutor not only in learning academic material but also in acquiring useful social skills and in gaining confidence. We conclude that cross-age tutoring often would be beneficial for the tutor but would not always be an efficient way to teach a younger pupil unless the tutor were above average in both intelligence and social skills. Older children—especially those who have younger siblings or who are leaders of informal groups—are more likely to have the characteristics required for effective tutoring.

Helping and Friendship

Previous research has shown the importance of imitation, reciprocity, and dependence of the other in affecting the motivation of the helper (Krebs, 1970; Macauley & Berkowitz, 1970). The social skills approach is basically concerned with the effectiveness of the helper. Consideration of a wide variety of skills leads to the conclusion that good intentions are not enough; in order to deal successfully with other persons, quite specific social skills are needed. These skills are not obvious to common sense and probably could not be acquired in the course of normal socialization (Argyle, 1972a). The possession of social skills affects motivation to help as well as effectiveness of the help. Burley (1976) found that willingness to take the blame for another person was predicted better by a "social intelligence" scale than by an "other-orientation" scale. One study found that children were more likely to help another child in distress if they had experienced the same trouble themselves (Lenrow, 1965). In the formation of friendship, nonverbal signals are important in communicating attitudes of liking via facial expression, proximity, and gaze. These signals are readily decoded and may be reciprocated. Social skills theory also emphasizes the need for smooth synchronizing of patterns of social performance in friendship. Schutz (1958), among others, has constructed compatible and incompatible combinations of persons (e.g., persons are compatible if only one is very dominant and if they have similar desires for intimacy). As two people come to know each other better and spend more time together, there must be an increasing degree of synchronizing. The social skills approach envisages the possibility of a wide range of relationships based on a variety of shared activities and types of mutual accommodation.

Behavioral Maladjustment

It is likely that social inadequacy is a primary source of difficulty in the case of neurotics. Social skills training might be a useful form of treatment for such persons. Bryant and Trower (1974) surveyed the intake of a mental hospital for a period of time, and assessed social skills of new patients. Of the non-psychotics, 20% were thought to be suffering primarily from social inadequacy; a further 20% were socially inadequate and had other symptoms. Psychiatrists and clinical psychologists thought that 30% would benefit from social skills training.

Forms of social inadequacy found in mental patients can be related to the components of social skills presented earlier. The main forms of failure were as follows: inexpressive or hostile nonverbal signals; failures of synchronizing of utterances (including interrupting, long pauses, and failure to "hand over" to the next speaker); low rewardingness; perception failure (including aversion of gaze), failure of common skill sequences, failure to handle common social episodes (such as getting to know people, and specific professional social skills); performance disrupted by anxiety; ignorance of rules governing common social situations; failures of self-presentation (e.g. presented bogus self-image or was overly concerned with self-presentation).

ACQUISITION OF SOCIAL SKILLS

If social behavior follows the same principles as motor skills, then learning of social skills should be similar to the learning of motor skills. Many of the professional skills needed on the job are acquired simply by doing them, no doubt by a process of trial and error assisted by modeling. We have studied a number of cases of such learning. For example, we found that the goods sold by new salesgirls increased by 40% to 60% in 8 months.

Certain aspects of social skills appear to have innate components. Thus, there seems to be an unlearned ability to send and receive facial signals and to use the eyes and respond to another's eyes as a stimulus. On the other hand, gestures are almost entirely learned. A similar form seems to exist in all cultures for greetings, as for language; there is also some evidence of universal rules and structures for social behavior.

Experiences in the family affect later social behavior in a number of ways. Early attachment to the mother appears to be necessary for later social attachments to take place, though it is not clear why this is so. Attachments involve closely coordinated skills in an intimate relationship that is highly rewarding. Parents are taken as models, especially when leader or dominant roles are played. Subordinate roles in the family are learned as well, and the style of behavior acquired is generalized to other similar situations. Relations with the opposite sex are affected by the observed relation between the parents (Argyle, 1969). The processes of role playing and modeling described above occur in other forms of social skills training, and will be described later.

From an early age children interact with peers; cooperative play is found by the age of two. Studies of helping behavior show that at age four or five about 25–30% of children will share food or toys with other children or help another in an emergency (Krebs, 1970). Flavell (1968) found that children of 3 or 4 years of age had little ability to take the role of the other (to realize that another person had a different visual perspective), but that role taking skills increased during childhood and adolescence. How much these changes are due to cognitive maturation and how much to some kind of social learning is not known.

Attachment to friends and groups increases during childhood and reaches a peak during adolescence. Skills of group behavior, including cooperation, making friends, and leadership, presumably develop via a number of processes of social learning. In a questionnaire study of reactions to social problem situations, McPhail (1967) found that crude, dominating solutions reached a height at the age of 13 and were rapidly replaced by more skilled, "mature" solutions.

SOCIAL SKILLS TRAINING

Special training in social skills is commonly given to teachers, interviewers, and many others who work with people. It is increasingly being given to mental patients. There are several widely used components of social skill training that will be discussed briefly.

Role playing is a technique used for training interviewers, teachers, mental patients, and others. It is commonly used in "assertiveness training." Role playing training usually consists of a series of sessions lasting from one to three hours. In each session a particular aspect of the skill or a particular problem situation is dealt with. The first phase of role playing includes a lecture, discussion, demonstration, tape recording or a film about a particular aspect of the skill. This is particularly important when an unfamiliar skill is being taught or when rather subtle social techniques are involved. In the second phase a problem situation is defined, and trainees role play with stooges for about 10 or 15 minutes each. The background to the situation may be supplied by written materials such as the application forms of candidates for interview or background information about personnel problems. The stooges may be carefully trained beforehand to provide various problems, such as talking too much or having elaborate and plausible excuses. The third phase consists of a feedback session that includes verbal comments by the trainer, discussion with the other trainees, and playback of audio- or videotapes. Verbal feedback is used to draw attention (constructively and tactfully) to what the trainee was doing wrong and to suggest alternative styles of behavior. Tape recordings provide clear evidence for the accuracy of the comments (Argyle, 1972a). The basic role playing procedures can be elaborated in various ways.

Many experimental before-and-after studies have evaluated this type of training. There is no doubt that role playing is effective in improving professional skills (Argyle, 1969). Various kinds of modeling, coaching, and role play have been found successful in assertion training for students (Friedman, 1972), though McFall and Twentyman (1973) found that audio or videotape models did not add to the effectiveness of role playing and coaching. Studies of the treatment of real mental patients by social skills training have usually studied a combination of role playing, coaching, and modeling, and this combination is more effective than psychotherapy (Argyle, Trower, & Bryant, 1974; Gutride, Goldstein, & Hunter, 1973). Sarason (1968) found that the combination of modeling and role playing was most effective for teaching delinquents social skills such as applying for a job and dealing with the boss.

Several other techniques are available for social skills training. Desensitization has been used to help persons with social phobias such as anxiety about public speaking (Paul, 1966). One aspect of social skills training is increasing one's sensitivity to social signals, which is a central aspect of T-group training (Bunker, 1965). It is also possible to increase sensitivity by shorter and simpler methods. Davitz (1964) succeeded in increasing sensitivity to emotions in tone of voice by several 15-minute sessions in which trainees listened to different emotions expressed on tapes, made similar tapes themselves, and then discussed them in a group. Jecker *et al.* (1965) increased teachers' accuracy of judging children's understanding by pointing out the facial and gestural cues in 45-second films of children. Less elaborate methods based on discussion and role playing are currently being used in schools. Methods are also being explored in which a person can teach himself social skills by providing his own feedback and reward.

REFERENCES

Abercrombie, K. Paralanguage. *British Journal of Disordered Communication,* 1968, *3,* 55–59.

Argyle, M. *Social interaction.* London: Methuen (New York: Atherton), 1969.

Argyle, M. *The psychology of interpersonal behavior.* London: Penguin Books, 1972. (a)

Argyle, M. Non-verbal communication in human social interaction. In R. A. Hinde (Ed.), *Non-verbal communication.* New York: Cambridge Univ. Press, 1972(b). Pp. 243–268.

Argyle, M. The syntaxes of bodily communication. *International Journal of Psycholinguistics,* 1973, *2,* 71–91.

Argyle, M. *Bodily communication.* London: Methuen, 1975.

Argyle, M., Alkema, F., & Gilmour, R. The communication of friendly and hostile attitudes by verbal and non-verbal signals. *European Journal of Social Psychology,* 1972, *1,* 385–402.

Argyle, M., & Cook, M. *Gaze and mutual gaze.* New York: Cambridge Univ. Press, 1975.

Argyle, M., & Dean, J. Eye-contact, distance and affiliation. *Sociometry,* 1965, *28,* 289–304.

Argyle, M., & Ingham, R. Gaze, mutual gaze and proximity. *Semiotica*, 1972, *1*, 32–49.

Argyle, M., Ingham, R., Alkema, F., & McCallin, M. The different functions of gaze. *Semiotica*, 1973, *7*, 19–32.

Argyle, M. & Kendon, A. The experimental analysis of social performance. In L. Berkowitz (Ed.), *Advances in experimental social psychology*. Vol. 3. New York: Academic Press, 1967. Pp. 55–98.

Argyle, M., Lalljee, M., & Cook, M. The effects of visibility on interaction in a dyad. *Human Relations*, 1968, *21*, 3–17.

Argyle, M., Salter, V., Nicholson, H., Williams, M., & Burgess, P. The communication of inferior and superior attitudes by verbal and non-verbal signals. *British Journal of Social and Clinical Psychology*, 1970, *9*, 221–231.

Argyle, M., Trower, P., & Bryant, B. Explorations in the treatment of personality disorders and neuroses by social skills training. *British Journal of Medical Psychology*, 1974, *47*, 63–72.

Argyle, M., & Williams, M. Observer or observed? A reversible perspective in person perception. *Sociometry*, 1969, *32*, 396–412.

Bales, R. The equilibrium problem in small groups. In T. Parsons, R. Bales, & E. Shils (Eds.), *Working papers in the theory of action*. Glencoe, Illinois: Free Press, 1953. Pp. 111–161.

Barker, R., & Wright, H. *Midwest and its children, the psychological ecology of an American town*. New York: Harper, 1954.

Birdwhistell, R. *Kinesics and context*. Philadelphia: Univ. of Pennsylvania Press, 1971.

Bonarius, J. Research in the personal construct theory of George A. Kelly: role construct repertory test and basic theory. In B. A. Maher (Ed.), *Progress in experimental personality research*. Vol. 2. New York: Academic Press, 1965. Pp. 2–46.

Bunker, D. The effects of laboratory education upon individual behavior. In E. Schien, & W. Bennis (Eds.), *Personal learning and organizational change through group methods*. New York: Wiley, 1965, Pp. 255–267.

Bryant, B., & Trower, P. Social difficulty in a student population. *British Journal of Educational Psychology*, 1974, *44*, 13–21.

Burley, P. M. The role of social intelligence in helping behavior. Unpublished D. Phil. thesis, Oxford Univ., 1976.

Clarke, D. D. The use and recognition of sequential structure in dialogue. *British Journal of Social and Clinical Psychology*, 1975, *14*, 333–339.

Crawford, D. G., & Signori, E. I. An application of the critical incident technique to university teaching. *Canadian Psychologist*, 1962, *3*, 1–13.

Crystal, D. *Prosodic systems and intonation in English*. London: Cambridge Univ. Press, 1969.

Davitz, J. *The communication of emotional meaning*. New York: McGraw-Hill, 1964.

Eibl-Eibesfeldt, I. Similarities and differences between cultures in expressive movement. In R. Hinde (Ed.), *Non-verbal communication*. New York: Cambridge Univ. Press, 1972. Pp. 297–312.

Ekman, P., & Friesen, W. The repertoire of non-verbal behavior: categories, usage and coding. *Semiotica*, 1969, *1*, 49–98.

Ekman, P., Friesen, W., & Ellsworth, P. *Emotions in the human face*. Oxford: Pergamon, 1972.

Feffer, M., & Suchotliff, L. Decentering implications of social interaction. *Journal of Personality and Social Psychology*, 1966, *4*, 415–422.

Flavell, J. *The development of role-taking and communication skills in children*. New York: Wiley, 1968.

Fleishman, E., & Harris, E. Patterns of leadership behavior related to employee grievances and turnover. *Personnel Psychology,* 1962, *15,* 43–56.

Friedman, P. The effects of modeling, role playing and participation on behavior change. In B. A. Maher (Ed.), *Progress in experimental personality research.* Vol. 6. New York: Academic Press, 1972. Pp. 42–81.

Garfinkel, H. Trust and stable actions. In O. J. Harvey (Ed.), *Motivational and social interaction.* New York: Ronald, 1963. Pp. 187–238.

Goffman, E. *The presentation of self in everyday life.* Edinburgh: Edinburgh Univ. Press, 1956.

Goffman, E. *Relations in public.* Harmondsworth: Allen Lane, 1971.

Graham, J. A., & Argyle, M. A cross-cultural study of the communication of extra-verbal meaning of gestures. *Journal of Human Movement Studies,* 1975, *1,* 33–39.

Gutride, M., Goldstein, A., & Hunter, G. The use of modeling and role-playing to increase social interaction among asocial psychiatric patients. *Journal of Consulting and Clinical Psychology,* 1973, *40,* 408–415.

Jecker, J., Maccoby, N., & Breitrose, H. Improving accuracy in interpreting non-verbal cues of comprehension. *Psychology in the Schools,* 1965, *2,* 239–244.

Kendon, A. Some functions of gaze direction in social interaction. *Acta Psychologica,* 1967, *26,* 1–47.

Kendon, A. The role of visible behavior in the organization of social interaction. In M. von Cranach & I. Vine (Eds.), *Symposium on human communication.* New York: Academic Press, 1971. Pp. 29–74. (a)

Kendon, A. Some relationships between body motion and speech: an analysis of an example. In A. Siegman, & B. Pope (Eds.), *Studies in dyadic communication.* Oxford: Pergamon, 1971. Pp. 177–210. (b)

Krebs, D. Altruism—an examination of the concept and a review of the literature. *Psychological Bulletin,* 1970, *73,* 258–302.

Lenrow, P. Studies in sympathy. In S. Tomkins, & C. Izard (Eds.), *Affect, cognition and personality.* London: Tavistock, 1965. Pp. 264–294.

Macauley, J., & Berkowitz, L. (Eds.) *Altruism and helping behavior.* New York: Academic Press, 1970.

McFall, R., & Twentyman, C. Four experiments on the relative contributions of rehearsal, modeling and coaching to assertive training. *Journal of Abnormal Psychology,* 1973, *81,* 199–218.

McPhail, P. The development of social skill in adolescence. Unpublished manuscript, Oxford Department of Education, 1967.

Osgood, C. Dimensionality of the semantic space for communication via facial expressions. *Scandinavian Journal of Psychology,* 1966, *7,* 1–30.

Paul, G. *Insight vs. desensitization in psychotherapy.* Stanford, California: Stanford Univ. Press, 1966.

Robinson, P. *The social psychology of language.* London: Penguin Books, 1972.

Ryans, D. *Characteristics of teachers.* Washington, D. C.: American Council on Education, 1962.

Sarason, I. Verbal learning, modeling and juvenile delinquency. *American Psychologist,* 1968, *23,* 254–266.

Scheflen, A. *Stream and structure of communicational behavior.* Commonwealth of Pennsylvania: Eastern Pennsylvania Psychiatric Institute, 1965.

Schutz, W. *FIRO: A three dimensional theory of interpersonal behavior.* New York: Holt, 1958.

II

Helping Relationships
with Children

An understanding of the processes and consequences involved in helping relationships with children can be reached only by way of a great deal of empirical research. The wide range of current research being conducted on questions related to tutoring by children is well represented by the studies reported in the second section of this book. The four chapters in this section describe several research studies conducted by the authors themselves. Studies reported in three of the chapters stem from questions asked about some aspect of teaching by children, but results of these experiments have general scientific significance as well. Findings from these studies contribute to our understanding of the psychological processes in tutoring, and also suggest ways that tutoring programs in the schools can be improved.

In the introduction to the first section it was emphasized that tutoring by children in the natural school setting is a very complex affair. A large number of psychological processes are involved, and many factors influence the ultimate outcome of the interaction. In the natural tutoring situation all these unknown factors are free to vary in an uncontrolled fashion. To reduce such complexity to more manageable proportions, the investigator often is forced to simplify the problem. An adequate understanding of a complex behavioral phenomenon often necessitates studying it experimentally under well controlled conditions. Following this strategy, authors of the first three chapters in this section designed research to test specific hypotheses relevant to tutoring by children. Only the last chapter in this section deals with research conducted in the natural school setting: The chapter by Cowen describes the rationale and results of several programs that provide helping relationships for children with academic or behavioral problems in school.

In the first chapter in this section, Feshbach reports research designed to study the process by which tutoring achieves its effects. Several experiments explored individual differences in the teaching style used by young children when teaching another child. Data recorded during the instructional session consisted of the spontaneous use of positive and negative verbal reinforcement by the child doing the teaching. A great deal of previous research has shown that social class membership and ethnic background are related strongly to academic performance in school; therefore, these variables were examined systematically in the research undertaken.

In Feshbach's studies a 4-year-old child taught a 3-year-old child how to solve a simple puzzle in a standardized instructional setting. Since children of this young age have not yet attended school, their reinforcement style should reflect primarily their socialization experiences in the home.

Results of these studies revealed clear and consistent differences in the teaching style used by children as a function of their social class and ethnic background. Of the four groups investigated (middle- and lower-class whites; middle- and lower-class blacks), middle-class white children used a greater number of positive reinforcements during the teaching than did any of the other three groups. Furthermore, the middle-class white group was the only one of the four groups that used a greater number of positive than negative reinforcements while teaching. The reinforcement style that mothers used when teaching their 4-year-old children disclosed the same pattern as found for their children: The amount and type of verbal reinforcement used in teaching was related to social class and ethnic background. Thus, the teaching style used by children seems to be modeled after the reinforcement style used by their parents.

In other research using the same standard teaching paradigm, the behavior of successful and problem readers was observed while they taught another child. The basic findings of Feshbach's research were extended further by observing teaching styles of children from social groups which differ in academic achievement within their own cultures, and by then comparing these results across three countries: United States, Israel, and Britain.

Feshbach's studies demonstrate that children's social class and ethnic background influence the style of reinforcement they use in an instructional situation. These results suggest that reinforcement style may mediate the relation typically found between a child's academic performance in school and his social class and ethnic background. The use of reinforcement by a child seems to reflect the characteristic learning environment that exists in his home. Some parents apparently use a small amount of positive reinforcement and a low amount of positive relative to negative reinforcement in connection with learning situations in the home. Socialization experiences of this kind in early childhood certainly would not seem to be the best preparation for future academic success in school.

In Chapter 6 Cicirelli discusses pertinent theory and research concerning older children teaching their siblings. In Chapter 1 Allen mentioned Bossard and Boll's (1956) study on the large family system; results of the study indicated that older children did help their younger siblings a great deal. Research on older children teaching their younger siblings has direct implications for the school, since a large proportion of children in elementary school do have one or more siblings attending the same school.

The first hypothesis advanced by Cicirelli asserts that siblings will be more effective in teaching each other than in teaching unrelated pupils. As a test of this hypothesis, third graders taught first graders a geometric concept in a single, short, face-to-face teaching session. Half the dyads were composed of older and younger siblings, and half the pairs were unrelated children. Results offered some support for the hypothesis that sibling pairs are more effective than nonsiblings, but results depended upon the sex of the tutor. In addition to the differential teaching effectiveness of sibling and nonsibling pairs, the teaching style used during the instructional session also differed for the sibling and nonsibling dyads.

The second hypothesis tested by Cicirelli's research states that certain sibling dyads within a family will be more effective in teaching than other sibling pairs. Results of an experiment conducted by Cicirelli supported this hypothesis. It was found that teaching results were more positive if the older sibling was a girl (rather than a boy) or if there was a wide spacing in age (rather than small) between the older and younger sibling. Several possible theoretical explanations for results of these studies were discussed, but no single explanation seems able to account adequately for all the data.

The studies on teaching by siblings demonstrate clearly that a valuable resource for teaching and socialization is available in the schools—older siblings. It would be quite feasible to utilize siblings as teachers or as other types of helpers. If a sibling tutoring program were developed in the school, its impact might be felt as well as in the relationship between the siblings at home. As Cicirelli mentions, at this point we can only speculate about such potential secondary effects of a sibling tutoring program in the schools. The research needed to answer the many questions that come to mind has not yet been conducted.

In Chapter 7 Allen and Feldman report a number of empirical studies designed to investigate psychological processes involved in tutoring; most of these studies focused primarily on the tutor. Two broad areas received attention in the studies reported: (1) factors responsible for the effects that tutoring has on the tutor; and (2) interaction processes or social skills used in tutoring. Two theoretical chapters in the first section are directly relevant to the research described by Allen and Feldman: the role theory perspective of Sarbin (Chapter 2) and the social skills model—particularly the discussion of nonverbal behavior—as expounded by Argyle (Chapter 4). These two theoretical chapters can be consulted profitably in conjunction with Allen and Feldman's presentation.

In attempting to account for the positive effects of tutoring on the tutor, Allen and Feldman invoke constructs from role theory. Enactment of a role usually produces modifications in self-perception, beliefs and attitudes, and overt behavior; the resultant changes are in the direction of greater consistency with expectations associated with the role. The effects of enacting the role of tutor (which has expectations similar to the attractive role of adult teacher) can be viewed as simply a specific case of this more general phenomenon.

The role theory framework proved its heuristic value by suggesting a series of studies to investigate the tutor's attributions and attitudes about the tutee as a function of the tutee's sequence of success or failure on the task. Across several studies, results consistently disclosed a strong primacy effect; that is, the earlier performance of the tutee more strongly affected the tutor's attitudes and attributions about ability than the same performance later in the tutoring session. This result is reminiscent of the "halo effect" found in other areas of psychology. It was discovered that the primacy effect does not occur if the tutor is allowed to inspect the completed record of a tutee's learning; in this case the tutor's attributions and attitudes about the tutee are more strongly determined by the tutee's terminal performance.

To be a successful tutor one must possess the verbal and nonverbal social skills required by the role. Allen and Feldman explored the social skills used in tutoring in several empirical studies, most of which emphasized nonverbal behavior. One experiment investigated the effect of minimal nonverbal cues from a stimulus child. Results revealed that third and sixth grade children were more accurate than adult teachers in discriminating level of understanding and lack of understanding of a lesson. In another study children were instructed to role play understanding or not understanding a lesson by using only nonverbal responses. Very different patterns of nonverbal behavior were emitted by children in the two conditions. Another study investigated nonverbal "leakage." Children's true affective reactions were revealed through their nonverbal responses even though a constant verbal response was always given. Thus, the tutors were not able to inhibit successfully inappropriate nonverbal responses.

The studies reported in this chapter call attention to a few of the elements that make up the repertoire of social skills needed by a tutor.

In the final chapter in this section Cowen takes a very general look at helping programs using nonprofessionals (both older children and adults) in the school. The use of older children to tutor younger children is part of a broader movement that advocates giving nonprofessionals a more important role in human-service helping programs. As noted in the first chapter in this book, evidence indicates that nonprofessionals can be effective help agents for other persons and may themselves receive some personal psychological benefits from the transaction.

To illustrate the range and variety of ways that nonprofessionals can be utilized effectively in helping children, Cowen discusses four human-service programs that he has initiated. Most attention in the chapter is devoted to a "child-aide" program in which housewives are employed to help elementary school children who experience problems of adjustment in school (either behavioral or academic problems). After a short training period, the housewives were able to provide a variety of human services including tutoring.

Thanks to the child-aide program many problem children received attention who would not have been reached by professional services. So woefully inadequate is the supply of trained professionals that they simply cannot respond to all schoolchildren who need help. It is noteworthy that nonprofessional child-aides were about as successful as professionals in dealing with children having adjustment problems in school. Interestingly, the most successful help agents possessed psychological characteristics (e.g., warmth and empathy) that traditionally have not been given much consideration in the selection of professional mental health workers.

In a separate but related program, Cowen enlisted retired persons as child-aides to help elementary students who were having problems in school. Consistent with the finding that tutoring helps the children who tutor, the retired persons also indicated that they benefited from working with the children. Results of a third program showed that alienated school students were helped by having tutored primary students. A fourth program used undergraduates as help agents to provide social and intellectual stimulation for slow-developing ghetto infants.

In all these human-service programs Cowen has employed nonprofessionals to perform tasks normally reserved for certified professionals. Abundant evidence supports the conclusion that young children in school can benefit academically and behaviorally from help given by a variety of nonprofessional help agents: housewives, retired persons, maladjusted high school students, and college students. Moreover, the help agents themselves seem to be helped psychologically; the "helper-therapy" principle is certainly not restricted to tutoring between children. This section ends, then, by reaffirming a point made in the first chapter: A helping program has mutual positive consequences for the helper and the person being helped. Tutoring by children seems to be only one special case of this more general phenomenon.

REFERENCE

Bossard, J. H. S., & Boll, E. S. *The large family system.* Philadelphia: Univ. of Philadelphia Press, 1956.

5

Teaching Styles
in Young Children:
Implications for Peer Tutoring[1]

Norma Deitch Feshbach
University of California, Los Angeles

One of the more innovative professional developments in child care and education is the discovery that children can participate in the delivery of socio-educational services. Children, traditionally viewed as recipients of these services, now are seen as a potential source of help and assistance. There are a number of current programs in the mental health area that train children to act as quasi therapists and counselors (Cowen, 1973). Of particular interest is the increasing number of programs in which children, including children at primary grade levels, function as educational therapists or tutors for same-age or younger

[1] The author acknowledges the following support: Studies I and II reported in this paper were supported by Contract 4-6-061646-1909 from the Office of Education, HEW, to the Research and Development Center, School of Education, University of California, Los Angeles. Studies III and IV were supported by Contract 4-447612-05547-7 from the Chancellor's Committee on International and Comparative Studies from the Ford Foundation International and Comparative Studies Grant, University of California, Los Angeles. Study V was supported in part by a Faculty Grant, University of California, Los Angeles, and in part by the Prediction and Prevention of Reading Failure Project, University of California, Los Angeles, National Institute of Mental Health USPHS MH-16796. Study VI was supported by the Prediction and Prevention of Reading Failure Project, University of California, Los Angeles, National Institute of Mental Health USPHS MH-16796.

pupils (Lippitt & Lohman, 1965; Shapiro & Hopkins, 1967; Frager & Stern, 1970).

In general, research on peer teaching and peer counseling interactions has focused on the effect on achievement level, self-esteem, and related behaviors in both the participants—the trainer and trainee or tutor and tutee (Gartner, Kohler, & Reisman, 1971; Melaragno & Newmark, 1968). A major concern has been evaluating the effectiveness of the various remedial and training procedures in which the child functions as the primary change agent (Ellson, Barber, Engle & Kamgwerth, 1965). A related question, and one that has received relatively little attention, is the process by which these changes are brought about. For the most part, the mechanisms that have been suggested, such as modeling, feed-back, social intimacy, and social approval, are similar to the mediating influences identified in the broader role of peers as socialization forces (Hartup, 1970).

Clearly, peers exert a powerful influence on children's development and performance, ranging from direct conformity pressures in group settings (Berenda, 1950; Harvey & Rutherford, 1960) to more subtle, indirect, but no less potent effects of peer models on the playground and in the classroom (Hartup, 1970). One of the more significant ways children influence each other in an interpersonal transaction is through administering rewards and punishment and providing information. A very clear demonstration of how peers shape behavior is provided in a series of studies concerned with preschool children's aggressive behavior (Patterson, Littman, & Bricker, 1967). These naturalistic studies showed how the reinforcing and punitive responses of preschool age mates to aggressive behavior gradually modified children's level of aggressive activity. Other studies have indicated that peer status and familiarity are relevant individual difference factors governing the effectiveness of peer reinforcements (Hartup, 1964; Hartup, Glazer, & Charlesworth, 1967).

REINFORCEMENT STYLES IN TEACHING

One of the major concerns of the studies presented in this chapter is with children's use of reinforcement. Whereas most investigations of peer reinforcement have been concerned primarily with the effects upon the recipient, the present studies emphasize individual differences in the dispenser's use of reinforcement. Reinforcement patterns that children spontaneously employ in their interaction can be viewed as a reflection of their mode or style of teaching and learning.

A series of investigations was carried out to assess individual differences in teaching styles in experimental situations in which a young child instructed a peer. The context for the initial research was an interest in children's teaching styles as a reflection of early socialization experiences in the home. From this perspective, the child's teaching behaviors are derived from parent models; that is, the reinforcement patterns displayed by the child when instructing other children were hypothesized to mirror the reinforcement contingencies that punctuated the parental training of the child. The child's instructional behavior was viewed as a mediator between socialization practices of the home and that of other socialization agents such as the peer group and school.

Individual differences in response patterns manifested in peer teaching situations are presumed to interact with variations in teachers' programs and instructional styles. The studies summarized here attempt to delineate dimensions of children's peer teaching behaviors relevant to this interactional mode. These relations are examined in the context of social class and ethnic difference within our own culture and in two other national settings.

The most important initial decision in planning these studies was the choice of the response dimension to be used. Positive and negative reinforcement was a basic response dimension that could be applied meaningfully to parent, teacher, and child behavior, and that also had explanatory value. A number of considerations went into the choice of this dimension. First, reinforcement is central in the learning process, having both motivational and informational functions. Second, there is clinical and experimental evidence suggesting that the effects of positive reinforcement upon learning and performance are qualitatively and quantitatively different from the effects of negative reinforcement (Rodnick & Garmezy, 1957; Weiner, 1972). Third, reinforcement is pervasive in social interaction. Teachers provide reward and punishment (praise and criticism) in diverse academic contexts. Similarly, parents use reward and punishment in training independence, disciplining aggression, and teaching a child how to button his clothes. Parental socialization practices and teacher instructional styles share important functions. The process of education and the process of socialization have some common characteristics, and sometimes the processes are indistinguishable.

In focusing on patterns of reinforcement behavior as a major parameter of social interaction having educational concomitants, minimization of the importance of other dimensions of social interaction is not intended. The utility of assessing reinforcement behavior lies in its reliability and ease of measurement, and, more important, in its well-established theoretical properties. Also, because of its affective and cognitive components, reinforcement style is likely to be correlated with other teaching interactions.

In addition to reinforcement style, social class and ethnicity were assessed in most of the studies. Social class was of interest because of empirical data linking social class differences to differences in academic performance (Deutsch, Katz, & Jensen, 1968; Jensen, 1969). At the same time there are many studies suggesting systematic differences in the socialization practices of different social classes (Becker, 1963; Bronfenbrenner, 1958; Kohn, 1963; Miller & Swanson, 1960; Sears, Maccoby, & Levin, 1957). One critical dimension of social class variation in the "ecology of socialization" that mediates cognitive performance may be class-linked reinforcement patterns.

The studies reviewed here, in which social class and ethnicity were key independent variables, were designed to determine whether these variables are systematically related to the pattern of reinforcement manifested by children in paradigmatic teaching situations. This problem was studied cross-culturally in the United States, England, and Israel. In many studies data also were collected on the teaching styles manifested by mothers of the child-tutor, but the maternal data will not be reviewed in detail. Rather, the major part of this chapter will focus on children's data. Most studies investigated teaching styles in preschool age children. The concluding study used a sample of older children varying in reading competency. With this overview, we turn now to our initial studies of socio-ethnic differences in reinforcement style.

Social Class and Children's Reinforcement

Our first step in this research program was to investigate patterns of reinforcement used by lower- and middle-class children in interaction situations involving cognitive learning concomitants (Feshbach & Devor, 1969). For these studies we needed a very young age group so that social class variations in behavior could not be attributed to school influences. Furthermore, the earlier the age at which social class and ethnic differences in reinforcement styles could be established, the greater our confidence that this variable contributes to cognitive differences between children of different social classes. Also, the children had to be at a level of social maturity and linguistic competence sufficiently advanced to permit the expression and assessment of positive and negative reinforcement. In addition, since imitation was a possible mechanism for the acquisition of reinforcement styles, the age level had to be one at which modeling effects had been demonstrated. For these reasons, we decided to study 4-year-old children for differences in patterns of reinforcement as a function of socioeconomic background.

The following experimental paradigm was used in the initial studies. Each 4-year-old child was asked to teach a 3-year-old child a simple eight-piece wooden puzzle. Prior to the peer teaching sequence, the experimenter demonstrated the puzzle to the 4-year-old. During this familiarization period, the 4-year-old teacher-child was given three trials to assemble the puzzle. During the first trial, the child was given active verbal assistance by the experimenter. During the second trial, the experimenter made one positive verbal remark, "That's very good," and one critical remark, "That's not right," about the child's performance. At the third trial, the child completed the puzzle while the experimenter left to get the 3-year-old pupil.

After being introduced to the younger child, the 4-year-old was given the following instructions: "Now it's your turn to be the teacher. You're going to teach Andy how to do this puzzle. What does 'teach' mean? It means 'to help.'

You may help Andy by using words but not your hands. Now you may begin by telling Andy how to do the puzzle."

The 4-year-old "teachers" had no difficulty in understanding the teaching task, and most of them entered into the teaching role with great seriousness. Like their parents and their teachers, they wanted their 3-year-old pupils to learn. One could see in these 4-year-old teachers reactions of frustration, pleasure, disappointment, and excitement as their pupils shifted back and forth from persistent errors to flashes of insight.

The children's active engagement in the teaching task resulted in verbal reinforcement behaviors that were recorded verbatim and could readily be scored as positive or negative. Positive and negative reinforcing statements were defined in terms of their encouraging and discouraging connotations rather than in the more formal sense of increasing or decreasing a specific response. The positive category included statements of praise, encouragement, and affirmation; the negative category included criticism, negations, and derogatory comments. Typical examples of positive comments were: "See, she can put it together"; "That's better"; "Yeah, like that"; "He did it." Frequent negative comments were: "Wrong way"; "Not that way"; "No, don't bang it"; "You stupid." To determine the reliability of this dichotomous classification, 80 randomly selected statements were scored by two independent raters. There was only one instance in which the raters disagreed. The total number of positive and total number of negative statements were determined for each child and constituted the basic dependent measure. In addition, the performance of the 3-year-olds was assessed in most of the studies by the number of errors made and time taken to complete the puzzle.

The 4-year-olds in our first study were 50 boys and 52 girls, approximately equally distributed by ethnicity and social class. There were four combinations of race and social class: middle-class whites; lower-class whites, middle-class blacks, and lower-class blacks. The middle-class groups attended private nursery schools and lived in neighborhoods identified as middle- to upper-middle class; their fathers' occupations were professional and managerial. The lower-class children were enrolled in children's centers and lived primarily in neighborhoods identified as disadvantaged; their parents were engaged in unskilled or semi-skilled occupations.

In all instances, ethnicity and social class of the 3-year-old pupil was the same as that of the 4-year-old teacher. In this first study, the sexes of the children were varied so that within each grouping half the pupils were of the same sex and half were of the opposite sex as their 4-year-old teachers. (The variation in sex of pupils did not affect the outcome, and consequently will not be elaborated in the presentation of the results.)

The mean frequencies of positive reinforcements used by each group are indicated in Table 1 (Study I). Middle-class white children used a significantly

Table 1

Mean Frequencies of Reinforcement Administered by American, Israeli, and English 4-Year-Old "Teacher" Children

Culture	Middle-class white	Middle-class black	Lower-class white	Lower-class black
Positive Reinforcement				
American (Study I)	2.30	.20	.80	.70
American (Study II)	2.40	.08	1.90	.08
Israeli (Study III)	1.80	–	.57	–
English (Study IV)	1.80	–	.70	–
Negative Reinforcement				
American (Study I)	1.60	1.30	1.70	2.10
American (Study II)	2.30	.40	2.60	1.60
Israeli (Study III)	1.20	–	1.00	–
English (Study IV)	2.40	–	2.50	–

greater number of positive reinforcements than did each of the other three groups. In contrast, the middle-class black children used significantly fewer positive reinforcements than either of the lower-class groups. The overall pattern of social class and race differences was reflected by both sexes, and the strikingly greater use of positive reinforcement by the middle-class white boys and girls was consistent with expectation. The results for the middle-class blacks are an interesting deviation from the hypothesized relationship between social class and use of positive reinforcement, possibly reflecting a form of constriction that derives from marginal social roles.

Differences in the mean frequency of negative reinforcement used by each group were not statistically significant. (Data are presented in the bottom half of Table 1.) If the two ethnic groups are combined and children are categorized as using or not using negative reinforcement, an interesting social class difference emerges. Of the 49 middle-class 4-year-old teachers, 21 did not use any negative reinforcement; only 10 of the 46 lower-class teachers used none. Another way of viewing the data is to examine the relative frequency of positive and negative reinforcement used by each group. The greatest difference is found between middle-class whites and lower-class blacks. The middle-class white sample was the only group to use more positive than negative reinforcements when instructing the 3-year-olds, whereas the lower-class black children displayed the largest preponderance of negative over positive reinforcements.

It is reasonable to ask whether these differences in children's teaching behaviors could be attributed to differences in their pupils' performance. An analysis of errors and time to solution failed to reveal any significant performance difference among the groups. In addition, pupil performance measures were not significantly correlated with the number of positive or negative reinforcements administered by the teacher-child.

The possible role of linguistic factors in the pattern of results is also of interest. There were no significant differences among the 4-year-old groups in number of words used to make a positive or a negative reinforcing statement nor in the grammatical complexity of the statements. A possible explanation in terms of greater verbal facility on the part of the middle-class white child is rendered particularly unlikely by the fact that the mean number of words used to make a negative comment (3.5) was greater than the mean number of words used to make a positive reinforcing statement (2.3).

The results of this first study of children's teaching styles suggests that as early as age 4, children display different reinforcement patterns as a function of their socio-ethnic background. The findings were generally consistent with the assumption that styles of reinforcement used by these 4-year-olds are modeled after the socialization practices they experience at home. The results also support the selection of reinforcement style as a fruitful dimension of individual differences that relates variations of socialization practices in the home and school with variations in cognitive performance.

Maternal Reinforcement Style

The initial study of teaching styles of 4-year-olds was repeated on a second American sample in the course of extending the investigation to include observations of maternal reinforcement styles (Feshbach, 1973b). The second study included 109 4-year-olds and their mothers; an equal number of 3-year-olds served as pupils. Subjects were again divided into 4 groups based on social class and ethnicity: middle-class white, lower-class white, middle-class black, and lower-class black. The mothers and children were drawn from 11 parent educational preschool centers distributed throughout Los Angeles. These are preschools conducted by the city, attended one day a week by the child and his mother. The middle-class sample in this second study was less privileged and the lower-class sample less disadvantaged than their counterparts in the first study.

For the initial instructional sequence, we followed the same procedure as before—the 4-year-olds were asked to teach a puzzle to 3-year-olds. In a second instructional sequence about an hour later, each mother was asked to teach her own 4-year-old a similar but more complex wooden puzzle. The same measures used to analyze the child–child interactions were used to analyze the mother–child interactions. The reliability of the categorization of reinforcements was again very high.

The mean frequencies of positive reinforcements used by the 4-year-old groups are presented in Table 1 (Study II). The pattern for these data (except for the relatively high number of positive reinforcements by lower-class whites) is similar to the pattern observed in the earlier study (Feshbach & Devor, 1969). Both middle- and lower-class white 4-year-olds used a significantly greater number of positive reinforcements than did either middle- or lower-class black children.

There was less consistency between the results of the first and second studies in use of negative reinforcements than in use of positive reinforcements. Yet the pattern of reinforcement—the relative frequency of positive as compared to negative reinforcement—was similar in both studies. The preponderance of negative over positive reinforcement was greatest for the lower-class black children and least for the middle-class whites.

Some insight into the functional significance of the greater use of positive and negative reinforcements by the white 4-year-olds is provided by an appraisal of the performance of the 3-year-old pupils. For both the middle-class and lower-class white samples an identical correlation of .71 was obtained between the 4-year-old teacher-child's negative reinforcement score and the number of errors made by his pupil. The corresponding correlations for the black samples were zero. The socio-ethnic differences in patterns of reinforcement used by the mothers corresponded to the socio-ethnic differences found for the 4-year-old "tutors." In general, middle-class white children and their mothers used relatively more positive than negative reinforcement; lower-class black children and their mothers used more negative than positive reinforcement; and the other two groups fell between these two extremes.

These data suggest that the learning environment of the lower-class black child is more stressful than the environment of his white advantaged counterpart. We can infer that the lower-class black child receives more negative reinforcement from his mother than other children and that the same child receives fewer positive reinforcements from his peers than the middle-class white child. Exposure to a primarily negative reinforcing environment can disrupt learning and depress cognitive performance. These potentially disruptive effects may operate in teaching situations designed to provide remedial instruction, such as peer teaching programs. The tutor's use of reinforcement is an important instructional device that the tutor can employ to facilitate learning.

CROSS-CULTURAL STUDIES OF REINFORCEMENT STYLE

Reinforcement style is only one of many behavioral dimensions of socialization that allows social class and ethnic differences to exert an influence on cognitive functioning and achievement. If the concept of reinforcement style is important, differences should be found in social groups that differ in academic achievement in other cultures. Thus, the next study was carried out in Israel, where one can find ethnic and economic divisions within the society associated with differences in children's academic levels.

Ethnic and Social Class Differences in Israel

The social division that exists in Israel between Israelis of Western origin and Israelis of Middle Eastern origin is somewhat comparable to socio-ethnic divisions in our own society. Middle Eastern Jews (whose dominant culture has been Arabic) are economically and socially disadvantaged in comparison with Israelis of Western origin (Smilansky & Yam, 1969). The discrepancy in academic achievement between Jews of Eastern and Western origins has been of great concern to the Israeli educators and governmental authorities. Special educational programs for disadvantaged Israeli children and their families (Lombard, 1971; Smilansky, 1968) have objectives similar to programs for disadvantaged groups in the United States. It was decided to replicate in Israel the study of reinforcement styles carried out with American 4-year-olds and their mothers (Feshbach, 1974).

The procedures developed for the American samples were followed as closely as possible in Israel. Our Israeli sample included 60 4-year-olds and their mothers (and an equal number of 3-year-olds), all from eight preschools in Jerusalem and its environs. The sample was equally divided by sex and social class. The lower-class children were predominantly from Yemenite and related ethnic backgrounds, whereas the middle-class sample was largely of Western origin.

The mean frequencies of positive and negative reinforcements used by the Israeli middle-class 4-year-olds are shown in Table 1 (Study III). The middle-class Israeli children displayed about three times the frequency of positive reinforcements as the lower-class children, a highly significant difference. On the other hand, they made little use of negative reinforcement, and the difference between socioeconomic groups was insignificant.

In terms of the observed pattern of reinforcements, the educational "ecology" of the Israeli lower-class child resembles that of the American lower-class black child; the Israeli middle-class child and the American middle-class white child appear to share common experiences. Israeli lower-class children (relative to middle-class children) receive fewer positive reinforcements from their peers, fewer positive reinforcements from their mothers, and (if they are male) more negative reinforcements from their mothers. These results support the hypothesis that reinforcement style is an important behavioral dimension linking socio-ethnic differences in socialization practices with socio-ethnic differences in cognitive performance.

Social Class Differences in England

England was selected as the third culture for studying reinforcement styles because of the reported achievement differences and linguistic pattern differences between English middle- and working-class (lower-class) children (Bernstein, 1961, 1962). Bernstein has proposed that social class differences in language exposure and usage are important determinants of social class differences in English children's cognitive performance and achievement. It is possible that social class differences in reinforcement style could mediate this differential achievement. The same procedures used in the United States and in Israel also were applied to research with an English sample (Feshbach, 1973a).

The English sample consisted of 50 middle- and working-class mothers and their 4-year-old children, and 50 3-year-old pupils. The children came from 7 preschools in the Greater London area. Father's occupation and residential area were used to assign a child to the middle-class or working-class group. Practically all of the English middle- and working-class samples were white and native to England; the distinctions were economic and social.

The mean frequencies of positive reinforcement used by the children are presented in Table 1 (Study IV). The middle-class 4-year-olds again used significantly more positive reinforcements than did the lower-class group. For the middle- and working-class children the mean frequency of negative reinforcement was almost identical. Thus, the social class differences in reinforcement patterns in English 4-year-olds are comparable to socio-ethnic differences in children's reinforcement styles in the Israeli and American samples.

Results for maternal use of reinforcements differed in several interesting respects from data obtained for the American and Israeli mothers. Middle-class English mothers appeared to shower their sons with positive reinforcement. In contrast to the Israeli and American mothers, there was no socioeconomic difference in the frequency of use of negative reinforcement by English mothers.

To compare reinforcement patterns more directly across cultures, the proportion of positive reinforcements relative to total reinforcements was determined for each American, English, and Israeli child. The proportional analysis also controls for differences in absolute number of reinforcements. A 3 X 2 (culture by social class) analysis of variance was carried out for the entire sample. A significant main effect was obtained for social class: The middle-class samples displayed a consistently higher proportion of positive reinforcement than the lower-class samples.

These cross-cultural socioeconomic differences in reinforcement styles are consistent with the socio-ethnic differences observed in academic achievement. It seems reasonable, then, to conclude that reinforcement style may be one important factor—though not the only factor or the most significant factor—mediating socio-ethnic differences in cognitive performance and academic achievement.

Reinforcement styles employed by parents and children can be viewed as reflecting pervasive features of family environments (Feshbach, 1973a). The lower-class family is subject to more privation, frustration, illness, and in general to more stressful events than is the middle-class family. Under these circumstances, we might expect the lower-class parent to be less tolerant and more critical of their child's errors and other deviant behaviors. Economic circumstances make it likely that the lower-class family will use more negative reinforcement than the middle-class family.

Perhaps the most unfortunate consequence of these socialization experiences is internalization by the child of response modes likely to interfere with the effective transmission of information. As early as age 4 the child seems prepared to duplicate the patterns of reinforcement of the parent in tutoring with peers—and perhaps in transactions with his or her own offspring in the future.

TEACHING STYLE AND COGNITIVE COMPETENCE

The theoretical implications of positive and negative reinforcement usage are by no means restricted to cognitive differences between poor and more advantaged children. Other possible antecedents of reinforcement style are variations in personality, situational stresses, and cultural mores. We should, therefore, expect variations in reinforcement patterns to be associated with variations in cognitive performance within a particular socio-ethnic group.

The relation between level of success in learning to read and various teaching behaviors (including reinforcement styles) was investigated in two studies. The first study examined the teaching behavior of mothers (Bercovici & Feshbach, 1973); the second dealt with peer–teacher interactions between children in early elementary grades. The independent variable of these studies was the reading competence of the child. Successful and problem readers were drawn from equally comfortable middle-class, advantaged, family backgrounds.

Mothers' Instruction and Reading

In the first study mothers of successful and problem readers were observed instructing their own and other children in several cognitive tasks (Bercovici & Feshbach, 1973). All children had normal intelligence and were matched on IQ, age, and sex. The Early Prediction and Prevention of Reading Disability Project (Feshbach, Adelman, & Fuller, 1974) collected data on the children's IQ, reading ability, and teachers' evaluation of competency and classroom performance. Children in both groups were completing first grade and were between 6½ and 7½ years old.

Each mother instructed three different children in two different cognitive tasks. The first child was the mother's own, the second had the same reading competence as the mother's own child, and the reading level of the third child differed from that of the mother's own child. The sample consisted of 40 mothers and 120 children. The range of dependent variables was broadened to include such maternal behaviors as controlling and directive statements, autonomy-fostering statements, and manual guidance in addition to reinforcing behaviors.

Analysis of the mother's teaching strategies indicated that mothers of problem readers used more negative reinforcement, were more directive and intrusive, and, in general, appeared to be less patient than mothers of successful readers when instructing both their own and other children. Mothers of problem readers were more interfering (telling the child what to do or completing parts of the task themselves). Their greater intrusiveness in the child's performance was accompanied by a significantly greater degree of critical, negative reinforcing statements (whether teaching their own child, a matched child, or a competent reader). In addition, on a separate measure, mothers of problem readers revealed more negative child-rearing attitudes than mothers of successful readers.

Perhaps the most interesting finding in this study was obtained on a post-test administered to the children. Children who had been taught by mothers of problem readers—whether problem or successful readers themselves—performed significantly more poorly on a post-test (the first cognitive task taught) than children taught by mothers of successful readers. This outcome was produced by an interaction ranging from 8 to 15 minutes in duration. One can only conjecture about the effects of sustained exposure to socialization experiences or teaching styles characterized by intrusiveness, impatience, and negative reinforcement.

Interaction during Peer Teaching

In a recent study, we investigated teaching styles in the problem and successful readers themselves as manifested in peer teaching situations. One purpose was to determine whether tutorial behaviors of successful and problem readers were similar to teaching patterns of mothers of successful and problem readers. A second purpose of particular relevance to peer teaching was to observe the behavior tutors displayed and the cognitive effects upon the learner of these behaviors.

This study employed a somewhat older population of boys and girls (Feshbach & Aschbacher, 1975). The sample consisted of 87 white, middle-class children (29 second graders and 58 first graders). The second grade children served as tutors; the first graders served as learners or tutees. All participants had average intelligence and no manifest neurological impairment. Half the children at each grade level were problem readers, and the other half (matched for IQ and sex) were successful readers. Each second grade tutor was assigned two same-sex first grade tutees (one a successful reader and one a problem reader).

The task consisted of four learning mazes and a fifth post-task maze. (Under each maze was a piece of carbon paper and a second sheet on which the solution path was printed.) The mazes varied in difficulty progressing from 4 critical turns to 10. After being taught the task, the tutor in turn taught two learners (tutees) individually (one from each reading group). The experimenter administered the post-test maze. Two observers recorded the following behaviors: pre-task orientation time, total interaction time, verbal prompting, nonverbal reinforcement, and negative verbal and nonverbal reinforcement. Each peer interaction was also videotaped.

The reinforcement data were rather complex, reflecting sex differences and interactions between the reading competence of the teacher and the learner. Frequencies of positive and negative verbal reinforcements in Table 2 reflect these interactions, particularly in the use of negative verbal reinforcement. The difference in use of positive reinforcement between the successful and problem readers was small, and none of the main effects and interactions were significant. The tendency of competent male readers to administer more positive reinforcement to tutees who are competent readers as compared to tutees who are problem readers, and the reverse trend displayed by the girls, approached statistical significance. Negative verbal reinforcement data yielded a significant triple interaction. Problem-reader tutors and female successful-reader tutors tended to administer more negative reinforcement to tutees who were competent readers than to tutees who were problem readers. But the male tutor who was a competent reader administered much more negative reinforcement to the tutee who was a problem reader than to the competent reader.

Differences in use of nonverbal positive and negative reinforcement by successful and problem readers were consistent with expectations. Data in Table 3 indicate that academically successful readers displayed significantly more posi-

Table 2
Average Frequencies of Verbal Reinforcements (Per Minute)
(Study VI)

	Tutor (Successful reader)		Tutor (Problem reader)	
	Learner (Successful reader)	Learner (Problem reader)	Learner (Successful reader)	Learner (Problem reader)
Positive Reinforcement				
Boys	.82	.45	.63	.66
Girls	.41	.61	.40	.47
Negative Reinforcement				
Boys	.28	.90	.66	.46
Girls	.36	.19	.33	.19

Table 3
Average Frequency (Per Minute) of Nonverbal
Reinforcements
(Study VI)

	Tutor (Successful reader)		Tutor (Problem reader)	
	Learner (Successful reader)	Learner (Problem reader)	Learner (Successful reader)	Learner (Problem reader)
	Positive Reinforcement			
Boys	.50	.50	.20	.10
Girls	.13	.11	0	0
	Negative Reinforcement			
Boys	0	0	.50	.10
Girls	0	0	0	.05

tive nonverbal reinforcements and significantly fewer nonverbal negative reinforcements than did the problem readers. Though the rate of nonverbal negative
reinforcement was low among girls, results were in the same direction and
approached statistical significance. A more detailed analysis was undertaken of
the videotape recordings of peer interactions. An elaborate coding scheme was
developed based, in part, upon extant classifications of nonverbal behaviors
relevant to teaching–tutoring interaction situations (Argyle, 1972; Duncan,
1969; Mehrabian, 1971, 1972), and, in part, upon our previous research (Bercovici & Feshbach, 1973). In all, 27 separate measures were coded.[2] Our
approach in analyzing these specific behavior items was primarily exploratory.
There were no specific expectations regarding differences between reading
groups in the frequencies of subtle bodily postures and movements. We were
searching for indirect behavioral indices that might discriminate between our
groups.

Mean scores were determined for the tutors for each of the 27 specific
behavior items. (For 15 items, response frequence was too low for analysis.)
Most of the significant effects were interactions. Three were triple interactions,
which indicates the subtlety and complexity of variables influencing these
nonverbal responses. Overall, it appears that male tutors who are competent
readers differed systematically (and in most cases significantly) from male tutors
who are problem readers when teaching learners who are problem readers. The

[2] Ms. Paula Sapon played a major role in the development of the scoring instrument and its
application. Deep appreciation and thanks are expressed for her skill and diligence.

competent male reader displayed more touching behavior, pointed more often in a facilitative way to the task, maintained a closer distance and displayed greater eye contact with the problem learner. On the other hand, female tutors displayed a reverse trend with problem readers. The female tutor who is a competent reader (in comparison with the female tutor who is a problem reader) displayed significantly less touching behavior, maintained a significantly greater distance from the tutee, and showed somewhat less eye contact when paired with a problem learner. Incidentally, there was only one main effect: a greater frequency of "hands on head" when tutors interacted with problem readers than with competent readers.

In summary, in interaction between tutors and tutees who are successful and problem readers the clearest tutor difference that emerges is in the use of reinforcement. Although the use of verbal reinforcement was not in accord with expectation based on maternal differences (Bercovici & Feshbach, 1973), the nonverbal reinforcement pattern was consistent with theoretical and empirical expectation. Moreover, an interesting pattern of verbal reinforcement emerges on inspection of sub-group means. Male tutors who are competent readers dispensed more positive verbal reinforcement to successful reader tutees. This group also demonstrated the highest frequency of nonverbal positive reinforcement behavior with an absence of nonverbal negative reinforcement. Thus, these competent boys were more discriminating in their administration of verbal reinforcement, while at the same time providing an overall encouraging positive environment.

The differential reinforcement patterns exhibited by tutors who varied in reading achievement probably reflects their learning environments. The successful reader has probably received more positive and fewer negative reinforcements in school than the less-competent reader. Given the young age of the "tutors," it is more likely that the learning environment in the home had primary influence on their reinforcement styles and reading ability. The findings from mothers of successful and problem readers support this interpretation (Bercovici & Feshbach, 1973). Longitudinal studies tracing the cognitive development of children, in conjunction with an evaluation of parental teaching behaviors, attitudes, and values, will be necessary to provide direct evidence for this proposed relation.

CONCLUSIONS

Several implications for the implementation and evaluation of peer teaching programs can be drawn from this series of studies. These studies of peer teaching have focused on the analysis of process; less attention was given to direct cognitive outcomes of different peer teaching styles. But the results indicate a consistent association between cognitive competence and tendency to use a positive pattern of reinforcement. Moreover, cognitive competence and the child's positive reinforcement style are related to positive maternal reinforcement style. It seems reasonable to infer that reinforcement style manifested in a teaching situation (by parent, teacher, or child tutor) has important cognitive consequences.

In programs that employ peers as tutors, it may prove useful to assess the reinforcement patterns displayed by children in the actual tutoring situation when evaluating effectiveness. Individual differences in tutor effectiveness (as assessed by tutee gains) may be correlated with tutors' reinforcement pattern. It would be productive to include dimensions of reinforcement in the training of peer tutors. The tutor's use of reinforcement would appear to be amenable to modification, training, and control; research indicates that parents, teachers, and therapists can be trained to apply particular schedules of reinforcement (Bandura, 1969; Berkowitz & Graziano, 1972; Fargo, Behrns, & Nolen, 1970). One finally may conjecture that the overall effectiveness of a peer tutoring will be related to the prevalent pattern of reinforcement characterizing the population of children in the program.

REFERENCES

Argyle, M. Non-verbal communication in human social interaction. In R. A. Hinde (Ed.), *Non-verbal communication.* Cambridge: University Printing House, 1972. Pp. 243–268.

Bandura, A. *Principles of behavior modification.* New York: Holt, 1969.

Becker, W. C. Consequences of different kinds of parental discipline. In M. L. Hoffman, & L. W. Hoffman (Eds.), *Review of child development research.* Vol. 1. New York: Russell Sage Foundation, 1963. Pp. 169–208.

Bercovici, A., & Feshbach, N. D. Teaching styles of mothers of successful and problem readers. Paper presented at the meeting of the American Educational Research Association, New Orleans, February 1973.

Berenda, R. *Influences of the group on judgments of children.* New York: Columbia Univ. Press, 1950.

Berkowitz, B. P., & Graziano, A. M. Training parents as behavior therapists: A review. *Behavior Research and Therapy,* 1972, *10,* 297–318.

Bernstein, B. Social class and linguistic development: A theory of social learning. In A. H. Halsey, J. Floud, & C. A. Anderson (Eds.), *Education, economy, and society.* New York: Free Press, 1961.

Bernstein, B. Social class, linguistic codes, and grammatical elements. *Language and Speech,* 1962, *5,* 221–240.

Bronfenbrenner, U. Socialization and social class through time and space. In E. E. Maccoby, T. M. Newcomb, & E. L. Hartley (Eds.), *Readings in social psychology.* (3rd ed.) New York: Holt, 1958. Pp. 400–425.

Cowen, E. L. Social and community interventions. In P. H. Mussen & M. R. Rosensweig (Eds.), *Annual review of psychology.* Vol. 24. Palo Alto, California: Annual Reviews, 1973. Pp. 423–472.

Deutsch, M., Katz, I., & Jensen, A. *Social class, race, and psychological development.* New York: Holt, 1968.

Duncan, S. Nonverbal communication. *Psychological Bulletin,* 1969, *72,* 118–137.

Ellson, D., Barber, L., Engle, T., & Kamgwerth, L. Programmed tutoring: A teaching aid and a research tool. *Reading Research Quarterly,* 1965, *1,* 77–127.

Fargo, G. A., Behrns, C., & Nolen, P. *Behavior modification in the classroom.* Belmont, California: Wadsworth, 1970.

Feshbach, N. D. Cross-cultural studies of teaching styles in four-year-olds and their mothers. In A. E. Pick (Ed.), *Minnesota symposia on child psychology.* Vol. 7. Minneapolis: Univ. of Minnesota Press, 1973. Pp. 87–116. (a)

Feshbach, N. D. Teaching styles in four year olds and their mothers. In J. F. Rosenblith, W. Allinsmith, & J. Williams (Eds.), *Readings in child development: Causes of behavior.* New York: Allyn & Bacon, 1973. (b)

Feshbach, N. D. Teaching styles of Israeli four year olds and their mothers: A cross-cultural comparison. In *The Hebrew T. Megamont Journal.* Jerusalem: The Henrietta Szold Institute, 1974.

Feshbach, N. D., & Ashbacher, P. Peer teaching styles of problem and successful readers. Unpublished manuscript, Univ. of California, Los Angeles, 1975.

Feshbach, N. D., & Devor, G. Teaching styles in four year olds. *Child Development,* 1969, *40,* 183–190.

Feshbach, S., & Adelman, H. Prediction and Prevention of reading failure Project. Univ. of California, Los Angeles, National Institute of Mental Health USPHS MH-16796, 1971.

Feshbach, S., Adelman, H., & Fuller, W. Early identification of children with high-risk of reading failure. *Journal of Learning Disabilities,* 1974, *7,* 639–644.

Frager, S., & Stern, C. Learning by teaching. *Reading Teacher,* 1970, *23,* 403–409.

Gartner, A., Kohler, M., & Riesman, F. *Children teach children: Learning by teaching.* New York: Harper, 1971.

Hartup, W. W. Friendship status and the effectiveness of peers as reinforcing agents. *Journal of Experimental Child Psychology,* 1964, *1,* 154–162.

Hartup, W. W. Peer interaction and social organization. In P. H. Mussen (Ed.), *Carmichael's manual of child psychology.* Vol. II. New York: Wiley, 1970. Pp. 361–456.

Hartup, W. W., Glazer, J. A., & Charlesworth, R. Peer reinforcement and sociometric status. *Child Development,* 1967, *38,* 1017–1024.

Harvey, O. J., & Rutherford, J. Status in the informal group: Influence and influenceability at differing age levels. *Child Development,* 1960, *31,* 377–385.

Jensen, A. How much can we boost IQ and scholastic achievement? *Harvard Educational Review,* 1969, *39,* 1–123.

Kohn, M. L. Social class and parent-child relationship: An interpretation. *American Journal of Sociology,* 1963, *68,* 471–480.

Lippitt, P., & Lohman, J. Cross-age relationships, an educational resource. *Children,* 1965, *12,* 113–117.

Lombard, A. D. Home instruction program for preschool children (Hippy). Interim Report 1969–1970, Center for Research in Education of the Disadvantaged, Hebrew Univ. of Jerusalem, Israel, March, 1971.

Mehrabian, A. *Silent messages.* Belmont, California: Wadsworth, 1971.

Mehrabian, A. *Nonverbal communication.* Chicago: Aldine-Atherton, 1972.

Melaragno, R. J., & Newmark, G. A pilot study to apply evaluation-revision procedures to first-grade Mexican-American classrooms. Unpublished report, 1968.

Miller, D. R., & Swanson, J. E. *Inner conflict and defense.* New York: Holt, 1960.

Patterson, G. R., Littman, R. A., & Bricker, W. Assertive behavior in children: A step toward a theory of aggression. *Monograph of Society for Research in Child Development,* 1967, *32,* 5–6.

Rodnick, E. H., & Garmezy, H. An experimental approach to the study of motivation in schizophrenia. In M. R. Jones (Ed.), *Nebraska symposium on motivation.* Lincoln: Univ. of Nebraska Press, 1957. Pp. 109–184.

Sears, R. R., Maccoby, E. E., & Levin, H. *Patterns of child rearing.* New York: Harper, 1957.

Shapiro, A., & Hopkins, L. Pupil-teachers. *Reading Teacher,* 1967, *21,* 128–129.

Smilansky, S. The effect of certain learning conditions on the progress of disadvantaged children in kindergarten age. *Journal of School Psychology,* 1968, *4,* 68–81.

Smilansky, S. & Yam, Y. The relationship between family size, ethnic origin, father's education, and student's achievement. *Behavioral Sciences Quarterly,* 1969, *16,* 248–273.

Weiner, B. Attribution theory, achievement motivation, and the educational process. *Review of Educational Research,* 1972, *42,* 203–215.

Siblings Teaching Siblings

Victor G. Cicirelli

Purdue University

In recent years there has been renewed interest in using children to teach each other as a supplement to regular educational programs. Many tutoring programs have been developed not only in the United States, but in Russia, Great Britain, Cuba, and other countries. Two principles of learning seem to justify these new programs.

First, young children can learn certain tasks more effectively if they are taught by a person closer to their age (who understands their problems and viewpoint, and can communicate at the same language level) than by an adult. This may be especially true for certain tasks such as games, youthful skills, taboo subjects, and for certain personal-social characteristics (such as sex-role identity) in which parents and other adults are unwilling to or incapable of helping children. Older children or peers may be more effective teachers for these tasks.

Second, an individual can learn through the process of teaching someone else. Learning through teaching can be an important way to understanding new material. In preparing to teach, one must develop examples, analogies, illustrations, and applications in order to help the learner grasp the material. In so doing, the teacher himself improves his understanding of the material. If it is possible to learn effectively by teaching someone else, then children should have the opportunity to learn through teaching other children.

These principles can justify tutoring programs in which younger children are taught by peers or older children. Going beyond these principles, the thesis of this chapter is that young children also can be taught by their siblings. More specifically, the thesis is twofold. First, siblings may be more effective as teachers than nonsiblings (peers and older children) under certain conditions and for certain tasks. Second, within families, certain sibling dyads are more effective in the teaching–learning situation than other dyads. Older siblings as teachers can be proposed as a supplement to programs using peers or older children in tutoring situations. A large percentage of young children in elementary schools have older brothers or sisters in the same school; hence, the use of siblings is quite practical in tutoring programs in the school.

INTERACTION WITHIN THE FAMILY

One can view interactions within the family as a larger system involving three subsystems: parent–parent interactions, parent–child interactions, and sibling–sibling interactions. For example, in a two-child family the possible interactions among family members are shown in Figure 1. One can visualize the subsystem that involves the siblings operating as an independent unit, and also as influencing and being influenced by the two other subsystems.

If one considers the siblings (at least those relatively close in age) as a peer group, then the "family peer group" can be compared with the nonfamily peer group. In many ways, there are similarities between the family and the nonfamily peer group systems. It can be hypothesized that the activities occurring in the peer group also will occur in a family peer group of equal size and age level. In both cases peers can be models, reinforcers, caretakers, confidants, and pacesetters, as well as teachers.

There are several differences, however, between family and nonfamily peers. First, there is a greater amount of interaction, or more frequently repeated interaction between family peer dyads than between nonfamily peer dyads. The sibling relationship is one of extensive intimate daily contact, thus a sibling pair establishes customary patterns of communication and responsiveness to each other. One aspect of this interaction pattern is an educative function in which information is transmitted from one sibling to another, gradually shaping abilities and styles of learning. Second, the group structure or association between family peer members is more durable than a voluntary association of nonfamily peer members. Third, ascribed (nonchosen) roles exist in a family peer group along with achieved (chosen) roles. Fourth, there is greater commonality in the family peer group since all the family peer members are socialized by the same two dominant members of the family interaction system (parents).

In sum, several differences exist between the family peer group and the nonfamily peer group. There is greater opportunity for family peers to provide reinforcement and modeling for each other. The closeness of the family leads to

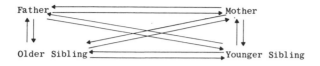

Figure 1 Interaction possibilities in a two-child family.

greater empathy, rapport, and communication. In the family, the child is better able to view things from his peer's viewpoint, speak the same language, and understand his problems and learning difficulties. Most important is the long-range advantage of siblings teaching siblings. If siblings teach each other, they will develop caring relationships and will turn to each other for help. Research has shown that siblings maintain fairly frequent contact throughout life, and that sibling rivalry or comparison between brothers remains important in adulthood (Adams, 1968).

RESEARCH ON SIBLINGS TEACHING SIBLINGS

At this point some empirical evidence relevant to sibling teaching will be examined. The available data will be organized around two major hypotheses, one dealing with siblings versus nonsiblings and the other concerned with the effectiveness of particular sibling combinations.

Siblings versus Nonsiblings as Teachers

The first hypothesis is as follows: Under certain conditions and for certain tasks, older siblings are more effective as teachers or helpers of their younger siblings than nonsiblings or even parents. Only a small amount of evidence bearing on this hypothesis is available, although a great deal of opinion and conjecture exists. In a survey of sociological literature on siblings, Irish (1964) pointed out that sibling bonds remain strong and positive throughout life, second in strength only to mother–child ties. Older siblings act as substitutes for parents under conditions when parents are "indifferent, harried, or uncomprehending (Irish, 1964)." They may be better teachers than parents when they have more direct knowledge about the subject (e.g., childhood skills or school problems), or when the subject is taboo (e.g., sex or death). Siblings also serve as role models for each other in many situations, particularly when the younger child can observe an older child of the same sex. Irish also views siblings as challenging and stimulating one another. Siblings are particularly important in large families of the urban poor, according to results of one study (Minuchin, Montalvo, Guerney, Rosman, & Schumer, 1967).

The sibling relationship is an especially influential one in view of the length of time siblings spend together and the extensive range and intimate nature of many activities involved (Bossard & Boll, 1954, 1960). The sibling relationship differs from other relationships by its "stark frankness"; dissembling and deception are impossible to maintain. According to Bossard and Boll (1954, 1960), siblings feel that they understand each other's problems better than parents, and are able to communicate more reasonable and meaningful disciplinary standards.

In one of the few quantitative studies of siblings in relation to nonsibling peers, Sutton-Smith (1966) asked fifth grade children about games they played with siblings and nonsibling playmates. First-born children took high-power roles with siblings and low-power roles with nonsibling friends; later-born children took low-power roles with older siblings but high-power roles with friends. This suggests that the younger siblings modeled their play behavior after older siblings.

Importance of peer interaction for adequate socialization in monkeys is demonstrated by Harlow's (1969) studies. Since "peers" in these experiments were age mates reared in a family-type group with the infant monkey, Harlow's results have implications for sibling studies as well. Cooperative behavior, control of aggression, and appropriate sex behavior developed optimally when both maternal care and peer play were available, in contrast to maternal care alone. Peer interactions (under optimum conditions) appeared to be able to compensate fully for lack of mothering.

One experimental study has investigated the effectiveness of older siblings and nonsiblings as teachers of a geometric concept to first grade children (Cicirelli, 1972). This study investigated the effect of older siblings and nonsiblings of both sexes as teachers of younger children on a concept-learning task. Each of the 120 first grade children in the study had an older sibling in the third grade. Samples of 30 sibling pairs were drawn from populations of boys with older sisters, boys with older brothers, girls with older sisters, and girls with older brothers. For half of the children in each group, the older sibling taught his or her younger sibling; the remaining half were re-paired so that the older child taught an unrelated first grade child.

The experimenter trained the older child in the trapezoid concept to a given learning criterion in a 30–45 minute session using a standardized teaching procedure. Then the older child taught the trapezoid concept to a younger child in a 10-minute session that was recorded. A concept attainment test was given to determine the learner's mastery of the trapezoid concept. An analysis of variance was conducted on the learner's concept attainment scores and Chi-square tests were calculated to determine the relation between variables measured in the teaching situation and the learner's concept attainment.

Results of the analysis of variance indicated a significant interaction ($p < .004$) between the sibling–nonsibling status of the child teachers and the teacher's sex. Interpretations of tests of simple main effects were as follows: First, sisters were more effective than brothers when teaching younger siblings, irrespective of the sex of the younger child. Second, sisters were more effective in teaching younger siblings than nonsibling girls were in teaching unrelated younger children. Third, boys tended to be more effective in teaching unrelated younger children than in teaching younger siblings. Fourth, boys and girls did not differ in effectiveness as teachers of unrelated younger children.

From observations made during the teaching session, it was evident that children teaching their own siblings differed in their teaching behaviors from children teaching nonsiblings. Chi-square tests were computed between each variable measured in the teaching situation and the compound variable "sex of teacher and sibling–nonsibling status of teacher" (categorized into male sibling, male nonsibling, female sibling and female nonsibling teachers). The following statistically significant associations appeared: First, girls teaching their siblings tended to use the deductive method more often than other teachers; boys teaching their siblings used the inductive method more often than other teachers. Second, girls teaching their siblings tended to do more explaining, describing, and defining of the concept than other teachers. Third, girls teaching siblings and boys teaching nonsiblings engaged in more demonstrating and illustrating of attributes of the trapezoid than other teachers–girls teaching nonsiblings did least of all. Fourth, teachers of siblings tended to be more selective in the examples presented than were teachers of nonsiblings. Fifth, girls teaching their siblings tended to give less feedback than other teachers, perhaps because their greater use of deductive method made feedback less relevant. Finally, girls teaching nonsiblings tended to give more incorrect feedback than other teachers.

It is apparent that the teaching behavior of an older child depends on the sibling relationship to the learner and is not a general characteristic of the child. For example, 14 of 30 older sisters used the deductive method while teaching their younger siblings and only 3 used the inductive method (the remainder used a mixed method); yet only 2 of 30 older girls used the deductive method while teaching nonsiblings (13 used the inductive method). (Recall that all the girls in this study were actually older sisters with younger siblings; half of the "sisters" were randomly re-paired to teach unrelated children of the same age and sex as their own siblings.) Shifting of one's teaching strategy according to the teacher's sibling relationship to the learner was likewise true of the older boys as teachers.

The shift in teaching approach and the variation in achievement by the learner depending upon the sibling relationship indicate that social interaction between siblings is an important determinant of their role behavior. The teaching role emerges out of the ongoing interaction between sibling pairs, which is characterized by pre-existing patterns of communication and responsiveness. By studying this interaction one might gain valuable insights into the manner in which siblings influence each other's learning.

Effectiveness of Different Sibling Dyads

The second major hypothesis of this paper asserts that certain sibling dyads are more effective than others in the teaching–learning situation. Previous research, and in particular the pioneering studies of Helen Koch (1954) and recent work of Sutton-Smith and Rosenberg (1969), amply demonstrates that the cognitive development of a child is related to his position in the sibling structure of the family. But the specific factors mediating such effects are not yet clear. Many investigators explain the relationship of sibling structure to cognition in terms of differential parental treatment or parent–child interaction. In addition, interactions among siblings may also be an important factor.

The model shown in Figure 2 may explain the outcomes to the child that derive from his sibling status. To elaborate on the model, one must start with some definitions. The *sibling structure* of a family is the network of positions for children in the family defined by the number of children, birth order, sex of the children, their ages, and age spacing between children. The *sibling status* of two or more children is their position within the network. (For some researchers, sibling status is identified with one dimension of the sibling structure, e.g., birth order. In my own work, sibling status is defined by age, sex, birth order, and age spacing taken simultaneously.) *Sibling interaction* refers to the reciprocal interchange of verbal and nonverbal communication between siblings.

In the model, interactions among family members are grouped into three subsystems: parent–parent, parent–child, and sibling–sibling. Children in different sibling status positions will receive varying responses from parents and other siblings in the family, which will be manifested in differential interpersonal behavior in the family interaction subsystems (parent–parent, parent–child, and sibling–sibling interactions). These subsystems in turn influence the child's behavior, personal characteristics, and development. It follows, then, that one would expect different sibling dyads (different sex, age, etc.) to interact differently and result in different outcomes.

Evidence in the literature indicates differential treatment by the parent of children in different positions in the family. For example, Bossard and Boll (1960) found distinct role expectations for children according to their position in the sibling structure. According to one study, mothers were less warm emotionally and more restrictive and coercive toward their first child than toward their second (Lasko, 1954). Rothbart (1976) reviewed existing studies in this area and concluded that greater intrusiveness and control by the mother of the first born's behavior (especially girls) was a general finding. These findings refer, however, to children below school age.

There has been little direct study of sibling interaction—although the negative effects of sibling rivalry have been discussed for many years. Sutton-Smith and Rosenberg (1969) reported results of an interview–questionnaire administered to upper grade elementary school children concerning tactics for getting their sibling to do what they wanted them to do. Boys used attack and offense more often; girls used reasoning, defense, and making the sibling feel obligated. First-born children were more likely to boss, attack, interfere, ignore, be offen-

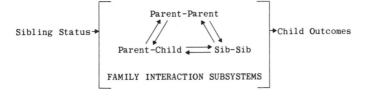

Figure 2   A model for the effect of sibling status on the child.

sive, or bribe their sibling; second-born children were more likely to attack property, plead, or reason with their sibling. Bossing, being offensive, sulking, and teasing were more likely to be used with a sibling of the same sex; being defensive and making-up were techniques used with an opposite sex sibling. First-born children used more powerful techniques in interactions with their siblings than did later-born children; also, siblings of the same sex used more powerful techniques. Koch (1960) found that a pair of brothers reported more quarreling than any other combination of siblings, which lends some support to the results of Sutton-Smith and Rosenberg (1969).

In the concept-learning study discussed earlier (Cicirelli, 1972), four types of sibling dyads were compared: older brother teaching younger brother, brother teaching sister, sister teaching brother, and sister teaching sister. In general, older sisters were more effective teachers of their younger siblings than were older brothers. Looking at the four sibling dyads, highest average concept attainment scores were found for boys taught by older sisters (23.20), followed by girls taught by older sisters (19.67) and boys taught by older brothers (18.07); poorest scores were made by girls taught by older brothers (17.07). (Correlations between the learners' concept attainment scores and teachers' IQ and reading achievement were close to zero, indicating the lack of importance of initial differences.) The two extreme sibling dyad groups were examined further. Older girls teaching younger brothers explained, described, and defined the trapezoid concept significantly more than did older boys teaching younger sisters.

Because the concept teaching task used in the first study was highly structured and allowed only a rather narrow range of behaviors in the teaching-interaction session, research was conducted using an object-sorting task having no "right" answers (Cicirelli, 1974). This should provide a better vehicle for studying sibling interaction, since the children would be freer to react to the task and to each other than in the concept-learning study.

Only children from two-child families were selected. Age of the siblings and spacing between them were varied in this study since these factors are important in research on sibling structure (Sutton-Smith & Rosenberg, 1969). One would expect on the basis of previous research that a child's siblings would have the greatest effect in the preschool and early elementary years, with the effect diminishing with age. Similarly, a close age spacing is presumably beneficial for girls but detrimental for boys, but when the older sibling is helping the younger on a cognitive task, the younger might well view the wide-spaced older sibling as a more effective source of aid.

A factorial design was used, with four sibling structure factors and one treatment factor. There were 160 sibling pairs in all, 40 from each of the following groups: kindergarten children with second grade siblings, kindergarten children with fourth grade siblings, second grade children with fourth grade siblings, and second grade children with sixth grade siblings. Each of these groups of 40 contained 10 sibling pairs from each of the 4 sex combinations (boys with older brothers, boys with older sisters, girls with older brothers, and girls with older sisters). The object-sorting task required children to form groupings of 50 pictures of familiar objects. Half the children in the study were assigned to an "alone" condition, in which the child made a practice categorization of the pictures from the object-sorting task while alone. The remaining half of the children were assigned to a "sibling" condition, in which the child made the initial categorization with the help of his older sibling. The experimenter observed and recorded interaction between the sibling pairs in the "sib" condition as they worked on the sorting task. Measures of the younger sibling's task performance were obtained from a subsequent "test" administration of an alternative form of the object-sorting task. These measures included categorization style (number and size of groups, number of ungrouped items), and conceptual style (type of category formed, such as descriptive, relational, and inferential).

Results provided evidence that older siblings did influence their younger siblings' performance on the object-sorting task, and that performance depended (at least in part) on sibling status. Concerning categorization style, children in the "sib" condition made more groups than did children in the "alone" condition. Similarly, on the average children in the "sib" condition left fewer items ungrouped than children in the "alone" condition; however, this finding depended on the age spacing between the siblings. Among children with siblings 4 years older, those in the "sib" condition left fewer items ungrouped than children in the "alone" condition; among children with siblings 2 years older, there was little difference between those in the "sib" and "alone" conditions. Regarding group size, among children with siblings 4 years older those in the "sib" condition made smaller groups than those in the "alone" condition. Looking at the conceptual style variables, the older sibling had no direct influence on the younger sibling's use of relational categories that depended on sibling status. Among kindergarten children, those in the "alone" condition used a higher percentage of descriptive categories than those in the "sib" condition, but among second grade children there was little difference between the two conditions. For children in the "sib" condition, girls used a higher percentage of inferential categories than boys when their siblings were 4 years older, but boys used a higher percentage than did girls when the sibs were 2 years older. Among children in the "alone" condition these relations were reversed.

An analysis was conducted on the behaviors observed while the siblings were interacting in the object-sorting task situation. The interaction was coded into 29 categories; 18 were significantly correlated with the object-sorting measures. These behaviors were: the older sibling explaining, telling the younger sibling what to do, giving cues, questioning, giving category name, encouraging, criticizing, giving confirmation of a group made by the younger sibling, adding to the younger sibling's group, making a group himself, nonverbally encouraging and criticizing, and rearranging groups made by the younger sibling; the younger sibling verbalizing his actions as he sorts, accepting direction from the older sibling (verbally and nonverbally), rejecting help, showing objects to the older sibling, and working independently.

Point-biserial correlations were computed between the sibling status variables and frequency of the sibling interaction behaviors. Sex of the younger sibling was significantly related to two of the older sibling's behaviors: The older sibling showed a greater tendency to give cues or hints and to verbalize his actions when the younger sibling was a girl. Sex of the older sibling was related in the following way: Older sisters showed a greater tendency to point to objects for grouping, to add objects to the younger sibling's grouping, and to observe the younger sibling working; older brothers showed a greater tendency to verbalize their actions. The younger sibling was more likely to accept nonverbal direction when the older sibling was a girl and more likely to work independently of the male older sibling. The older sibling was more likely to make groups himself when the younger sibling was of kindergarten age rather than a second grader, and the second grade child showed a greater tendency to verbalize his actions than did the kindergarten child. Finally, the younger sibling showed a greater tendency to accept direction when the older sibling was 4 years older than when he was only 2 years older.

In an attempt to simplify the sibling interaction data, a principal components factor analysis was conducted. The first five factors accounted for 80% of the variance, and suggest meaningful patterns of sibling interaction. In the first, the older sibling is highly directive of the younger sibling's sorting activities without being explanatory. In the second, there is some explanation along with a good deal of verbalization of activity. The third and fifth factors involved nonverbal interaction between the siblings, the third being a directing pattern and the fifth a criticizing, interfering pattern of behavior. The fourth factor is of particular interest since it is reminiscent of the deductive teaching style in the concept-learning study. It is an explanatory teaching pattern, with the older sibling giving category labels, giving cues, asking questions, and so on, and the younger sibling accepting this help and verbalizing his own sorting actions. (These behaviors were associated with the younger sibling's use of the developmentally more advanced inferential categories.)

THEORETICAL EXPLANATIONS

Looking back over the studies completed thus far, it seems clear that older siblings do have an effect on their younger siblings' performance on cognitive tasks, that this effect differs from their effect on nonsiblings, and that the effect depends on sibling status positions. If the older sibling is a girl or widely spaced in age from the younger sibling, effects are more positive than if the older sibling is a boy or close in age. A common pattern of teaching or helping behavior in the studies is the older sibling giving explanations, making verbal labels (of concept attributes and object categories), and asking pertinent questions. In concept learning, this provides the child with labels that might not be in his repertoire and helps him to become aware of attributes that he might be unable to abstract for himself from the examples provided.

How can such results be explained? Why are sisters more effective than brothers in teaching younger siblings? Why are sisters more effective in teaching their younger siblings than in teaching unrelated younger children? Why are older siblings more effective in helping younger siblings when there is a wider age spacing between the sibling pair? Several different explanations can be offered.

Sibling rivalry has been advanced as one possible factor accounting for some research findings of sibling effect. Boys tend to react more intensely to sibling displacement; sibling displacement by a newborn within an age spacing of 2 to 4 years is most intense (Koch, 1960; Rosenberg & Sutton-Smith, 1969). Thus, older brothers close in age to younger siblings should demonstrate more hostility, competitiveness, and jealousy than older sisters. Such sibling rivalry also could lead younger siblings to be defensive and resist learning from an older brother. Both Sutton-Smith (1966) and Adams (1968) speak of the effects of sibling rivalry between males of college age or older, and Sutton-Smith and Rosenberg (1969) reported that older boys typically used "attack and offense" as tactics in interactions with their younger siblings. Perhaps when siblings are in a teaching–learning situation a male older sibling is less motivated to teach his younger sibling, and the younger sibling is more resistant to learning.

Role theory provides another possible explanation (Sarbin, 1964). Girls tend to identify more with their mothers and with their female schoolteachers than boys (Koch, 1960; Sutton-Smith & Rosenberg, 1969); thus, they are more ready to assume a teaching role. Moreover, an older sister tends to have more responsibility for care of younger siblings than an older brother, often being delegated caretaking or teaching roles (Bossard & Boll, 1960; Mead & Heyman,

1965). Sisters consequently develop the role of teacher of younger siblings to a greater extent than older brothers. By similar reasoning, older siblings with a wide age spacing also tend to be delegated more teaching and caretaking roles than a closely spaced older sibling.

Sutton-Smith and Rosenberg (1969) have theorized that interaction between siblings is characterized by both modeling and reactive components, with second-born children relying more heavily on modeling of the older sibling. Direct modeling of the older sibling's performance does not seem to have been an important factor in the sibling teaching studies since the older sibling generally did not perform the tasks himself. On the other hand, such reactive behaviors as dependency on the older sibling and conformity to his suggestions also appear to be of minor value in explaining the outcome as evidenced by the weak correlations between behaviors and outcomes. (The fact that the younger siblings accepted help and direction more readily from a sibling who was 4 years older does provide some evidence for a reactive component of the interaction, however.) It is possible, of course, that subtle modeling of the older sibling's task-appropriate behaviors occurred even though the older sibling did not actually model the task. If some sort of modeling is responsible, it is quite reasonable that the widely spaced older sibling would be viewed as a more powerful and competent model. Although children close in age spacing tend to show more spontaneous interaction in the home situation, perhaps one should distinguish between quantity and quality of sibling interaction. Widely spaced older siblings might be more effective as models on cognitive tasks even though the actual amount of interaction between siblings might be less than if the children were closely spaced.

Social facilitation theory suggests other possible explanations (Cottrell, 1968; Zajonc, 1965). The mere presence of the older sibling in the task situation might arouse or energize the younger sibling, leading to greater task involvement on his part. If the presence of another is a learned source of drive, where a positive or negative evaluation by the "spectator" is anticipated, the older sibling as a spectator would be a well-learned source of drive for the young child and thus might produce a more definite and intense effect on the young child's task behaviors than the presence on a nonsibling. If the older sibling is viewed as nurturant and supporting—as the older sister or widely spaced older sibling might be—the child's general arousal level should be less than if the sibling is viewed as negatively evaluating or threatening. And performance on a learning task, where dominant responses are incorrect, should be better when arousal is at an intermediate level.

Studies of social reinforcement (Stevenson, 1965), though not involving a teaching–learning situation, have shown that social reinforcement by peers is effective in increasing task performance. Such effects were greater when reinforcement was delivered by a disliked, rather than by a liked, peer. Social reinforcement also was found to be more effective when delivered by strangers than by parents. If one considers the older child in the teaching situation as having some of the properties of a social reinforcer, then one might predict that the familiar sibling would be less effective than a nonsibling teacher. Unfortunately, results did not bear out such a prediction.

No single explanation seems to account for the results of the sibling teaching experiments, although each position applies to a portion of the findings. This may be reasonable, since a sibling or peer teaching situation is a highly complex interaction. In addition to the influence of more formal teaching variables (kinds of explanation, learning cues, feedback, etc.) that may involve appropriate role behaviors by teacher and learner, other factors such as social reinforcement, social facilitation, modeling, rivalry, and competition may all be involved.

IMPLICATIONS FOR RESEARCH AND PRACTICE

The present state of knowledge about sibling teaching is so limited as to make recommendations for practice highly tenuous. For example, if sibling teaching programs were instituted in schools, what would be the effects at home? Nevertheless, present results suggest that certain sibling dyads would be especially effective in school peer tutoring situations—more effective than other sibling dyads or nonsibling pairs. A first recommendation, then, might be to select as tutors pairs of children that would be expected to yield favorable results: widely spaced siblings, and older sisters. A second recommendation would be to emphasize in training programs for prospective child tutors those behaviors characterizing the more effective sibling dyads: explanation, verbal labeling, and questioning. Present results suggest that a "deductive" teaching style is more effective than "inductive" or laissez-faire methods. It may be that "discovery" or self-guided instruction requires a highly knowledgeable and sophisticated teacher for effective implementation, and is not suitable for child tutors.

The study of sibling interaction leads to the conclusion that a child's siblings are indeed important agents of socialization. When peer tutoring programs are contemplated in the schools, the use of such a valuable resource as a child's own siblings should be given careful consideration.

REFERENCES

Adams, B. N. *Kinship in an urban setting.* Chicago: Markham, 1968.

Bossard, J. H. S., & Boll, E. H. Security in the large family. *Mental Hygiene,* 1954, *38* 529–544.

Bossard, J. H. S., & Boll, E. H. *The sociology of child development* (3rd ed.). New York: Harper, 1960.

Cicirelli, V. G. The effect of sibling relationships on concept learning of young children taught by child teachers. *Child Development,* 1972, *43,* 282–287.

Cicirelli, V. G. Effects of sibling structure and interaction on children's categorization style. *Developmental Psychology,* 1973, *9,* 132–139.

Cicirelli, V. G. Relationship of sibling structure and interaction on younger sib's conceptual style. *Journal of Genetic Psychology,* 1974, *125,* 37–49.

Cottrell, N. B. Performance in the presence of other human beings: Mere presence, audience, and affiliation effects. In E. C. Simmel, R. A. Hoppe, & G. A. Milton (Eds.), *Social facilitation and imitative behavior.* Rockleigh, New Jersey: Allyn & Bacon, 1968. Pp. 91–110.

Harlow, H. Age-mate or peer affectional system. In D. Lehrman, R. Hinde, & E. Shaw (Eds.), *Advances in the study of behavior.* Vol. 2. New York: Academic Press, 1969. Pp. 333–383.

Irish, D. P. Sibling interaction: A neglected aspect in family life research. *Social Forces,* 1964, *42,* 279–288.

Koch, H. L. The relation of primary mental abilities in five- and six-year-olds to sex of child and characteristics of his sibling. *Child Development,* 1954, *25,* 209–223.

Koch, H. L. The relation of certain formal attributes of siblings to attitudes held toward each other and toward their parents. *Monographs of the Society for Research in Child Development,* 1960, *25,* 1–124.

Lasko, J. K. Parent behavior toward first and second children. *Genetic Psychology Monographs,* 1954, *49,* 97–137.

Mead, M., & Heyman, K. *The family.* New York: Macmillan, 1965.

Minuchin, S., Montalvo, B., Guerney, B. G., Rosman, B. L., & Schumer, F. *Families of the slums.* New York: Basic Books, 1967.

Rosenberg, B. G., & Sutton-Smith, B. Sibling age spacing effects upon cognition. *Developmental Psychology,* 1969, *1,* 661–668.

Rothbart, M. K. Birth order and mother-child interaction in an achievement situation. *Journal of Personality and Social Psychology,* 1971, *17,* 113–120.

Rothbart, M. K. Sibling position and maternal involvement. In K. F. Riegel & J. A. Mecham (Eds.), *The developing individual in a changing world.* Vol. III: *Social and environmental issues.* The Hague: Mouton, 1976.

Sarbin, T. R. Role theoretical interpretation of psychological change. In P. Worchel & D. Byrne (Eds.), *Personality change.* New York: Wiley, 1964. Pp. 176–219.

Stevenson, H. W. Social reinforcement of children's behavior. In L. P. Lipsitt and C. C. Spiker (Eds.), *Advances in child development and behavior.* Vol. 2. New York: Academic Press, 1965. Pp. 97–126.

Sutton-Smith, B. Role replication and reversal in play. *Merrill-Palmer Quarterly,* 1966, *12,* 285–298.

Sutton-Smith, B., & Rosenberg, B. G. Modeling and reactive components of sibling interaction. In J. P. Hill (Ed.), *Minnesota symposia on child psychology,* Vol. 3. Minneapolis: Univ. of Minnesota Press, 1969. Pp. 131–152.

Zajonc, R. Social facilitation. *Science,* 1965, *149,* 269–274.

7

Studies on the Role of Tutor

Vernon L. Allen Robert S. Feldman

University of Wisconsin   University of Wisconsin

In this chapter we shall discuss some empirical findings from an ongoing series of studies dealing with cross-age tutoring. The general purpose of the research program is to provide a better understanding of the underlying psychological factors mediating any changes in academic achievement and social behavior due to children teaching other children. Although we are interested in the effect of tutoring for both the tutor (the child doing the teaching) and the tutee (the child being taught), the primary focus of research reported in this chapter will be on the child who serves as the tutor.

In the following pages we shall summarize briefly our research in two areas: (1) factors responsible for the positive psychological effects of tutoring on the tutor; and (2) interaction processes occurring in cross-age tutoring dyads, with special emphasis on nonverbal behavior. The strategy of our research is intended to maximize the benefits derived from a reciprocal relation between theory and empirical findings. To this end, diverse though complementary research methods have been used, including field research in the school, questionnaire studies, and controlled experiments in the laboratory.

Role theory is employed as the general conceptual orientation in the present research project because it appears to be particularly appropriate for analysis of cross-age tutoring. The macro-social roles of teacher and student are also involved in the micro-social system of tutoring. The molar units of analysis used by role theory render it particularly amenable to the analysis of complex, ongoing social behavior and applied research problems in general. Moreover, role theory explicitly recognizes the interactive and complementary nature of social behavior. The theory has the further advantage of linking the individual to the social system by means of the concept of social position.

Before proceeding, a few comments about the use of theory in applied research are appropriate. We maintain that it is better to approach an applied problem with a general theoretical framework than without one. A theory identifies relevant independent and dependent variables for investigation; proceeding with such guidance usually will be more productive than selecting variables unsystematically or intuitively. A theory also specifies intervening psychological processes—thereby suggesting explanations for the behavior in question. Finally, a theory provides a conceptual framework and terminology for communicating about a problem in a systematic and unified manner.

CONSEQUENCES OF ENACTING THE ROLE OF TUTOR

One of the most interesting results to emerge from research on tutoring concerns its effects on the child who teaches or helps another child. Even more intriguing than improvement in learning are the changes in social behavior, motivation, attitudes, and self-concept occurring in the child doing the tutoring (Gartner, Kohler, & Riessman, 1971). The tutor frequently shows a better attitude toward school and teachers, becomes more responsible, and thinks more highly of himself. The positive effects of tutoring have impressed teachers and other observers over the years. Turning to the nineteenth century for an example, Joseph Lancaster stated in his book published in 1803: "... I have ever found, the surest way to cure a mischievous boy was to make him a *monitor.* I never knew anything succeed much better, if as well" (p. 31, italics in the original). (By the term "monitor," Lancaster meant "tutor.") And Lancaster did have some extreme cases. In one instance a boy's truancy was so severe that "his father got a log and chain and chained it to his foot, and in that condition, beating him all the way, followed him to school repeatedly" (Lancaster, 1803, p. 32).

The Teacher Role

Let us explore the role of teacher from the vantage point of a role theoretical analysis.. It is a basic tenet of role theory that enactment of a role produces changes in behavior, attitudes, and self-perceptions consistent with expectations associated with the role. Empirical data demonstrate that role enactment does indeed produce behavioral and attitudinal changes in the person enacting a role (Lieberman, 1956; Waller, 1932). In the case of the child who enacts the role of teacher for another child, the role represents prestige, authority, and feelings of competence; it would seem reasonable to expect that enacting the role of teacher would increase self-esteem and produce a more positive attitude toward school and teachers. In short, the effects of tutoring on the tutor can be understood as being the consequence of enacting the role of teacher, in much the same way that enacting any role produces behavioral and cognitive changes that are consistent with role expectations.

How can one maximize the positive consequences of tutoring for the child enacting the role of teacher? According to role theory, a number of factors contribute to the degree of change produced by enacting a role, including involvement in the role, clarity of the role expectations, accuracy of role location, and so on (Sarbin & Allen, 1968). Following the implications of role theory, in our long-term studies on tutoring in the schools we attempted to incorporate into the program those factors predicted to enhance the positive effects of tutoring for the tutor. To increase involvement and provide greater clarity of role expectations, we supplied appropriate symbolic cues to increase the visibility of the tutor role for the tutor, tutees, and other children. Distinctive appurtenances were incorporated into the program, such as a certificate designating the tutor as a "student teacher," a portfolio for keeping a daily log and lesson plans, and other record-keeping paraphernalia typically possessed by a teacher. Furthermore, tutors consulted with their classroom teacher about their tutee's needs; they were given some responsibility for developing curriculum for their tutee; they had disciplinary responsibility for their tutee; tutoring sessions were not closely monitored. All these "symbols and tokens of position" should enhance involvement in the role and help clarify role expectations—factors that, according to theory, should increase the likelihood of behavioral and attitudinal changes consistent with expectations for the role of teacher.

It is interesting to note in this connection that children who have participated in our tutoring programs have expressed a very consistent and almost unanimous positive reaction to it. Older children almost invariably have reported that they enjoyed teaching younger children; and the younger children also say that they liked being taught in the one-to-one situation by a student who is 2 or 3 years older. Both tutors and tutees always wanted to participate in a similar program in the future. Many older children, in particular, were very enthusiastic about being allowed to teach younger children. It is not hard to understand why children are so enthusiastic about being able to teach other children. The teacher role consists of many very attractive elements: increased responsibility and prestige in the eyes of other students, additional attention and reward from adults, and respect from the younger child being taught.

Our studies in the school also provide suggestive data indicating that tutors judge themselves as being more competent in intellectual and school-related areas after teaching another child. Because of the remarkable positive impact of tutoring on the tutor, some schools have used the technique as a means of improving the academic and social behavior of underachieving or recalcitrant children. One should be very cautious, however, about the possibility of concentrating too much on benefiting the tutor at the possible expense of the tutee, as illustrated in our study described below.

We conducted a short 2-week study in which low-achieving children taught younger children in several subject areas (Allen & Feldman, 1973). As a control for the sheer additional time the children spent studying the material, on alternate days the tutor either taught a younger child or spent the equivalent amount of time studying alone. Likewise, the tutees were taught by an older child or they studied alone. (This is, incidentally, one of the few studies that has included this essential control condition.) Results showed that the low-achieving tutors initially learned somewhat more when studying alone than when teaching a younger child, but by the end of the 2-week period, tutoring was producing better learning than studying alone. Perhaps the social aspects of the tutoring situation provided motivation and interest for these low-achieving children that was lacking when they worked alone. In the case of the learners (tutees) a weak interaction was found: Initially the tutees learned more when being taught, but by the end of the 2-week period they did slightly better when studying alone. These data certainly are not conclusive by any means, but they do at least suggest that while striving to obtain optimal benefits for problem children by using them as tutors, the gains may be purchased at the cost of their tutees.

Tutors' Evaluation of Tutee

As part of our role theory orientation to understanding the effect of tutoring on the tutor, we measured role perceptions and expectations by assessing the preferences of 800 children for a variety of tutoring arrangements. Among other findings, children preferred to teach children younger than themselves and to be taught by children older than themselves. Both boys and girls preferred same-sex tutors and tutees. For one interesting and central aspect of the role of teacher, evaluating and grading one's student, the data indicated that children wanted to evaluate and give marks to their learners quite frequently. It may be that evaluation and power over the student are attractive components of the teacher role. But such statements of preference should not be accepted at face value in the absence of congruent behavioral data.

To examine the tutors' behavioral reactions to evaluating their tutees, a tutoring situation was devised which varied the degree of evaluation required of the tutors across experimental conditions. Results revealed that tutors did not enjoy evaluating their tutees (Towson & Allen, 1970). When the evaluation had important consequences for the tutee (i.e., it determined the number of candies received), the evaluation was especially unpleasant for the tutor. In the evaluation conditions, the tutors indicated that they enjoyed tutoring less, believed that they did less well as a tutor, and thought that teaching was more difficult. Hence, tutors discovered that having the power to influence outcomes for another person was, in fact, less enjoyable than they might have anticipated. Certainly not all elements of the role of teacher are pleasant!

Being a Role Model

The concept of role model is a second factor that may be responsible for the impact of tutoring on the tutor. The use of tutor as a role model for the tutee may be a very important variable in some cases, but it will be discussed only briefly. The behavior of the older child who serves as tutor for a younger child can influence the tutee directly both in cognitive and social areas. The tutor may serve as a role model for the younger child; that is, the younger child may imitate the tutor, identify with him, and try to be like him. If the older child realizes that his own behavior is affecting the younger child's behavior—that is, that the younger child is using him as a model—the older child may feel obligated to behave in socially desirable ways. With greater age discrepancies between the older and younger child, the effect on the older child of being a role model should be stronger.

We attempted to investigate experimentally the effect on sixth grade tutors of their being imitated in varying degrees by their young tutees. Results showed that female tutors increased the amount of liking for their same-sex tutees the more they were imitated, but male tutors liked their tutees less when the tutees imitated them a great deal (Allen & Devin-Sheehan, 1974a). In a school situation providing opportunity for considerable out-of-class contact between older and younger children, being a role model for the younger child to imitate and "look up to" may exert a very powerful influence in constraining the tutor's behavior along socially desirable channels. From research on one-teacher schools we found that both teachers and children indicated that older children felt a high degree of responsibility for the younger ones (Allen & Devin-Sheehan, 1974b).

Attributions and Attitudes toward the Tutee

Reactions of the tutor toward his tutee (such as judgments about the tutee's ability and likeability) may have important effects on both the tutor and the tutee. In a series of studies, we investigated one factor likely to influence the attitudes and attributions of ability made by the tutor: the apparent success of the tutee in learning the material.

Both reinforcement theory and role theory suggest that the degree of a student's success over a period of time will affect the tutor's perception of the student's ability and also his liking for the student. Thus, a student who does consistently well should be perceived as more intelligent and likeable than one who does consistently poorly. Likewise, a tutor should like the teaching experience more when his student does consistently well than when he does consistently poorly. These predictions are straightforward and not surprising. Role theory suggests further, however, that a critical determinant of the tutor's perceptions is the order or sequence of a tutee's success or failure over a period of time.

In the tutoring situation it is congruent with the role of teacher for a student to do poorly on a task initially, but to show improvement in his performance later; that is, the teacher's efforts are supposed to help the student improve his learning. To enact appropriately and effectively the role of teacher, one's student should show an improvement in performance over time. The converse of this pattern of performance for one's student—initially doing well but then deteriorating over time—should be perceived as an ineffectual and inappropriate enactment of the role of teacher. Thus, for an equivalent amount of objectively successful learning the direction of change in the tutee's performance should lead to different consequences with regard to the tutor's satisfaction with the role enactment.

In our first study, the pattern or sequence of performance of a learner in a tutoring situation was varied in terms of degree of congruence of the learning to expectations about the teacher role (Allen & Feldman, 1974). In a one-session teaching situation, an 11-year-old tutor taught a concept-formation task to an 8-year-old (a confederate) whose performance over a series of trials created four sequences: success throughout, failure throughout, success in the first half followed by failure in the second half, or the reverse. In the condition that is congruent with the role of teacher (poor initial performance followed by an improvement), one would expect the tutor to react more positively about the tutoring experience and to express more positive attitudes and attributions about the learner.

Results showed clearly that the sequence of the tutee's success or failure, rather than the absolute amount of learning, per se, determined the tutor's reactions. Figure 1 shows that the tutor's attributions about the tutee's intellectual ability, liking of the tutee, and general reactions to the situation were disproportionately influenced by the tutee's performance early in the session. In other words, a strong and consistent primacy effect was found. Thus, contrary to our prediction, results showed that the condition that more closely approximated the role of teacher (poor learning followed by improvement) did not result in more positive responses from the tutor. Even so, this finding led us to conduct several other studies on the primacy effect in ability attributions and attitudinal response.

One might ask whether the primacy effect would have occurred if the parts of the lesson were separated by a period of time, say, an interval of a few days.

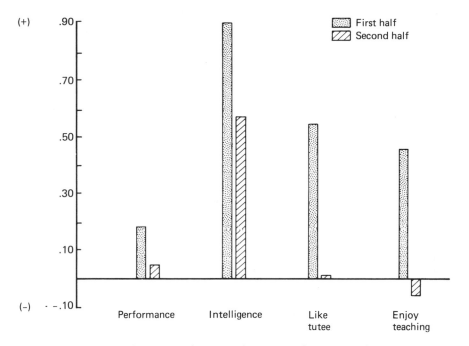

Figure 1 Reactions of tutor as a function of sequence of ongoing performance by tutee (success minus failure).

Many tutoring programs in the schools are arranged on a schedule of two or three meetings a week; such temporal separation of phases of learning might be sufficient to destroy any initial expectation about the tutee that had been established by the tutor. In a recent study we separated the parts of the lesson by a substantial period of time—2 days (Feldman & Allen, 1975a). Results still clearly disclosed a strong primacy effect, which attests to the strength and persistence of the tutor's initial expectations about the tutee.

Practical implications of these findings for cross-age tutoring in the schools are obvious. It is important that the first learning task be easy enough to ensure that the tutee can perform well, since initial learning strongly affects the tutor's attributions about the tutee's ability, liking of the tutee, and reaction to tutoring another child. We know from other research that a teacher's expectations about a student can influence learning (Rosenthal & Jacobson, 1968).

In subsequent research we discovered that it is possible to eliminate the primacy effect by devising a completely different type of situation (Feldman & Allen, 1975b). Four graphic charts were constructed, each of which portrayed the sequence of correct–incorrect responses made by a student over a series of trials. A subject was shown one chart representing a student's learning record, and then evaluated the quality of performance and the intelligence of this student. Since the complete record of the learner's performance was available to the subject, it is unlikely that an initial expectation about the learner could have been established; nor could the subject in any way distort his memory of the student's later performance.

As we expected, under these conditions the primacy effect was not manifested (Feldman & Allen, 1975b). To our surprise, however, we obtained a recency effect instead! That is, the level of second-half learning exerted a significant impact on judgment of performance and attributions of ability, although first-half learning did not. To assure ourselves that this finding was a reliable phenomenon, we replicated the experiment. Results again showed a strong recency effect.

In sum, it appears that the tutor is susceptible to either a primacy or a recency effect in his judgments about the learner, depending upon the nature of the situation. Observation of ongoing behavior as it unfolds on a trial-to-trial basis results in early performance exerting a greater impact than later performance on the attitudes and attributions made about the student. By contrast, when the record of the learner's sequence of completed performance is available for inspection, the level reached on later performance is taken as most indicative of amount of learning and underlying ability of the student. The present findings should reduce concern about the practical implications of the primacy effect found in attributions of ability. According to these data, a primacy effect will not appear if the cumulative record of a person's performance is available.

SOCIAL INTERACTION PROCESSES

To enact a role effectively and convincingly, an individual must possess the requisite role skills. For example, in the case of the tutor it is necessary to monitor the behavior of the tutee during the teaching session to determine whether the tutee is understanding the material being taught. Both verbal and nonverbal social skills are useful in interacting with the tutee. Several of our studies have dealt with the role skills relevant to the tutoring situation; in this section we shall focus primarily on studies concerning nonverbal behavior.

Tutee Performance and Tutor's Behavior

Studies reported earlier showed clearly that the degree of success or failure displayed by a tutee will be reflected in the attributions and reactions made by his tutor. Yet it is likely that overt behavioral responses as well as attitudinal reactions and attributions will occur. To extend research into the area of overt responses made by the tutor, we designed a study investigating behavioral concomitants of the tutor's affective reactions toward the tutee. Our earlier findings indicate that when the tutee performs well, the tutor is more satisfied with the role of teacher than when the tutee performs poorly. These attitudes held by the tutors might also be reflected in verbal and nonverbal behavior directed toward the tutee. Other empirical evidence shows that the nonverbal behavior of adults reflects their affective state (Argyle, 1969; Mehrabian, 1972). For instance, smiling, nodding, and greater eye gaze are generally found to signify positive affect; conversely, negative affect is indicated by frowns, grimaces, and headshaking. Thus, success or failure of the tutee should lead to differential nonverbal behavior from the tutor.

In addition, verbal behavior should be affected by the performance of the tutee. Instances of failure no doubt will lead to corrective verbal statements and further explanation; success probably will elicit responses of a different sort. It is reasonable to assume that the affective tone of the tutor's verbal responses, quite apart from the specific demands of the teaching situation, will also be affected by the tutee's performance.

Subjects were some of the children who participated in the first attribution study (Allen & Feldman, 1974). While a child interacted with his tutee (a confederate), we recorded the behavior on video- and audiotape. The tutee was coached to perform either well or poorly on the two halves of the 24-item test. For purposes of the present study, only results from the first half of the test were used. Thus, there were two conditions: (*1*) successful performance (the tutee answered correctly on 75% of the 12 items) and (*2*) failing performance (the tutee answered incorrectly on 75% of the questions).

Affective content of the tutor's speech was determined from typed transcripts of the tutoring sessions. Three categories of affective tone were used: positive, negative, and neutral. The unit of analysis was a logical phrase. Examples coded as representing positive affect are: "That's right" or "You're really catching on." Examples of phrases coded as negative are: "You're wrong," "It isn't," or "You better try getting these." Nonverbal behavior of tutors was analyzed by trained coders.

Results showed that tutors in the successful performance condition used a significantly higher proportion of positive affective phrases than tutors who taught children who performed poorly (Feldman & Allen, 1974). Conversely, tutors in the successful performance condition used significantly fewer negatively toned phrases than did subjects in the failure condition. Thus, the affective tone of tutors' verbalizations were affected by experimental manipulation. Nonverbal behavior also differed according to the tutee's performance. In conditions of tutee success the tutors exhibited significantly fewer instances of pursing lips, headshakes, forward learning, reaching toward tutee, and fidgeting; but there was a significantly greater frequency of headnoding and erect posture.

Frequency of eye gaze was also affected by tutee performance: tutees who did poorly were looked at a greater proportion of the time (.42) than tutees who did well (.34).

The results show quite clearly that both the verbal and nonverbal behavior of a tutor is affected by the performance of his tutee. Thus, not only do tutors like tutees who perform well, but they also behave differentially toward tutees according to their performance. It is reasonable to believe that the tutor's verbal and nonverbal affective responses will have an impact on the tutee's motivation and enjoyment of the tutoring experience.

Our research also shows that the nonverbal behavior of the tutor is influenced by the race of the tutee (Feldman, 1976). White and black college-age subjects taught either a third grade black or white tutee (who was actually a role-player). The tutors were led to praise the tutees verbally; the spoken content of this praise was identical for all subjects. Videotapes were made of the tutor's face as she administered the learning test to the tutee. Judges later rated how pleased the subjects appeared to be, based on nonverbal cues alone. Results showed that white tutors appeared significantly more pleased when praising a white tutee than a black. There was no difference for black tutors as a function of the race of the student. These results suggest that the nonverbal behavior of tutors is indeed affected by race of the learner. The white tutors, though verbally reinforcing their student, were judged as being more displeased when the tutee was black than when he was white.

Decoding Nonverbal Behavior by Children and Adults

In a teaching situation it is often necessary for the teacher to rely heavily on nonverbal cues to determine how much the student really understands about the material being taught. Little is known, however, about the accuracy of an observer's estimate of degree of understanding of another person on the basis of nonverbal cues alone. How accurately can one person decode another's nonverbal behavior? Both peer tutors and adult teachers who work with younger children should be adept in decoding nonverbal cues. Although some interest has been shown recently in research on decoding and encoding of nonverbal behavior, there is a paucity of evidence concerning the development of such behavior. The few studies that have directly investigated developmental trends in decoding ability have found that accuracy increases with age (Dimitrovsky, 1964; Gates, 1923). Since these studies used adults as stimulus persons, it is unclear whether the same results would hold if the stimulus persons were children.

A study was designed to examine systematically the accuracy of children and adults in decoding of nonverbal behavior, that is, in drawing inferences about the underlying cognitive state on the basis of children's overt non-verbal responses (Allen & Feldman, 1975). A set of 20 silent samples (30 seconds each) were prepared of stimulus persons who had been video taped while listening to 2 4-minute lessons. Stimulus persons were 10 third graders (5 males and 5 females). One lesson was very easy for the child (first grade level) and the other was very difficult (fifth grade level). The 2 samples from each stimulus person were arranged in random order on a new videotape. Thus, the final videotape consisted of 20 short segments: 10 stimulus children, each listening to a difficult lesson.

These samples of nonverbal behavior on the video tape were then shown to groups of adults, sixth graders, and third graders. The adult observers (12 males and 24 females) were almost all experienced teachers enrolled in graduate education classes at the University of Wisconsin. The 51 sixth grade children (26 males and 25 females) and 45 third-grade children (28 males and 17 females) all attended suburban elementary and middle schools in Wisconsin.

The observers were told that they would see several short film segments of children who were listening to an arithmetic lesson. It was explained that each film segment would be shown without any sound, and that after seeing each 30-second film clip they would estimate how much the student understood about the lesson. Hence, on the basis of the meager nonverbal cues available on the film the observers rated degree of understanding of the stimulus person. Data were analyzed by an analysis of variance that took into account the age and sex of subject, difficulty of the lesson, and sex of the stimulus persons.

Although results were complicated by a number of higher-order interactions, the main findings were quite clear. The most important result was the significant interaction involving age of observer and type of lesson (easy or difficult), indicating differential accuracy for age of observer in estimates of amount of understanding by the stimulus persons. As can be seen in Figure 2, observers in all age groups rated the stimulus persons who were listening to the easy lesson as understanding more than stimulus persons listening to the difficult lesson. But the third and sixth graders were more accurate—more discriminating—in their ratings than the adults. Analysis of the ratings of understanding within each age group showed that only the third and sixth graders significantly perceived differences in degree of understanding of the stimulus person as a function of level of difficulty of the lesson (third graders, $p < .005$; adults, ns). Thus, only the children were able to decode accurately the nonverbal behavior of the stimulus persons. Although there were other significant main effects and interactions, the basic finding that children were superior to adults in decoding nonverbal cues was not modified.

Although the decoding results were very clear, alternate explanations can be offered. First, children's nonverbal encoding may be different from that of adults, and perhaps frequent interaction with peers facilitates children's ability to decode the nonverbal behavior of other children. Alternatively, it is possible that adults may have misinterpreted the meaning of the children's nonverbal

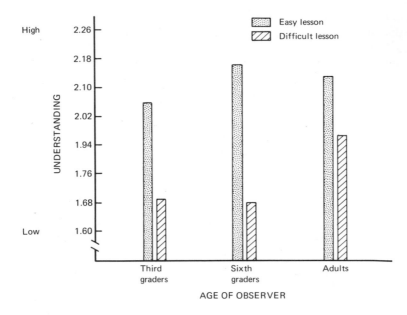

Figure 2 Ratings of understanding by age and lesson type. (Higher numbers indicate greater inferences of understanding.)

behavior because of the belief that adults and children encode differently. Although the precise explanation for the finding is not certain, it is clear that children were better than adults in decoding nonverbal cues indicative of another child's comprehension.

The decoding of nonverbal behavior exhibited by high- and low-achieving children was investigated in a subsequent study by using the same paradigm as described above (Allen & Atkinson, 1976). Observers viewed the nonverbal behavior of high- and low-achieving children (fourth and fifth graders) that occurred while they listened to a very easy and a very difficult lesson. Results showed that observers (college students) perceived that the high-achieving children understood significantly more than the low-achieving children in all conditions, and that females understood significantly more than males. Moreover, a difference was found in the perceived level of understanding between the easy and difficult lesson for the high-achieving males, but not for the low-achieving males. These results suggest the very interesting possibility that high- and low-achieving children differ in the nonverbal cues they emit during learning. Thus, the decoding of these nonverbal cues by others may lead to incorrect conclusions concerning the degree of understanding by low-achieving children.

Encoding of Nonverbal Behavior by Children

A question closely related to the accuracy of nonverbal decoding by children is whether they are able by role playing to encode successfully a given cognitive state by using nonverbal responses alone. The children who served as stimulus persons in the encoding study discussed above responded quite naturally, without being aware of emitting the nonverbal behavior. Would the nonverbal behavior have differed if the children had made an intentional effort to convey their degree of understanding?

Whether children are able to convey comprehension by the intentional deployment of nonverbal responses holds both theoretical and practical interest. Difference in nonverbal behavior under natural and role play conditions would carry implications about the role of self-awareness and self-monitoring of behavior. The practical implications are obvious. If children are able successfully to simulate degrees of understanding, the teacher's perception could be manipulated quite readily. Stated more generally, can a child successfully "present self" in a cognitive sense as well as in his social behavior?

To investigate this question we used as subjects the same third graders who were stimulus persons in the decoding study (Allen & Feldman, 1976). After having listened to the easy and hard lessons, the children were told first to pretend they were listening to a very hard lesson that they did not understand, and then to pretend they were listening to a very easy lesson. (The order of role playing was balanced across subjects.) The children were not allowed to respond verbally; rather, by nonverbal behavior alone they tried to indicate that they did or did not understand the lesson. The children actually listened to a tape-recorded story during this time, and their nonverbal responses were recorded on videotape.

The nonverbal behavior occurring during role play was coded into 15 categories by experienced coders. Nonverbal responses of the stimulus children under the role play condition were analyzed and compared to data from the natural response condition. On each of the 15 categories of nonverbal behavior, significant differences were found between the natural and role play conditions. For example, there was less body fidgeting under difficult than easy conditions when role playing, but the opposite was found in the natural condition; there was less roaming of the eyes in the difficult than in the easy condition when role playing, but the opposite when nonverbal behavior was natural. In general, when engaged in role playing the children's nonverbal responses seemed to be exaggerated and emitted at a higher rate than when responding naturally. Based on these results we can say, then, that if a child attempts purposely to convey to another person (e.g., a teacher) that he does or does not understand the material, the resulting pattern of nonverbal responses will differ from nonverbal responses expressed naturally.

Decoding Role Play Behavior

Role playing and natural behavior resulted in different nonverbal responses at the encoding state; nevertheless, the decoding stage should still be examined. Do the nonverbal responses produced by role playing convey to observers the distinction between cognitive states that was intended by the children? This question was investigated by showing third grade children twenty 30-second samples from the videotapes of the children who attempted to convey degree of understanding by role playing. The subjects rated each videotape sample on a six-point scale measuring amount of understanding.

Results showed that stimulus persons who role played understanding were rated by observers as understanding significantly more than stimulus persons who role played lack of understanding. The mean score for stimulus persons pretending to understand was 3.16; the mean rating for persons role playing not understanding was 2.73. In spite of objective differences in nonverbal responses under natural and role play conditions, there was apparently enough veridical behavioral redundancy in the response pattern to convey the intended cognitive state to other children.

Involuntary Nonverbal Responses

Another aspect of role skills connected with tutoring requires the tutor to differentiate and control the relation between his verbal and nonverbal behavior. In tutoring programs, tutors typically are instructed to praise and encourage their tutees at all times, regardless of actual performance. If the learner performs poorly, positive verbal responses from the tutor are inconsistent with his private knowledge. Under such circumstances the tutor's true feelings might be revealed through nonverbal cues and such cues could be detected by the learner. That is to say, nonverbal "leakage" may occur that reveals the true nature of one's underlying belief or affect. Children are capable of controlling their nonverbal responses to a certain extent, as indicated by the role play study above. At the same time, data indicate that a person sometimes, through nonverbal responses, reveals information that he had not intended to reveal. For instance, the study by Ekman and Friesen (1969) showed that individuals unintentionally disclose their untruthfulness through nonverbal behavior.

An experiment was designed to test more directly the "nonverbal leakage" hypothesis (Allen, Feldman, & Devin-Sheehan, 1976). A situation was arranged in which 45 male and female tutors (8- and 11-year-olds) were told that they should always say "good" after responses made by the younger tutee on a 20-item test—regardless of whether the tutee's responses were actually correct or not. In every case the tutee was a confederate who performed either very well (90% correct answers) or very poorly (90% wrong). Thus, tutors were either being truthful (successful performance) or untruthful (failing performance) when they always said "good" to their tutees. Appropriate role skills in this situation require that the tutor monitor his own verbal and nonverbal behavior, and be able to inhibit nonverbal cues indicating negative reactions to the tutee's poor performance. Can tutors of 8 and 11 years of age conceal nonverbal cues that express their true dissatisfaction with the tutee's poor performance? In other words, will nonverbal "leakage" occur?

Videotape recordings were made of each tutor's nonverbal behavior while giving positive verbal feedback to the tutee. Experienced coders categorized the tutors' nonverbal responses. Results disclosed a number of statistically significant differences in the objective nonverbal responses of the tutor across the good and poor performance conditions. Tutors in the poor performance condition exhibited, for example, fewer smiles, more stares, more pauses in speech, and more raising of eyebrows. These data are presented in Figure 3. Thus, nonverbal "leakage" did occur, revealing the discrepancy between the tutor's overt verbal responses and his own private knowledge.

Are other children capable of discerning the tutor's underlying affective reactions to the tutee on the basis of the "leaked" nonverbal cues? To answer this question we constructed a new videotape by using samples from two conditions of the nonverbal leakage experiment. The tape was comprised of 32 (silent) 30-second samples of the tutors' nonverbal behaviors. Each segment was shown to 55 observers (8-year olds); they were asked to indicate for each how "satisfied" the tutor appeared to be with his tutee.

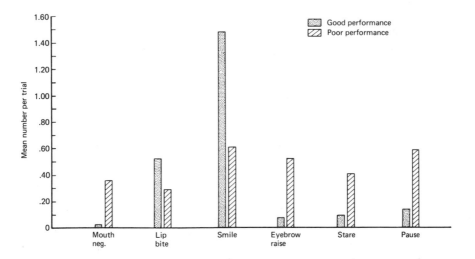

Figure 3 Nonverbal leakage by tutors.

Results revealed that tutors in the poor performance condition (where the tutor's positive feedback was inconsistent with the tutee's performance) were judged to be significantly less satisfied with their tutees than the tutors in the good performance condition. Thus, not only does nonverbal "leakage" occur in objective behavior but other children can detect these negative reactions based only on the tutor's subtle and unintended nonverbal responses. These data indicate that when the tutor's praise is not veridical, nonverbal signs of dissatisfaction will appear that can be accurately decoded by the tutee. Therefore, constant praise from the tutor which disregards the tutee's actual performance—as recommended by some tutoring programs—may have a detrimental effect on the tutee's motivation and feelings of satisfaction about the tutoring situation.

Conclusions

The research reported in the present chapter has been directed toward increasing our understanding of the psychological processes involved in tutoring of children by other children. A particular focus of the research has been on those factors responsible for the positive changes resulting from being a tutor. We have utilized role theory in our research primarily as a heuristic device—as a conceptual framework for suggesting questions and as a tool for analyzing the components of the tutoring situation.

Tutoring by children is a very complex psychological situation: It involves elements of cognitive, social, and affective behavior from both the tutor and the tutee. Perhaps further systematic analyses of the social interaction occurring between the tutor and tutee—including patterns of verbal and nonverbal responses—will provide a more penetrating insight into the dynamics of the tutoring process. Such information gleaned from controlled research would have direct applicability to the problems faced by practitioners attempting to design effective tutoring programs. It is obvious that a great deal of additional empirical research is necessary in order to answer the many important theoretical and practical questions associated with the situation of children tutoring children.

REFERENCES

Allen, V. L., & Atkinson, M. L. The decoding of nonverbal behavior emitted by high- and low-achieving children in learning settings. Unpublished manuscript, Wisconsin Research and Development Center for Cognitive Learning, Madison, Wisconsin, 1976.

Allen, V. L. & Devin-Sheehan, L. The tutor as a role model: Effects of imitation and liking on student tutors. Technical Report No. 304, Wisconsin Research and Development Center for Cognitive Learning, Madison, Wisconsin, 1974. (a)

Allen, V. L., & Devin-Sheehan, L. Cross-age interaction in one-teacher schools. Unpublished manuscript, Wisconsin Research and Development Center for Cognitive Learning, Madison, Wisconsin, 1974. (b)

Allen, V. L., & Feldman, R. S. Learning through tutoring: Low-achieving children as tutors. *Journal of Experimental Education,* 1973, *42,* 1–5.

Allen, V. L., & Feldman, R. S. Tutor attribution and attitude as a function of tutee performance. *Journal of Applied Social Psychology,* 1974, *4,* 311–320.

Allen, V. L., & Feldman, R. S. Decoding of children's nonverbal responses. Technical Report No. 365, Wisconsin Research and Development Center for Cognitive Learning, Madison, Wisconsin, 1975.

Allen, V. L., & Feldman, R. S. Nonverbal cues to comprehension: Encoding of nonverbal behavior naturally and by role-play. Working Paper No. 147, Wisconsin Research and Development Center for Cognitive Learning, Madison, Wisconsin, 1976.

Allen, V. L., Feldman, R. S., & Devin-Sheehan, L. Nonverbal indicators of behavioral inconsistency by tutors: Nonverbal leakage. Working Paper No. 143, Wisconsin Research and Development Center for Cognitive Learning, Madison, Wisconsin, 1976.

Argyle, M. *Social interaction.* Chicago: Aldine-Atherton, 1969.

Dimitrovsky, L. The ability to identify the emotional meaning of vocal expressions at successive age levels. In J. Davitz (Ed.), *The communication of emotional meaning.* New York: McGraw-Hill, 1964.

Ekman, P., & Friesen, W. Nonverbal leakage and clues to deception. *Psychiatry,* 1969, *32,* 88–109.

Feldman, R. S. Race of student and nonverbal behavior of teacher. Unpublished manuscript, Virginia Commonwealth Univ., Richmond, Virginia, 1976.

Feldman, R. S., & Allen, V. L. Effect of tutee performance on tutor's verbal and nonverbal behavior. Technical Report No. 305, Wisconsin Research and Development Center for Cognitive Learning, University of Wisconsin, Madison, Wisconsin, 1974.

Feldman, R. S., & Allen, V. L. Determinants of the primacy effect in attribution of ability. *Journal of Social Psychology,* 1975, *96,* 121–133. (a)

Feldman, R. S., & Allen, V. L. Attribution of ability: An unexpected recency effect. *Psychological Reports,* 1975, *36,* 55–66. (b)

Gartner, A., Kohler, M. C., & Riessman, F. *Children teach children: Learning by teaching.* New York: Harper, 1971.

Gates, G. S. An experimental study of the growth of social perception. *Journal of Educational Psychology,* 1923, *14,* 449–461.

Lancaster, J. *Improvements in education as it respects the industrious classes of the community.* London: Darton and Harvey, 1803.

Lieberman, S. The effects of changes in roles on the attitudes of role occupants. *Human Relations,* 1956, *9,* 385–402.

Mehrabian, A. *Nonverbal behavior.* Chicago: Aldine-Atherton, 1972.

Rosenthal, R., & Jacobson, L. *Pygmalion in the classroom: Teacher expectation and pupils' intellectual development.* New York: Holt, 1968.

Sarbin, T. R., & Allen, V. L. Role theory. In G. Lindzey, & E. Aronson (Eds.), *The handbook of social psychology.* vol. 2. Reading, Massachusetts: Addison-Wesley, 1968. Pp. 488–567.

Towson, S., & Allen, V. L. The effect of evaluation of tutee on tutor's reaction to tutoring. Unpublished manuscript, Univ. of Wisconsin, 1970.

Waller, W. *The sociology of teaching.* New York: Wiley, 1932.

8

Nonprofessional Human-Service Helping Programs for Young Children[1]

Emory L. Cowen

University of Rochester

For more than a decade, a group at the University of Rochester has been involved in conceptualizing, conducting, and evaluating some 25 programs using nonprofessionals as human-service help agents—most for young children experiencing adaptive problems. Since many of these already have been described (e.g., Cowen, 1967, 1970, 1972), the present account is limited to several programs that reflect the range of opportunities and the challenges of this emergent field. These programs imply a conceptual stance that differs from the ideologies that have guided past mental health practice. One purpose of this chapter is to describe and interrelate several of our nonprofessional human-service programs. This may be achieved best by first indicating how we began these programs and then discussing future directions suggested by our experiences.

A RATIONALE FOR NONPROFESSIONAL HUMAN-SERVICE INTERVENTION

It has been clear for some time that even in a relatively affluent society such as ours the demand for mental health services exceeds resources (Albee, 1959,

[1] This chapter was prepared with support from an NIMH Experimental and Special Training Branch grant, MH 11820-04. This support is gratefully acknowledged.

1969). Mental health resources have been most available to wealthier, better educated inhabitants of major urban centers. A regrettable distributional law seems to be that where help is most needed, it is least available.

The mental health effort also has failed to deal effectively with major disturbances, the clearest (but not the only) example being schizophrenia. Few indictments are as harsh as Scheff's (1966) assertion that 50 years and 5000 studies have resulted in "virtually no progress" with respect to "cause and cure" of schizophrenia. Scheff implies that we have asked the wrong questions and followed the wrong approaches in trying to cope with this disorder. Limitations of psychotherapy also have been obvious in recent years. The most sober appraisal available from individuals deeply immersed in the field (Bergin, 1971; Rotter, 1973) is that psychotherapy is, at best, a procedure of modest exactness and limited effectiveness. Its social effectiveness has been challenged even more severely (e.g., Hollingshead & Redlich, 1958; Lorion, 1973). Certain helping techniques that evolved and flourished in middle-class milieus have not generalized well to other groups, such as the poor.

Two concerns appear repeatedly in discussions of existing problems in the helping professions. First, we have too long been under the influence of an "end-state" mentality (Cowen, 1973; Zax & Cowen, 1972). The job of the helping professions is presumed to begin when well-entrenched dysfunction is first identified. Under such circumstances, the professional's task proves to be largely a counterattack against rooted disorder. A second recurrent theme is that demand for helping services clearly outstrips available resources.

Conceptual alternatives to past, popular practices are required. The possibility of prevention implies at least two major roles for mental health professionals. The first role—social system analyst or modifier—changes the classic mental health question, "How can we repair damage?" to its opposite, "How can we build health or resources in the first place?" This question leads to describing the salient dimensions of social systems and determining how they affect development and adjustment. To study such questions properly calls for new alliances of skills and the involvement of specialists heretofore not involved in the mental health field.

A second new role for mental health professionals is directed toward the problems of manpower shortages and is termed the "mental health quarterback" (Cowen, 1967). Through mental health consultation, early detection, crisis intervention, and training and supervision of nonprofessionals, the scope and impact of mental health helping services can be extended geometrically. Preventive payoff from this approach will depend on the specific directions chosen; for example, work with children offers the possibility of ontogenetically early secondary prevention.

Both the social system modifier and mental health quarterback roles are alternatives to traditional ways of doing things, but they entail different assumptions, objectives, and techniques and require different backgrounds and experiences. The social system is the more elusive and complicated, and depends on skills not usually included in the training of mental health specialists. Though the quarterbacking role also differs from traditional ones, many of the basic skills come from standard clinical training, with new emphases and recombinations of elements in actual practice.

I am persuaded that the systems role is the more important of the two for achieving primary prevention, but many factors work against it. Not the least is the mental health professional's lack of experience in system definition and analysis of entrenched social systems. It is also difficult to relate system analysis to "real," day-to-day problems because of its abstractness. By contrast, some of the skills required for the quarterback role are available to mental health professionals, and programs derived from this role can be related to immediate problems of human distress.

Having reached this point in conceptual focusing, and recognizing the need for viable alternatives to traditional delivery systems, it seemed more pragmatic to follow the quarterbacking branch at the critical crossroad. This way of viewing mental health problems, defining alternatives, and interpreting realities led us to begin active exploration of nonprofessional human-service helping programs. The next major section of this chapter describes 4 such programs (selected from an array of 25) to illustrate the range of program possibilities and some associated problems of nonprofessional development.

HOUSEWIVES AS CHILD-AIDES

Our initial venture in nonprofessionalism was with a child-aide program. It has received the greatest investment of time and effort of any of our nonprofessional programs. It also has been our best source for understanding the potentials and pitfalls of the approach, and the most concentrated focus for research. Although it was the first programmatic expression of the thinking reviewed in the previous section, it was not a starting point in our work; rather, it grew out of still earlier program efforts. The latter need to be summarized briefly to set the stage for the aide program.

Our basic Primary Mental Health Project began primarily because of two common clinical observations in the schools. The first was the oft-heard complaint of teachers that "kid troubles" are not spread evenly across children. A widespread teacher observation was that a large fraction (perhaps 40–60% of her time was preempted by a small number of children in the class (i.e., 3 or 4 out of a group of 30). As a consequence of this "inequity," the affected children did not develop optimally. The attention they required also detracted from the education of other children and created frustration for the teacher.

A related observation was that referrals to mental health professionals peaked during the transition period between elementary and high schools. Inspection of the cumulative records of referred youngsters revealed that many had a chronic history of ineffective school behavior dating back to fifth, third, and even first grade or kindergarten. Either helping resources had not been available or people had incorrectly supposed that the troubles would vanish. Rather than vanishing, in many cases the problems broadened and worsened over time.

These concrete concerns, far more than theorizing, led to the Primary Mental Health Project in 1958. The project's first 5 years can be summarized briefly. During that period we developed procedures for early identification of school dysfunction and a primitive program for early intervention (Cowen, Izzo, Miles, Telschow, Trost, & Zax, 1963; Cowen, Zax, Izzo & Trost, 1966). About one in three primary graders was experiencing at least moderate school maladaption. That figure closely approximates the 30% school maladjustment figure later reported by Glidewell and Swallow (1969) based on a national survey conducted for the Joint Commission of the Mental Health of Children.

The value of early detection has been limited in the past by the system's inability to provide the necessary help. Nowhere is this concern more critical than in the area of school adjustment problems. The situation we faced in the early 1960s was bleak. The Rochester City School District, though relatively well provided with mental health services, was nevertheless unable to help many children who could profit from assistance. Professional manpower shortages indicated that satisfactory solutions would not be found at that level.

This dilemma of bringing effective help to children who desperately needed it forced us to review past thinking and, ultimately, to join a small band of workers (e.g., Holzberg, Knapp & Turner, 1967) who were re-examining assumptions about what is required for one person genuinely to help another. Previously, such requirements were defined in intelligence, educational background, specific course work, supervised clinical experience, and advanced degrees. There were, however, reasons to question this simple view. Most of us certainly have found interpersonal help through understanding people who were not mental health professionals. Undoubtedly, many human problems have been resolved this way. Furthermore, mental health professionals are not equally adept as help agents; even the most highly sophisticated are not completely effective. Overriding all other concerns was the realization that the collective effort of mental health professionals was markedly restricted in the more critical social sense. Thus, society's mental health problems seem more likely to result from things not done than from errors of commission or technique.

It became more plausible to us that variables such as personality attributes, interest patterns, life styles, and prior experience could be even more important than traditionally defined professional desiderata for determining whether a person could help others. The magnitude of the school adjustment problems we had identified and the lack of resources for dealing with them, together with several encouraging pilot studies using nonprofessionals, led to the operating hypothesis that using nonprofessionals as help agents was a sensible alternative that merited exploration.

Because our target group was young children experiencing school adjustment problems, the first help agent "species" we selected was the genus "Housewifus Americanus"! We assumed that many housewife-mothers had prior experience with children that would transfer to helping interventions with maladapting primary graders. In selecting an initial group of six aides in 1964 we exercised all imaginable biases consistent with the thinking summarized above. Thus, we looked for characteristics such as warmth, empathy, effectiveness in interpersonal relations, openness to psychological thinking, interest in children, and evidence of effective mothering. Selection bypassed the usual criteria of education and advanced degrees.

Our training stance was fully consistent with the views thus far developed. The training experience for the initial group consisted of 6 weeks at less than half time each week. Principles of child development, behavior and adjustment problems in children, early learning and blocks to learning, and parent–child relations were considered, though not in a standard lecture paradigm. Rather, after limited information was presented, these topics became foci for discussion. Classroom observation and film-viewing sessions were also part of the curriculum, each followed by discussion. Two of the most important objectives of this compact training sequence were less obvious. One was to catalyze a way of defining and approaching problems. The second (and even more important) was to help reduce the anxiety that these women were experiencing because they were about to tread on terrain previously reserved only for mental health professionals.

From those modest origins our child-aide program has evolved to a much larger enterprise in which 80 trained aides now are placed in 16 schools located in 4 school districts (the Rochester City School District and 3 nearby county districts). Omitting several interesting evolutionary steps, let me focus on the structure of the program, how it actually works, and the things we have learned from it.

Each elementary school currently is staffed professionally by portions of the time of a school psychologist and social worker, and by five half-time child-aides. These 16 current schools are remarkably varied. They include urban, inner-city (90% nonwhite) and relatively affluent suburban settings; primary (K–3) and elementary (K–6) schools; large (1000) and small (100) neighborhood schools; and broad socioeconomic differences. Prospective aides learned about the project from sources ranging from word of mouth to reports in the public media. They first are interviewed by project staff,[2] at which time a global suitability-judgment is rendered. As specific openings occur, candidates are

---

[2] Mary Ann Trost, Chief Social Worker for the Primary Mental Health Project, has done these interviews in the past.

made available to school personnel who do a second interview and select the women they want for their settings.

We know a fair amount about the characteristics of these women. On the average they are in their early 40s, married, and have three children. Although most have middle-class backgrounds, there are also some low-income black and Spanish-speaking aides. Compared to demographically similar women or to other women volunteer groups, they rate high in characteristics such as warmth, sensitivity, and effectiveness of interpersonal relations (Cowen, Dorr, & Pokracki, 1972), score high on personal characteristics such as nurturance, affiliation, empathy, and succorance, and low on aggression, have strong interests in social service and teaching, and have very positive attitudes toward children and schools (Dorr, Cowen, Sandler & Pratt, 1973; Sandler, 1972).

New groups of aides are trained each year. Core training of about six sessions is conducted by project staff. For several reasons the job is much easier today than it was initially. We have written training manuals and have a TV tape library with film clips for all basic project functions (e.g., referral conferences, progress conferences, termination conferences, aides seeing children individually and in groups, individual and group supervisory sessions, consultation visits, etc.). Most important of all, school settings now have high proportions of veterans who can readily communicate the project's ways to the newcomer. We also have created the role of senior (supervisory) aide, filled by aides who have risen through the ranks (Cowen, Trost, & Izzo, 1973), who are very helpful in familiarizing new aides. Much of the aides' real learning, however, takes place on the job through consultation and participation with peers in a continuous process of working with children. Even for such a highly select group, data indicate that continuing growth in understanding and sensitivity results from working in the project (Dorr, Cowen, & Sandler, 1973).

Early each school year referrals are received (primarily from teachers). When a child is referred, the teacher submits several brief, objective, behavior checklists describing his situation. The school social worker meets with the child's mother to learn more about him and to obtain background information about the family. All the information is reviewed in a referral conference involving mental health professionals, teacher, and prospective aide. Decisions are made about whether the child should be seen by an aide, and, if so, what the major objectives should be. Children are seen for a variety of reasons, including educational and behavior problems ranging from aggressive, acting-out difficulties to shy, timid, undersocialized responses, to learning disabilities (Clarfield, 1972).

Aides see children after the referral conference and regularly thereafter. Most children are seen individually, although some aides conduct small groups (Terrell, McWilliams & Cowen, 1972). There is great variability in what aides actually do with youngsters. Activities include cooperative play, competitive play, tutorial activities, expressive play, social conversation, and problem conversation.

Relatively little thus far has been done to train aides to use specific techniques for specific problem constellations.

Aides are supervised by the school professionals. Visits from staff consultants often focus on difficult or perplexing cases or on special problems that arise in working with particular children. Typically, concerned parties, including professionals, aides, teachers, and other school personnel come together around the midyear to assess children's progress, clarify goals, and consider alternative ways of working with the child if objectives have not been met well. On the average, children are seen for about 35 sessions of about 30 to 40 minutes each during the school year; thus, contacts are not superficial.

The child-aide program can be evaluated from multiple standpoints. Clinically and impressionistically, it makes good sense. Program visitors, school professionals, and teachers are impressed with the aides (Dorr, Cowen, & Kraus, 1973). Cost—benefit analysis of the aide program indicated that a 40—50% increase in program costs can increase the services tenfold (Dorr, 1972). Given the national estimate of 30% maladjustment in schools (Glidewell & Swallow, 1969), a crucial variable in considering social effectiveness is the number of children contacted (Cowen, Dorr, Sandler, & McWilliams, 1971). Working with an average of 75 aides in 1972—73, our program brought intensive helping services (i.e., more than 22,000 contacts) to 709 children—11% of the primary enrollment of participating schools. Included were the hard core of school maladjustment problems along with large numbers of children who otherwise would go unattended. If the process also short-circuits downward educational spirals and other socially adverse consequences that follow early school difficulties, it more than pays for itself in economic, human, and societal terms.

We have undertaken several evaluations of the aide program, with encouraging findings. An early study showed both that aides helped children significantly and that they were more effective than a comparison group of student helpers (Cowen, 1968). An interview follow-up study with mothers of children who were seen through the aide program 2—5 years earlier demonstrated that the children's initial educational and interpersonal gains remained stable over time (Cowen, Dorr, Trost, & Izzo, 1972). In another investigation aides themselves judged that highly significant across-the-board gains took place in children they had seen (Dorr & Cowen, 1973). Finally, in a recent comprehensive outcome study (Cowen, Lorion, Dorr, Clarfield, & Wilson, 1975), significant academic and personal growth again was found in children seen by aides. These studies offer heartening early returns, though they are based largely on "soft" data, such as teacher and aide ratings of behavior.

The preceding summary of program-outcome findings is generally accurate, but it is misleading in one way. Several recent studies show that the program is not equally effective for all children. An instructive case in point is our "pure types" study (Lorion, Cowen, & Caldwell, 1974). The term "pure types" is a convenient shorthand term that describes children's initial referral problems. Although some children defy neat packaging, a majority (71%) can be classified into three groups: act-outers, shy-withdrawn, and those having learning problems. As an undifferentiated group these children improve significantly; however, the shy-withdrawns do much better than either of the two other types. This finding forced us to rethink several assumptions and practices. We had selected warm, loving women as aides and had emphasized heavily relational factors in their training. Such aides are apparently most helpful to shy-withdrawn, cuddly, motherable children. A clearer understanding of the nature of the behavior of aides that differentiates successful from unsuccessful outcomes would provide a basis for more technique-oriented aide training.

Before leaving the aide program, let me note several problems. Our first program, which placed aides full time in the classroom, was a failure; chronic teacher–aide conflict was created around the problem of authority. In that program the isolation of teachers and aides in their training promoted paranoia in both groups and blocked the development of a team orientation (i.e., "We're here to help kids") (Zax & Cowen, 1967). As we have moved from a small program to large ones, communication nets have become more complex, and there have been more communication breakdowns. Failure to supervise aides adequately, especially in understaffed settings, has upset aides and has restricted their potential for growing with the job. Nevertheless, aides enjoy their work and are challenged by it. All are paid according to district-determined pay scales, several of which are sufficiently low that aides would surely quit unless the experience was very rewarding.

Other problems come from the weak financial basis of the aide program. In a climate of ever-shrinking educational dollars, it is more difficult each year to maintain even a tenuous solvency. Two points can be made in this regard. First, the child-aide program could not have developed without constant, heroic effort by a supporting citizens' group that assumed the major fund-raising and public relations responsibilities required for the program to survive. Second, because of city–county differences in school-aid formulae and tax levels, the program has a better prognosis for survival in suburban districts than in urban ones. This is probably true for most geographic areas in America today.

Program continuity and ultimate independence should be matters of continuing concern. Good communication, program evaluation, and formal planning with districts for transfer of program responsibilities favor program survival. Currently, we are in various stages of "transferring the helm" with participating districts. Our role is shifting more and more to training trainers, modeling, and moving on to explore new approaches. Changes in the nature and details of the program are to be anticipated as districts assume control and responsibility.

The child-aide model has been an exciting one that offers a sensible, effective, socially utilitarian alternative to traditional school mental health delivery systems. Although we initially were attracted to using nonprofessionals for practical reasons such as fiscal shortages and limited professional manpower, experience suggests that carefully selected, well-trained aides more than justify themselves. Indeed, in some ways they do as well or better than professionals in direct child-serving roles in the schools.

RELATED PROGRAMS

Most of our background and experience with nonprofessionals comes from the child-aide program. Descriptions of three other nonprofessional helping programs will therefore be briefer.

Retired Persons as Child-Aides

As we gained experience with the child-aide program and developed some confidence with the approach and optimism about its potential, we realized that it was merely one special instance of a broader, more generic approach having many untapped parameters. Because we were operating from a university base, several of our earliest extensions used college students as help agents with young maladapting school children (Cowen, Zax, & Laird, 1966; Cowen, Carlisle, & Kaufman, 1969).

Around this time Riessman (1965) articulated the "helper-therapy" principle, based on his experience with indigenous, low-income, neighborhood workers as human-service help agents in storefronts. Riessman contended that society harbors many alienated, disenfranchised groups for whom the process of being genuinely helpful to another person in distress might be the most rewarding of all possible experiences. If this is so, a single, properly engineered program could contribute simultaneously to the resolution of several social problems.

Retired people attracted our interest because they are among the most clearly disenfranchised of all social groups. Retirement is often an abrupt life-transition when individuals move from active, participant, contributory social roles to passive, ignored ones. Some retirees have the interests and resources to cope with their new circumstances, but for many others the transition exacts a heavy psychological toll. Moreover, when retirees are functionally ignored, their wisdom and experience are lost to society. Developing a human-service program using retired people as help agents could be of value to the retirees themselves in addition to benefiting the target groups they served. Since our prior experience and contracts were in the primary grades of schools, we decided to train older people for helping roles with children.

Some details of how we located our retirees have been reported elsewhere

(Cowen, Leibowitz, & Leibowitz, 1968). Ultimately we selected four women and two men, ranging in age from 67 to 82 years, and used a training format similar to the one used with our initial group of child-aides. Training consisted of 11 1½-hour sessions which included rudimentary consideration of personality development, behavior problems in children, and parent–child relations. Discussion sessions, the use of film materials, and actual classroom observations also were used extensively. Despite ominous forebodings from colleagues, we found the group to be reasonably flexible and comfortable with psychologically oriented views of behavior.

Retirees were assigned in teams of three to two elementary schools, each team under the supervision of an advanced clinical psychology Ph.D. candidate. They worked three half-days a week and were paid a token sum of $5.00 for each half-day session. Again, contrary to prevalent stereotypes, they appeared on the job faithfully, even on some especially harsh wintry days that Rochester so ably produces. Weekly group supervisory meetings conducted by graduate student leaders provided opportunity to review progress and problems with children, techniques, and role concerns of the retirees.

Two limited types of program evaluations were undertaken. The first, based on several objective rating scales, focused on the retirees' attitudes toward the experience. All reported having enjoyed the experience "very much" and had strongly positive feelings about continuing in the program. They felt that they had learned a "good deal" from the program and they they had been "reasonably helpful" to the children. A second set of ratings from teachers and retirees evaluated the progress of the 25 children seen through the program. These two sets of judgments corresponded well, indicating an average improvement for the children that centered between "somewhat" and "quite a bit." While these data were beset by classic problems of small samples, rater bias, and nonindependence, they do support the helper-therapy concept. There is reason to suppose that maladapting schoolchildren were helped in the program, and that the retiree help agents profited personally from the experience.

This program defies widespread stereotypes about the rigidity of the elderly and the belief that their "infirmities" make them unreliable. It reminds us that all communities have broad potential for developing diverse pools of help agents.

An interesting, if serendipitous, fringe benefit of the retiree program also can be noted. One nearly universal attribute of the world of primary graders is its predominant femaleness. Contrast this to the fact that most childhood behavior problems and referrals occur in frequency ratios of 2:1 or 3:1 of boys to girls. In many clinical reports dealing with early childhood problems in males, one can find a diagnostic statement such as "absence of male identification model." Using retirees as help agents is one of the few ways to bring male identification models into the otherwise feminine primary grade world. This point was intuitively grasped by school people; the positive reception teachers accorded to "grandfather"-figures was considerable.

"Tuned-Out" Secondary Students as Help Agents

This program is conceptually related to the two preceding ones, yet it differs in origin and in the help agents used. A shifting emphasis in our training program in clinical psychology prompted us some years ago to introduce a year-long practicum in community mental health into the doctoral curriculum. Through this course advanced trainees engage real world problems not adequately addressed by existing trainings. Programs using tuned-out secondary students as help agents grew out of this practicum and reflect, primarily, the work of several Rochester doctoral candidates in clinical psychology (Clarfield & McMillan, 1973; McWilliams & Finkel, 1973).

Virtually any high school or junior high school in the United States contains some students who are there in body only—often only because the law requires their presence. These youth are characterized by little (if any) motivation to succeed, chronic histories of academic underachievement, and lack of interest in traditional school curriculums and programs. They reach this state by various routes: some because of longstanding, uncorrected skill deficits, some because of climates of family lack of interest in education, some because they elect to meet fear of failure by tuning out, and some who see school work as irrelevant. Whatever the reason, the consequences of this "alienation syndrome" can be severe. Since modern society places heavy emphasis on education as a gateway to later achievement, those who fail to adapt educationally find many life opportunities blocked. Such students may express feelings of inadequacy, low self-esteem, and alienation from and bitterness regarding educational systems and society at large. Adverse social consequences such as unemployment or delinquency can ensue.

The students described above are not hard to locate. Typically, the barest description of the "tuned-out" syndrome is sufficient to allow teachers or guidance personnel to provide an impressive list who qualify. Such youngsters may have had (or been offered) counseling that was not used effectively because it was seen as part of an alien establishment. The challenge is to engage the students meaningfully, to help them find bona fide gratifications, and to help identify realistic career directions. One can again see in this situation a potential instance for the operation of Riessman's helper-therapy principle. By providing these youngsters with opportunities to help others experiencing distress, we hoped that benefits also might accrue to the help agent.

We again selected maladapting primary graders as the target group for the helping intervention. This program has been conducted for three consecutive years in two suburban school districts that have cluster schools (high school, junior high, middle school, and primary school). We have used both high school (McWilliams & Finkel, 1973) and junior high school (Clarfield & McMillan, 1973) students as help agents, with some preference for the latter because of earlier preventive potential. Guidance personnel, teachers, and principals identified as potential candidates students who were visibly underachieving, lacked motivation, and were socially withdrawn from the mainstream peer group. Helpers were given a description of the proposed program and its purposes. The following points were made: (*1*) We are moving rapidly toward becoming more of a leisure time society in which human-service activities will take on greater importance. (*2*) High schools, with their traditional "three Rs" orientation have not yet accommodated to this change. (*3*) An experimental program was to be started to provide training and experience in human-service activities. (*4*) Finally, a brief description of the projected program activities was given. Students who expressed interest in the program (and received parental approval) became the prospective help agents.

Brief training programs (6–8 sessions) were conducted, emphasizing development of relations with younger children, role playing, strategies for working with primary graders, and appropriate games and activities for the interaction. Target children (particularly those with problems of shyness, withdrawal, and under-socialization) were referred to the program by primary grade teachers. Helpers met with the children for 20 to 30 contact sessions. Weekly supervisory meetings for helpers were conducted by the graduate student program-leaders. These meetings dealt with concrete issues of how best to work with children, and with helpers' concerns about their roles or effectiveness. Later meetings covered the meaning of the experience for the help agent himself, and how this affected his sense of being worthwhile and his future career plans.

Each program has been set in a research context. Using teachers' behavioral judgments as criteria, the target children were found to have been helped absolutely and in comparison to nonprogram controls with similar problems (Clarfield & McMillan, 1973; McWilliams & Finkel, 1973). McWilliams and Finkel (1973) also reported behavior-change ratings by helpers for target children which included significant decreases in negative qualities such as being withdrawn, sad, and frightened, and significant increases in positive attributes such as being warm, trusting, and friendly. Help agents also reported significant increase in their understanding of young children and said they enjoyed the program more than any other aspect of their school experience (McWilliams & Finkel, 1973).

The program for tuned-out secondary students points once again to the social potential of using nonprofessionals and to the specific attractions of projects that offer mutually supportive solutions to unresolved problems. One suburban district now formally recognizes the program and offers academic credit to students participating in it.

Infant Stimulation

The last of the four programs to be considered here differs from the others in terms of who the helpers are, what they do, and, most importantly, the targets and locus of the intervention. This is our enrichment–stimulation program for slow-developing ghetto infants. As an aspiring community psychologist with programs in the primary grades of schools, I reported periodically to various community groups about "progress and fantasies." One such group was the Department of Pediatrics staff at the University Medical Center. In reporting early detection findings I made the rash statement that we really should start such programs with much younger children than kindergartners or prekindergartners (the youngest at that time). At that time several pediatricians in the group were involved in establishing an all-purpose Neighborhood Health Center in the heart of Rochester's inner-city ghetto. One of their most important objectives was to develop an active, preventively oriented, well-baby clinic. As the latter program became operational, several pediatricians with heretofore exclusively middle-class practices noted a clinical phenomenon of some concern. Among the infant clientele seen through the well-baby clinic, there was an alarmingly high proportion of 1- to 2-year-olds who were developing very slowly, but who had no identifiable neurological or physiological problems. The possibility that this was related to early environmental conditions was considered. This observation was related by one pediatrician to my earlier remark about the need to push back early detection much further in time.

This led to a series of exploratory contacts during which we tried to learn more about the potential target group by talking to Health Center personnel. Eventually we undertook a series of formal test evaluations using available scales of infant development with a sample of clinically identified early slow-developers. Some initially "detected" kids proved to be false alarms; still, there was a substantial subsample showing an average of 30% retardation. Test assessment indicated an unusual early developmental pattern in these children. Development was uneven across subareas: an average 10% slowdown in ambulatory, coordinative, and manipulative functions, but a 50% slowdown in language and social development.

From these experiences came the notion of an intervention designed to forestall and reverse the early slowdown. Such a program has now been in operation for 5 years. Help agents in the infant stimulation program come from our undergraduate community mental health practicum (Cowen, 1969; Cowen, Chinsky, & Rappaport, 1970). Students in that practicum are given general background about the community mental health area, programs using nonprofessionals, and early development and developmental problems of inner-city children. Recently, the student group has included Black and Spanish-speaking undergraduates.

The program begins after the infants have been identified and assessed and the students are selected and trained. Students band together in car pools and pick up the children three times weekly at their homes, thereby establishing family contacts. Children are brought to the Health Center and are typically seen in 1½- to 2-hour group sessions over a 5-month period. Thus, the program allows for about 50 to 60 contact sessions in all. Major program ingredients are intellectual enrichment and stimulation, language modeling, and shaping prosocial behavior, all within the context of a warm, friendly relation with the children. The meeting room is well stocked with books, games, toys, and objects. Children's actions are continually labelled, language is modeled, imitative behavior is encouraged, and child–child as well as child–adult social interactions are shaped and reinforced.

Notwithstanding the limitations imposed by small sample and difficulties in establishing control groups, there have been several research evaluations of the program's effects (Jason, Clarfield, & Cowen, 1973; Specter & Cowen, 1971). These evaluations are less than fully rigorous, but the sense of the findings is sufficiently stable and replicable to permit some confidence in them. It is clear both clinically and empirically that the children thrive and blossom in this program. The average Development Quotient gain over a 5-month period is about 16 to 18 points, most due to acceleration of language and social development. Observers—whether the help agents themselves, parents, health assistants, or pediatricians—are quick to see these changes; they are dramatic rather than miniscule. Indeed, if there is such a thing as a hypothetical time investment—payoff ratio, none of the 25 or so human-service help programs with which I have been associated rivals the infant stimulation program in immediate, observable payoff. Unfortunately, however, that is not the full story. According to clinical observation and limited objective follow-up data, it is clear that the rapid and dramatic gains are susceptible to erosion. When the program ends and the child returns to his normal environment, he begins to revert to his earlier developmental pattern.

This fact has led us to try to develop ways for maintaining the early gains. The Health Center, for example, has instituted a Step-Up program which continues enrichment for 2½- to 3-year-old Infant Stimulation alumni. We have tried to get family members to observe the program in action, sought to train several indigenous health assistant members of the Center's staff in the ways of Infant Stimulation, and, most important of all, have conducted stimulation sessions in the children's homes on a rotating basis so that parents could see how the program functions. After 5 years of program development (and in close liaison with the Neighborhood Health Center staff) the Center has now developed the knowledge and resources to conduct this program on its own.

DISCUSSION, IMPLICATIONS, AND CONCLUSIONS

The use of nonprofessional help agents in educational and interpersonal activities is a development in response to obvious pressing social needs. Burgeoning growth in this area in the past decade is reflected in the recent appearance of an impressive series of volumes devoted to the topic (e.g., Bowman & Klopf, 1971; Carkhuff, 1971; Goodman, 1972; Guerney, 1969; Sobey, 1970). The present chapter has made no attempt to review these reviews. Instead, it started with the factors that moved us to explore the use of nonprofessionals as human-service help agents and described four specific programs that we have developed during the past decade. These four programs well betray our emphases and biases; nevertheless, they represent only 4 of about 25 conceptually linked nonprofessional human-service programs we have organized. Rigid though we may be, we are not sufficiently rigid to have gone that far without the strong conviction that the basic approach is sound and socially utilitarian.

Several considerations growing out of our experience deserve emphasis in this concluding section. One, quite obviously, is the tremendous variability of the nonprofessional thrust along several salient dimensions (Cowen, 1973). Help agents in our programs have varied in age from 8 to 82, in socioeconomic status from the extremely poor to the affluent, and in education from virtually none to those with advanced degrees. Included among our help agents are several otherwise anomic or disenfranchised groups such as retirees, ghetto youth in difficulty, and tuned-out secondary students. Our experience is that factors other than the historically valued ones of intelligence, advanced degrees, and prior educational experience relate importantly to whether or not one human being can help another.

Many of our helping programs have by choice been targeted to maladapting primary graders; we have also developed programs for other target groups including slow-developing ghetto infants, prisoners, hospitalized schizophrenics, adolescents psychiatrically exempted from the schools, inner-city youth, and geriatric patients in nursing homes. Modern society includes many social groupings that stand to profit from the interested, dedicated, help of people; there is thus great diversity in potential target group applications.

As target groups for helping interventions have varied, so have the settings in which our programs have been conducted. These range from classic "total" institutions (Goffman, 1961) such as mental hospitals and prisons, to schools, neighborhood settlement homes and health centers, to storefronts and community centers. Such programs have the potential to operate effectively in many different locations.

There also has been much variability in how nonprofessionals are trained for human-service roles. Factors that influence training include the background, experience, and "style" of the helper group, the nature of the target group, the actual role to be carried out, and the predilections of those who run the program. For example, training inner-city adolescents as companion help agents with inner-city children was, for us, a more concrete, action oriented process than training middle-class housewives as help agents for maladapting primary graders. Training obviously should proceed differently for a primarily relational program than for one in behavior modification.

We have made a serious effort from the start to evaluate our nonprofessional human-service programs. It is important to do so, lest the nonprofessional movement, like some crusades that have preceded it, be elevated by enthusiasm rather than by empirical fact. Our research has been constrained by the realities of "real world," service oriented settings and programs (Cowen, Lorion, & Dorr, 1974). Nevertheless, at least in primitive ways we have shown for the four programs reviewed in this chapter that there are positive program effects for target groups along relevant criterion dimensions (e.g., better school adjustment and performance or accelerated intellectual development for infants). We also have demonstrated that there is direct value for the help agents in several programs built around the helper-therapy principle.

The development of nonprofessional helping programs necessarily implicates new roles for mental health professionals. The types of nonprofessional programs reviewed do not at all imply what some professionals fear—that is, their own potential obsolescence. Rather, they suggest new and more socially utilitarian professional functions that can expand mental health's reach. An inviting aspect of some nonprofessional human-service programs is that they simultaneously support three interlocking objectives: (*1*) solutions to pressing community problems, (*2*) more effective mental health manpower utilization, and (*3*) new directions in graduate (and undergraduate) training in the health professions.

There is nothing sacrosanct about the specifics of any program reviewed in this chapter. Specifics of our programs reflect the particulars of the types of settings that exist in our community—the resources, interests, and ways of perceiving problems in local settings—and the lines of contact between "us and them." We feel comfortable in assuming some cross-community generality in such matters, yet each community has its own special set of problems, needs, and style.

The use of nonprofessionals as mental health workers should not be regarded as a panacea. Whatever its potential values and benefits, it remains largely a reactive effort designed to deal with existing problems. Engineering settings and institutions that promote health in the first place is an even more attractive social alternative. But lacking the knowledge, resources, or mandate for primary prevention at this time, realistic approaches such as nonprofessional helping programs should be encouraged. Much remains to be learned about such programs. Under some circumstances nonprofessionals may render even more effective service than professionals. We need to understand better the limitations of nonprofessionals, problems associated with their gaining acceptance in established settings, mechanisms for their growth and advancement, and related matters. The point to be underscored is that the press of social reality and encouraging early results justify further serious exploration of the usefulness of nonprofessional workers in mental health programs.

REFERENCES

Albee, G. W. *Mental health manpower trends.* New York: Basic Books, 1959.

Albee, G. W. Emerging concepts of mental illness and models of treatment: The psychological point of view. *American Journal of Psychiatry*, 1969, *125*, 42–48.

Bergin, A. E. The evaluation of therapeutic outcomes. In A. E. Bergin & S. L. Garfield (Eds.), *Handbook of psychotherapy and behavior change: An empirical analysis.* New York: Wiley, 1971. Pp. 217–270.

Bowman, G. W., & Klopf, G. J. *New careers and roles in the American school.* New York: Bank St. College of Education, 1971.

Carkhuff, R. R. *The development of human resources.* New York: Holt, 1971.

Clarfield, S. P. An analysis of referral problems and their relation to intervention goals in a school based mental health program. Unpublished Ph.D. dissertation, Univ. of Rochester, 1972.

Clarfield, S. P., & McMillan, R. C. Tuned-out secondary school students as mental health aides in an elementary school. *American Journal of Community Psychology*, 1973, *1*, 212–218.

Cowen, E. L. Emergent approaches to mental health problems: An overview and directions for future work. In E. L. Cowen, E. A. Gardner, & M. Zax (Eds.), *Emergent approaches to mental health problems.* New York: Appleton, 1967. Pp. 389–455.

Cowen, E. L. The effectiveness of secondary prevention programs using nonprofessionals in the school setting. Proceedings, 76th Annual Convention. *APA*, 1968, *2*, 705–706.

Cowen, E. L. Combined graduate-undergraduate training in community mental health functions. *Professional Psychology*, 1969, *1*, 72–73.

Cowen, E. L. Training clinical psychologists for community mental functions: Description of a practicum experience. In I. Iscoe, & C. D. Spielberger (Eds.), *Community psychology: Perspectives in training and research.* New York: Appleton, 1970. Pp. 99–124.

Cowen, E. L. Primary Mental Health Project. In R. Quinn, & L. M. Wegener (Eds.), *Mental health and learning.* Washington, D.C., U.S. Dept. of H.E.W. 1972, Publ. No. (HSM) 72–9146, 27–36.

Cowen, E. L. Social and community interventions. In P. Mussen, & M. Rosenzweig (Eds.), *Annual Review of Psychology*, 1973, *24*, 423–472.

Cowen, E. L., Carlisle, R. L., & Kaufman, G. Evaluation of a college student volunteer program with primary graders experiencing school adjustment problems. *Psychology in the Schools*, 1969, *6*, 371–375.

Cowen, E. L., Chinsky, J. M. & Rappaport, J. An undergraduate practicum in community mental health. *Community Mental Health Journal*, 1970, *6*, 91–100.

Cowen, E. L., Dorr, D., & Pokracki, F. Selection of nonprofessional child-aides for a school mental health project. *Community Mental Health Journal*, 1972, *8*, 220–226.

Cowen, E. L., Dorr, D., Sandler, I. N., & McWilliams, S. A. Utilization of a nonprofessional child-aide, school mental health program. *Journal of School Psychology*, 1971, *9*, 131–136.

Cowen, E. L., Dorr, D., Trost, M. A., & Izzo, L. D. A follow-up study of maladapting school children seen by nonprofessionals. *Journal of Consulting and Clinical Psychology*, 1972, *36*, 235–238.

Cowen, E. L., Izzo, L. D., Miles, H., Telschow, E. F., Trost, M. A., & Zax, M. A mental health program in the school setting: Description and evaluation. *Journal of Psychology*, 1963, *56*, 307–356.

Cowen, E. L., Leibowitz, E., & Leibowitz, G. The utilization of retired people as mental health aides in the schools. *American Journal of Orthopsychiatry*, 1968, *38*, 900–909.

Cowen, E. L., Lorion, R. P., & Dorr, D. Research in the community cauldron: A case report. *Canadian Psychologist*, 1974, *15*, 313–325.

Cowen, E. L., Lorion, R. P., Dorr, D., Clarfield, S. P., & Wilson, A. B. Comprehensive evaluation of a preventively oriented school based mental health program. *Psychology in the Schools*, 1975, *12*, 161–166.

Cowen, E. L., Trost, M. A., & Izzo, L. D. Nonprofessional human service personnel in consulting roles. *Community Mental Health Journal*, 1973, *9*, 335–341.

Cowen, E. L., Zax, M., Izzo, L. D., & Trost, M. A. The prevention of emotional disorders in the school setting: A further investigation. *Journal of Consulting Psychology*, 1966, *30*, 381–387.

Cowen, E. L., Zax, M., & Laird, J. D. A college student volunteer program in the elementary school setting. *Community Mental Health Journal*, 1966, *2*, 319–328.

Dorr, D. An ounce of prevention. *Mental Hygiene*, 1972, *56*, 25–27.

Dorr, D., & Cowen, E. L. Nonprofessional mental health workers judgments of change in children. *Journal of Community Psychology*, 1973, *1*, 23–26.

Dorr, D., Cowen, E. L., & Kraus, R. Mental health professionals view nonprofessional mental health workers. *American Journal of Community Psychology*, 1973, *1*, 258–265.

Dorr, D., Cowen, E. L., & Sandler, I. N. Changes in response styles and attitudes of nonprofessional mental health workers as a function of experience. *Journal of School Psychology*, 1973, *11*, 118–122.

Dorr, D., Cowen, E. L., Sandler, I. N., & Pratt, D. M. The dimensionality of a test battery for nonprofessional mental health workers. *Journal of Consulting and Clinical Psychology*, 1973, *41*, 181–185.

Gildewell, J. C., & Swallow, C. S. *The prevalence of maladjustment in elementary schools: A report prepared for the Joint Commission on the Mental Health of Children.* Chicago: Univ. of Chicago Press, 1969.

Goffman, E. *Asylums.* Garden City, New York: Doubleday, 1961.

Goodman, G. *Companionship therapy.* San Francisco: Jossey-Bass, 1972.

Guerney, B. G. (Ed.) *Psychotherapeutic agents: New role for nonprofessionals, parents and teachers.* New York: Holt, 1969.

Hollingshead, A. B., & Redlich, F. C. *Social class and mental illness: A community study.* New York: Wiley, 1958.

Holzberg, J. D., Knapp, R. H., & Turner, J. L. College students as companions to the mentally ill. In E. L. Cowen, E. A. Gardner, & M. Zax (Eds.), *Emergent approaches to mental health problems.* New York: Appleton, 1967. Pp. 91–109.

Jason, L., Clarfield, S. P., & Cowen, E. L. Preventive intervention with young disadvantaged children. *American Journal of Community Psychology*, 1973, *1*, 50–61.

Lorion, R. P. Socioeconomic status and traditional treatment approaches reconsidered. *Psychological Bulletin*, 1973, *79*, 263–270.

Lorion, R. P., Cowen, E. L., & Caldwell, R. A. Problem types of children referred to a school based mental health program. *Journal of Consulting and Clinical Psychology,* 1974, *42,* 491–496.

McWilliams, S. A., & Finkel, N. J. High school students as mental health aides in the elementary setting. *Journal of Consulting and Clinical Psychology.* 1973, *40,* 39–42.

Riessman, F. The "helper" therapy principle. *Social Work,* 1965, *10,* 27–32.

Rotter, J. B. The future of clinical psychology. *Journal of Consulting and Clinical Psychology,* 1973, *40,* 313–321.

Sandler, I. N. Characteristics of women working as child-aides in a school-based preventive mental health program. *Journal of Consulting and Clinical Psychology,* 1972, *36,* 56–61.

Scheff, T. J. *Being mentally ill: A sociological theory.* Chicago: Aldine, 1966.

Sobey, F. *The nonprofessional revolution in mental health.* New York: Columbia Univ. Press, 1970.

Specter, G. A., & Cowen, E. L. A pilot study in stimulation of culturally deprived infants. *Child Psychiatry and Human Development,* 1971, *1,* 168–177.

Terrell, D. L., McWilliams, S. A., & Cowen, E. L. Description and evaluation of group-work training for nonprofessional child-aides in a school mental health program. *Psychology in the Schools,* 1972, *9,* 70–75.

Zax, M., & Cowen, E. L. Early identification and prevention of emotional disturbance in a public school. In E. L. Cowen, E. A. Gardner, & M. Zax (Eds.), *Emergent approaches to mental health problems.* New York: Appleton, 1967. Pp. 331–351.

Zax, M., & Cowen, E. L. *Abnormal psychology: Changing conceptions.* New York: Holt, 1972.

III

Tutoring Programs in Schools

The third major section of this book comprises six chapters; an intensive examination of tutoring programs as they actually exist in the schools is the primary purpose of these chapters. Having established a basic foundation in theory and research by material in the previous two sections, we are now prepared to move directly to a consideration of a variety of tutoring programs that use children as teachers. A wide array of such tutoring programs are currently in operation in schools throughout the United States.

Types of tutoring programs described in this section differ along several dimensions: They range from the structured to the unstructured, from emphasis on personal—social growth to stress on academic achievement, from small supplementary programs to extensive involvement by all students in the school, from providing help for low-achieving students to being used as enrichment, and from a focus on very young children to concern with older students. Chapters in this section give the rationale for several programs that now exist in the schools. On the basis of their own personal experience with ongoing tutoring systems, some of the authors offer suggestions and guidelines for initiating a successful program. They point out the benefits to be realized and the pitfalls to be avoided in school based tutoring programs. The final two chapters in this section report evaluation research in which the outcome of large, school based tutoring projects are carefully scrutinized. These analyses focus on the differential outcome of tutoring for tutors and tutees as a function of the psychological characteristics of the tutors.

The first chapter in this section describes the cross-age tutoring program developed by Lippitt and associates. As Lippitt observes, cross-age helping by students incorporates many of the features that are predicted to be the educational trends of the future: individualized instruction, use of nonprofessionals (including older students), and initiative by students for their learning. For all parties associated with a cross-age tutoring program, there are potential advantages and disadvantages. In the final section of her chapter, Lippitt presents a table that summarizes the possible positive and negative aspects of a tutoring program for the various groups affected: teachers of the older and younger students, older and younger students (tutors and tutees), administrators and the school system, and the community and family. Lippitt argues very forcefully that the potential advantages to participants in a tutoring program outweigh by far any problems that might result.

Lippitt states that several ingredients go into making a successful tutoring program; these include the staff, teachers, and parents, and the training of tutors in content matter as well as in relating constructively with younger children. The author describes the tutoring program developed by the Michigan group. Tutoring programs based on this design have produced improved performance in academic subjects (e.g., reading and language) for both older and younger participants (tutors and tutees). Several variations in the basic tutoring design are presented by Lippitt; among these variations are different types of staff organization, school and community service programs for children, credit for selecting tutoring as a subject in school, cross-age helping in a summer camp, and using parents to instruct older children about helping younger children at home.

Up to this point tutoring has been discussed in a rather general way, without devoting much attention to teaching methods or to the subject matter being taught. But instruction by the tutor on a specific academic subject is the raison d'être of most tutoring programs. In the next two chapters Harrison and Niedermeyer focus more directly upon subject matter and instructional techniques. Their basic concern is with problems connected with the development and use of curricular material rather than with the social relationship between tutor and tutee.

In his chapter Harrison argues that tutoring represents the best solution for dealing with the problems of low-achieving students: A highly structured instructional method can be combined with a sensitive and personalized learning environment. Harrison asserts that tutoring can be a particularly effective technique for helping low achievers, provided that the tutoring is highly structured and the tutors are well trained to teach specific skills. It is not true, according to

Harrison, that a low-achieving student will be helped simply by bringing him together with a tutor.

After an analysis of the basic tutorial skills needed for instruction, Harrison created a program for training tutors in the use of these skills. four major categories of skills are necessary for tutoring: general skills applicable to any content, material-specific skills (e.g., mathematics or reading), task-specific skills, and record-keeping skills. Tutors were able to learn to use these instructional skills effectively in a short training program. Nonprofessionals were about as successful as professionals in training the tutors.

Harrison strongly advocates the structured tutoring approach and has developed a training package that contains all the necessary materials (e.g., trainer's guide, practice booklet and tape, etc.) required for training tutors to employ specific instructional skills needed in tutoring mathematical concepts and basic reading skills. In extensions of the structured tutoring program parents have been trained as tutors, adults have taught Indian children, basic reading skills have been taught to illiterate adults, reading has been taught in Spanish (in Latin America), and English has been taught as a second language. Without doubt the structured tutoring program has been successful in teaching basic skills to low achievers and to naive learners. It should be remembered, however, that Harrison's structured tutoring program is designed to help the tutee learn; the program does not try to provide help for the tutor.

Chapter 11 presents seven considerations that Niedermeyer says the practitioner should use in selecting or developing an effective tutorial system. The components that should be taken into account in a complete tutorial instructional system include specification of expected outcomes of tutoring, periodic assessment of achievement, coordination of instructional materials with program objectives, provisions for training the tutors, close observation of the program once it is under way, collection of data regarding the users' satisfaction, and costs of the program.

In illustrating some of these guidelines, Niedermeyer refers to the program he developed that uses parents to tutor their kindergarten children in reading at home. The kindergarten teacher sends exercises home to the parents, and they practice these lessons with their child. Special instructional materials were developed for use with this in-home tutorial system. The components of an effective instructional program described in this chapter can be useful as a checklist when making decisions about selecting, establishing, and operating a tutorial program.

The title of the next chapter in this section, "The Tutorial Community," exemplifies an extension of the tutoring concept towards its furthest implications: the involvement of an entire elementary school in a comprehensive and interlocking system of tutoring among the students. The Tutorial Community described by Melaragno contains several innovative features, but the widespread use of tutoring is its most central and important characteristic. Tutoring is an integral and essential part of the school's curriculum; it is not used merely to provide remedial work, nor is it a minor supplement to regular classes.

Four types of tutoring are employed in the arrangement developed by Melaragno: (1) intergrade tutoring, in which upper grade students tutor primary students; (2) interschool tutoring, in which junior high students teach upper grade elementary students; (3) intraclass tutoring, in which students in the same class assist each other in the classroom; and (4) informal tutoring, in which older students serve as playleaders for younger students on the playground, help with projects, and accompany them on school trips. It is obvious that the entire student body is actively engaged in helping others or being helped; thus, tutoring is a pervasive part of the school experience for these students. Evaluation of the tutorial community program has shown positive results: Students have improved their academic skills and have displayed better attitudes toward school.

As Melaragno points out, tutoring programs are relatively easy to start; but it is much more difficult to maintain them effectively once the initial enthusiasm has abated. A tutoring program requires a heavy commitment of time and energy from the school community—and especially so if a large program is to sustain its initial momentum. Melaragno discusses the sources of teachers' resistance to tutoring programs and offers suggestions for dealing with such problems.

Most tutoring programs either do not continue over a long period of time or do not continue for long with the same students participating. By contrast, in the tutorial community tutoring is a standard feature of the school. As a result of long-term involvement in the program by tutors and tutees, special needs arise for them that usually would not develop in a typical short-term program. After having been taught for a long period of time, the tutees improve their learning and thereafter require instruction at a higher level. Sooner or later the teaching sessions begin to tire or bore the tutors—sooner if the instructional material is simple and the teaching is highly structured. It can be seen that the needs of tutees and tutors begin to change as a result of their extended experience in the tutorial community program. Both tutors and tutees require a richer teaching experience than is necessary in a tutoring program lasting only a short time. Melaragno suggests several ways of meeting the changing needs of tutors and tutees.

The last two chapters in this section are primarily concerned with evaluation research on tutoring. In neither chapter is the research directed toward merely observing simple overall effects; rather, more sophisticated analyses are conducted to determine the differential consequences attributable to particular combinations of psychological variables. The chapter by Strodtbeck, Ronchi, and Hansell presents the theoretical rationale and results of a study dealing with the Neighborhood Youth Corps tutoring program. In this program inner-city youths performing below grade level were paid for tutoring younger children in school.

In assessing this program Strodtbeck and associates included three basic sets of measures designed to ascertain the effects of tutoring on important aspects of psychological functioning of the tutor: level of ego development, self-esteem, and belief about locus of control of reinforcement (internal versus external). Additional data available concerning the tutor were grammar and spelling facility (scored from the sentence completion test that measures ego development), attendance in school, and other information from school files.

The most interesting findings of the study emerged from the cross-tabulation analyses. For instance, tutoring resulted in a greater sense of efficacy (internal control) when the tutor's involvement was either high or low. That is, efficacy scores were better either when the tutor's school attendance and learning were high or when both were low. The effect of tutoring on other psychological variables was strongly related to the tutor's score on the ego development scale. For tutors who scored high on ego development, the tutoring contributed to their sense of efficacy; but this was not true for tutors who had low ego development scores. Moreover, tutors high on ego development had better school attendance records and were rated as being better tutors by the classroom teachers. From this type of complex analysis, one can discover the type of variables that operate to modulate the effect of tutoring on the tutor. Perhaps further research of this kind will lead to a better understanding of the wide range of individual differences typically found in studies observing the effects of tutoring on the tutor.

Strodtbeck, Ronchi, and Hansell raise some very interesting questions concerning values, social change, and philosophy of science. These important issues rarely are made explicit, but evaluation research dealing with any program committed to facilitating social change must ultimately face fundamental questions of the kind alluded to in this chapter.

The final chapter in this section reports an evaluation study concerned primarily with predicting the academic gains of tutors and tutees who participated in tutoring programs under the direction of the Mobilization for Youth organization. Results of the study revealed that both tutees and tutors gained in reading scores, although the tutors improved even more than the students they had taught. In further analyses Cloward attempted to discover which factors would predict the outcome of tutoring. A total of 28 measures were available from the tutor for use in predicting the dependent variable—gain in reading skills. Stepwise multiple linear regression analyses were conducted on these data. The first analysis was concerned with determining the variables (or combination of variables) that best predicted reading gains made by the tutor. Results indicated that two personality scales were the best predictors of improvement in reading made by tutors as a consequence of their tutoring experience. A second analysis was conducted to determine which variables were the best predictors of gains in reading made by the tutees. In other words, which variables separate the effective tutors from the ineffective ones? Results of this analysis were entirely negative: None of the 28 variables were significantly correlated with teaching effectiveness of the tutors. Thus, for example, tutors with high scores on intelligence and academic ability had no greater effect on the reading scores of their tutees than tutors who had low scores on these measures.

Results of Cloward's research have very interesting implications for the selection of tutors. It would appear that academic credentials—the most common criterion used in selecting tutors—may be of only negligible value. Perhaps it would be preferable not to select tutors with a view toward their effectiveness as teachers; instead, those students could be selected as tutors who would themselves benefit most academically from teaching other children. According to Cloward's data the type of person who gains most from tutoring is the high-ability student who is a low achiever in school. Before acting on these results, however, a word of caution is in order. One must remember that in Cloward's analyses all the variables used as predictors were stable characteristics of the tutor. As Sarbin suggested in Chapter 2, perhaps the best prediction of tutoring outcomes will come from measures using the tutor–tutee interaction as the unit of analysis.

9

Learning through Cross-Age Helping: Why and How

Peggy Lippitt
University of Michigan

Cross-age helping is a dynamic teaching–learning process in which older students help younger ones with learning problems or offer enrichment opportunities. At the same time, the older students have a chance to use their knowledge and to feel they are making a tangible volunteer service contribution to others. Cross-age helping is an extension of the old one-room school practice of having students help less capable or younger peers. Often the one-room school practice did not work very well. The younger was sometimes quick to acquire the older's negative attitude toward school, but slow to learn what the older was trying to teach. Often when the older became frustrated with the slow pace of his younger, he would either ridicule him for being stupid or do the work himself.

Problems that fostered the old one-room school practice are still with us today: a wide variation in ability and too many students in each classroom. The basic problems with the old practice can be greatly reduced by appropriate training. The older's negative attitude toward school can be reversed, and he can make school more attractive to the younger. The older child can be taught what younger children are like, and can acquire techniques that improve the younger child's learning.

RATIONALE AND GOALS

Both younger and older children can profit from special attention to their particular needs. Younger children can benefit from individualized instruction and personal encouragement offered by peers who are old enough to be credible models, but still young enough to be "in connection." Friendship is an important factor for children in feeling good about themselves and being motivated to develop their potential to learn. A friend who is 2 to 4 years older can have a working relationship that is less "distant" and fragmented from the rest of a younger child's life than can an adult. A child alienated from adults can sometimes be reached by another, slightly older, child.

The positive examples of older children can be a major constructive influence on young ones. Teachers who use older students to help youngers report that time spent in the program pays for itself in time saved by not having to settle as many altercations between older and younger children on the playground. Older children are trained to find ways of helping younger children feel important and useful. Such behaviors by older children, together with the success the youngers achieve in learning, are potent factors in increasing the younger children's self-esteem. Having a big friend who cares gives a younger child an added feeling of worth and perpetuates a caring climate. Modeling the behavior of their older friends, the youngers begin to act toward even younger children the way the olders act toward them. The positive circular process can spiral downward even to the very young members of the children's own families.

Older students can improve many of their own skills by helping youngers. A new appreciation of what one has learned is gained when its significance for others is discovered. Older children willingly review areas they have never mastered thoroughly in order to explain the material to younger children. Human relations techniques and problem-solving methods are learned happily in order to do a better job for the youngers. The helping program gives the older children an apprenticeship in a service oriented job. Self-confidence is increased when a child discovers that he can be useful and responsible. Moreover, by helping younger children the older students can work through at a safe emotional distance some of their own problems in relating to others.

A sure way to empathize with one's own teacher is to be placed in the role of teacher. Instead of being told he will feel differently about things when he grows up and has children of his own, an older student helper has the experiences that will make him feel differently now. The involvement of older students in a collaborative program with adults to help younger students gives both the children and adults a new opportunity to be appreciated by the other. One of the most decisive factors in establishing harmony between groups is the existence of superordinate goals that have appeal for both, but which neither can achieve without the help of the other (Sherif, Harvey, White, Hood, & Sherif, 1961). Knowing one is a needed member of a significant team contributes greatly to a feeling of self-worth regardless of one's age.

One of the important assets of the program is that it allows students who are performing poorly in their own class to have the joyful experience of being recognized as experts by children who truly need their help. A sixth grader operating at a fourth grade level can be an excellent helper of a second grader who is also operating below grade level. An older student who has had trouble mastering material is often more understanding and patient than someone who has not experienced problems in learning. Bright older students also can help other bright students in a lower grade. For example, a special math unit in fractions designed by advanced math students in the sixth grade for advanced math students in the fourth grade provides stimulation and challenge for both groups.

The teaching staff also benefits from cross-age helping. Teachers report that when older students learn how to relate well to smaller children behavioral problems on the playground between the different ages are drastically reduced. Both helper and learner are placed in a position of trust and responsibility, thereby invoking change in behavior. When students are motivated and learn more, the teachers feel more successful too. In addition, the program facilitates a more positive and problem-solving attitude on the part of participating staff members.

INGREDIENTS FOR A SUCCESSFUL PROGRAM

To ensure the success of any cross-age helping program, several ingredients are necessary. These now will be described briefly.

Staff, Teachers, and Parents

The first important element of an effective program is staff members who have the skills to implement the program and who are dedicated to making it successful. Members of the staff should include a supportive administrator, at least one volunteer receiving-teacher who wants the older students' help, at least one volunteer sending-teacher from whose class older students go to help youngers, and someone to conduct seminar sessions for older student helpers in how to relate constructively to younger children. The seminar leader may be a counselor, a principal, school social worker, the sending or receiving teacher, or other available teacher who is interested in human relations.

Before older helpers actually work with their youngers, there should be some preservice training. This includes sessions for observation to find out what younger children are like, practice in how to relate to them constructively, and how to help them experience successful learning and a positive self-concept.[1]

Continued in-service training and support should be provided for the older helpers after they begin the program. Helpers need time to talk with each other and with their supervising staff members about on-the-job problems and joys. Provision should be made to supervise the helping sessions and to report successful practices and suggestions for alternative behavior. Feedback about the helpers' behavior and how they can improve is very useful. Teaching techniques for meeting new situations and time to practice them should be provided. All this the helpers can obtain in regularly scheduled in-service seminar sessions.

Student helpers working in pairs can provide older students with someone their own age with whom they can become better acquainted. Cross-age helping should be used to strengthen "own age" peer relationships as well as those with youngers. Besides being enjoyable, paired assignments can be useful in reporting on-the-job experiences during the seminar sessions. Moreover, pairing prevents the older student from regarding a receiving teacher's suggestions to helpers as a personal criticism.

Often the most significant person in the program for the older helpers is the teacher of the youngsters they are helping. The receiving teacher is equivalent to the person who hired them—the person for whom they are working. Helpers judge how well they are doing by the reactions of their receiving teacher to their efforts. Time should be allotted for helpers to meet with receiving teachers once a week to exchange ideas, discuss results, and plan new strategies. This can be planned for all the helpers of one receiving teacher at the same time; before school, after the helping session, or over lunch are satisfactory times for scheduling these conferences.

Training the Helpers

Training of helpers is extremely important for the program; it cannot be overestimated. Two types of training are necessary: content training in the area in which the older student is helping, and training in relating constructively to younger children (how to help them feel important, useful, accepted, and that they are growing in skill). The teacher whose children are receiving help from older students may have definite ways that he wants the material to be presented, for example certain methods of teaching remedial reading. If this is the case, the older helper should receive careful instructions, which are generally

---

[1] A cross-age helping package of dissemination materials by Peggy Lippitt, Ronald Lippitt, and Jeffrey Eiseman is published now by Xicom, R.F.D. #1, Sterling Forest, Tuxedo, New York. These materials include 12 seminar sessions for older helpers that can be adopted or adapted.

given during a conference with the receiving teacher or at a special time reserved for content training. An older helper may want to learn some specific methods, such as how to present subtraction facts or how to read stories to preschoolers. Often an expert in the content area can give training as part of the group seminar period.

Merely bringing older and younger students together does not ensure that they will get along well; forces working in the opposite direction should also be taken into consideration. Peer group norms often indicate that the appropriate way for older students to treat younger ones includes behavior such as exploiting, avoiding, and derogating. Youngers are very inventive in retaliating for such behavior by teasing, tattling, destroying olders' property, and otherwise being a nuisance. Training can teach the olders how to reverse this negative circular process. Legitimizing the olders' taking a nurturing, appreciative attitude toward youngers creates a great readiness to change. They easily empathize with a younger child's difficulties and are ingenious in thinking of ways to help the younger succeed.

Human relations training is essential to success for another reason. Many untrained older students who are placed in a position of authority resort to practices they have personally experienced. They may not like such practices, but equate them with the teacher role and have no alternatives to substitute in an emergency. Bribery, threats of punishment, "cut-downs", and guilt induction techniques will be used because these methods are familiar to everyone. This is only natural; many persons have not received much help in the area of liking themselves or caring about others, but we all have experienced what it is like to be criticized, punished, and belittled. Training in relating well to youngers includes practice in ways to avoid "cut-downs" and punishment, and how to give encouragement and build self-esteem.

Training is best given in seminar sessions, where students can identify with one another as a group making an important contribution to education. Suggestions can be given and received for alternative ways of being helpful, and new behaviors can be tried. In role playing episodes helpers can explore techniques before using them in actual work with their younger students. Older students have a chance to explore human relation techniques, invent games to motivate learning, find out more about children, about themselves, and the growing-up process.

DESIGNS FOR CROSS-AGE HELPING PROGRAMS

The Michigan Design

In our pilot studies in cross-age helping at the University of Michigan we always include the components summarized here. Initially, a meeting is held with persons who express interest in the program. Time is provided for the volunteer staff team to talk about goals and make design decisions (e.g., who will be paired with whom, for how long, location of the sessions, etc.). Preservice training is then given to the older (helper) students consisting of 4 to 12 seminars of 30 to 50 minutes each. The seminars deal with human relations problems such as how to relate positively to youngers and how to turn the mistakes of youngers into successful learning experiences. In-service training of one seminar per week (30–50 minutes) also is provided for older children. Once a week teacher conferences (15–30 minutes) are scheduled. Though the receiving teacher sets the goals to be achieved by the younger children, both the teacher and the helper plan the steps to reach the goals. Three or four helping sessions a week (30–40 minutes) are scheduled with the younger children. Sometimes students are given explicit and precise methods for helping, but often the helpers use their creativity to make their own lesson plans.

A pilot program in Detroit using this design involved three adjacent public schools in Detroit's inner-city: a high school, a junior high school, and an elementary school. The older helpers assisted across buildings as well as across grade levels. Upper elementary school students helped in primary grades; junior high students worked with upper elementary pupils; high school helpers worked in elementary and junior high. Each semester 68 student volunteers participated, providing service to children of 33 different receiving teachers. School staff members were trained to function as trainers of the olders and coordinators of the program.

Evaluation of the project focused on its feasibility for all age levels, attitude toward learning, and academic achievement. Data were obtained by teacher interviews and questionnaires from the older helpers. Results showed that teachers and older students both reported changes by the youngers in academic performance, turning in assignments, settling down to work, greater interest, greater class participation, better attitude toward receiving help, greater self-confidence, greater self-respect, and better attitude toward others.

One of the first school systems to use the cross-age helping procedures and materials developed in our pilot work was the Ontario–Montclair School District in Ontario, California. For the full year, 60 youngers from fourth, fifth, and sixth grades participated in the program. The helpers were eighth grade students who took a one-semester class called "Cross-Age Teaching." The olders were transported three times a week to the elementary schools for a tutoring period. Each older child was matched with a younger for specific help in content areas and interpersonal relationships.

Evaluation conducted during the second year involved 120 eighth grade helpers and their students (Poole, 1971). On academic performance, the helpers (older students) exceeded the control group by two months or more in reading, math, and language during the 7-month period. Similarly, the students receiving help significantly exceeded the control group in language and reading. Results also showed that self-concept scores for older and younger children in the program exceeded that of comparison groups. On sociometric ratings both older and younger children in the cross-age program increased in acceptability to peers, although comparison groups declined.

Other Designs for Cross-Age Helping

One innovative program in Los Angeles has used the remedial reading teacher as coordinator.[2] In this program, a group of 10 to 12 fifth and sixth grade students have a remedial reading period 5 days a week. For the first 10 days the remedial reading teacher trains these students in techniques of helping younger children who are having difficulties. After preservice training, they help younger children (first, second, and third graders) on a one-to-one basis. Directly after their own remedial reading period 3 days a week, the older helpers work with the youngers on a one-to-one basis. The reading teacher supervises the operations but does not interrupt during the helping sessions. Any comments are reserved for the seminar session on remedial reading held with the older helpers. Every 10 weeks these groups change to allow more students to give and receive help.

Various staff members can serve as seminar leaders. One crisis teacher in the Ypsilanti, Michigan schools schedules seminar sessions for the older helpers in four 45-minute groups on the day the social worker is at the school.[3] By teaching these sessions together, groups can be kept small (7–12) and still allow the social worker to cover a large case load in her day at the school. Older helpers of different types are included in each group—boys and girls, marginal children, behavior problems, isolates, peer leaders, underachievers, and good students. This is one of the few opportunities (besides gym) where alienated children have a chance to work closely with others who have a different outlook. No one is pressured to join the group. In schools where a seminar leader is not available, sending and receiving teachers have teamed up in permanent pairs. Between them they conduct their own seminar sessions for the olders.

Cross-age helping has been offered by both elementary and high schools as an elective subject. In one elementary school in the Ontario–Montclair, California, school system the helping program was included in the regular sixth grade curriculum. The program was voluntary; students who did not choose to be in it could join another sixth grade class during the cross-age helping period. In this design the sixth graders helped the youngers three days a week, had a feedback seminar session once a week, and had specific content training once a week during the helping period. The teacher who conducted the seminar was free to

---

[2] This program was developed by Herbert Rosner, working with parochial schools.
[3] William Atwell was responsible for organizing this program.

supervise the olders' interaction with their youngers 3 days a week. To help olders improve their teaching and relating skills, videotapes were made of tutoring sessions. Several high schools now offer tutoring as an elective course. In the Cherry Creek, Colorado, high school, students in math, science, social studies, art, and French are coached by department heads in these subjects 1 day a week. They help nearby elementary school children in these content areas 3 days a week.

In the Livonia, Michigan, school system one high school has an extensive community service program that offers students opportunity for volunteer school and community service as an experience in citizenship education.[4] Students can help during free periods or after school at nearby institutions, including elementary schools. This program places 500 high school students in volunteer community jobs. Training of the older helpers is done by the teachers receiving their services.

We are currently exploring two other types of cross-age programs. Studies are now underway using cross-age helping training in a methodical fashion in organizations serving youth and in summer camps. We are also investigating the feasibility of parents learning cross-age helping training techniques so they can help older children find ways of helping youngers at home. Cross-area helping programs have done a great deal to introduce constructive alternative behaviors to competition and denigration in schools. It will be interesting to see if trained parents can help older siblings promote an atmosphere of trust, responsibility, love, and concern between children of different ages that characterize many cross-age helping programs within schools.

CONCLUSIONS

Many advantages of cross-age helping have been mentioned in this chapter, but when one considers initiating such a program, it is useful to look at the possible disadvantages as well. Some of the advantages and problems connected with participation in a cross-age helping program—from the point of view of all concerned parties—are listed in Table 1. Unless potential problems are made explicit and dealt with before a program begins, they may emerge later and create havoc, even given the best of intentions. Considering problems before starting increases the likelihood of coping with them successfully. Cross-age helping should be a volunteer program for everyone taking part in it. Unless reasons for resistance are discussed and clarified, wholehearted volunteering may not occur. In attempting to increase involvement in the program, resolving barriers has proved more effective than increasing advantages. Sometimes barriers represent personal needs that can be met once they are known.

[4] This program was developed by John Graves.

Table 1

Participation in a Cross-Age Tutoring Program From the
Point of View of All Participants

Advantages	Barriers
The Sending Teacher (Older Students)	
1. The program can raise students' self-esteem and teach leadership skills.	1. Students will have less time in teacher's class.
2. It increases empathy for teacher role.	2. It takes time to schedule and organize.
3. Taking a position of trust and influence will evoke behavioral change.	3. How can I "control" things to run smoothly?
4. It offers an apprenticeship in service-oriented jobs.	4. Will someone else teach "my" children more, how will I feel about it if they do?
5. It is an incentive to catch up on knowledge gaps.	5. Will I get credit if it works or only blame if it doesn't?
6. It gives students a chance for more appreciation from others.	6. Will students' interest in another subject lessen their likelihood of achieving in mine?
7. Gives older student helpers a chance to learn human relations techniques.	
8. Less time needs to be devoted to discipline and settling playground problems.	
The Receiving Teacher (Younger Students)	
1. It will individualize instruction and reach more children.	1. It will take time to plan, assume division of labor, train students, and attend meetings.
2. It will increase motivation to learn and reduce behavior problems.	2. I like this-age-students, and don't understand older ones.
3. It gives me more time to help individuals, too.	3. I don't want to share my power.
4. It provides a way to extend my influence outside of my class.	4. I think older students are bad for younger ones.
5. It provides meaningful interaction with other staff members.	5. Can I prevent things from getting out of hand?
6. It helps bridge gap between student and teacher.	6. What can I do about feelings of professional jealousy if olders do a better job?
7. It will increase "my" childrens' self-esteem and social and academic skills.	7. I don't have human relations skills; how can I teach the helpers?
8. It will make school more fun for my children.	8. How can I train olders to use power wisely?

Table 1 (continued)

Advantages	Barriers

The Older Student

1. It provides an apprenticeship in helping jobs: a chance to learn techniques of caring.
2. It offers meaningful interaction with adults.
3. It's a chance to catch up on knowledge gaps.
4. It's a way to work through my own hang-ups at a safe emotional distance.
5. It offers a chance to feel influential, appreciated, needed.
6. It gives heightened self-esteem—a change in self image.
7. It's a chance for me to use my knowledge and put my ideas into practice.
8. It's an opportunity to do meaningful work with friends of my own age.

1. Fear of being unsuccessful.
2. Fear of not being given interesting work (relegated to janitorial-custodial help).
3. Fear of nonacceptance by teacher.
4. Fear of nonacceptance by younger.
5. Being nurturant to youngers violates peer norms.
6. No way to use youngers as scapegoats.
7. Fear of having no time for own peer group.

The Younger Student

1. Individualized learning, joy of learning and accomplishments.
2. Pleasure of having a "big" friend who cares.
3. Gives a better chance of success.
4. Removal of learning from the "authority figure" relationship; defensive games become unnecessary.
5. Older friend provides encouragement, support, incentive to work, and a feeling of worth.
6. Olders can interpret teacher's ideas in children's language.

1. Fear of being singled out as needing help.
2. Fear of olders if one has had a bad experience with "big kids" before.
3. Fear of failure.

Table 1 (continued)

Advantages	Barriers

The Administrators and School System

Advantages	Barriers
1. It's economically beneficial: taps available resources at little cost.	1. It takes time to explain and do a public relations job.
2. Provides a mechanism for in-service staff training.	2. It requires a willingness to negotiate scheduling for staff and students.
3. It's an adjunct to counseling and academic program.	3. It takes some money for: staff team, released time for supervision, workshop training, leading seminars, etc.
4. It lessens need to use energy in discipline, and leaves administrator more time to take a guiding role with staff and students and parents.	4. It requires dedicated commitment of staff and program coordinator and support by the administrator.
5. It provides participants opportunities to be more successful, appreciated, learn meaningful interaction and deal constructively with use of power.	5. There is a risk in trusting students with power.

The Community and the Family

Advantages	Barriers
1. It provides participants opportunities to be more successful, appreciated, learn meaningful interaction and deal constructively with use of power.	1. Desire to retain power by adults or leaders.
2. It fosters greater appreciation of all ages for all ages.	2. Fear of things getting out of control.
3. It is a more creative use of "people" resources.	3. Satisfaction from children and youth being in a dependent role.
4. It provides an educated group of volunteers in service-oriented professions.	4. Lack of knowledge about alternative methods of behavior.
5. It creates a community educated to use volunteers.	5. Absence of support for risking new behavior.
	6. New methods not seen as having any advantages over present methods.

167

Many good reasons can be cited for introducing cross-age helping programs into the lives of our youth. There are benefits to be gained for the younger children, the older children, and the teaching staff. It is clear that cross-age helping is an innovation that is consistent with many of the educational trends predicted for the future: individualization of instruction, participation by older students, collaboration with adults, use of volunteers in educational settings, and taking initiative for one's own learning (Joint Commission on Mental Health of Children, 1968).

REFERENCES

Joint Commission on Mental Health of Children. *A prediction and analysis of some of the major changes that will take place in the next fifty years.* Report of Task Force VI. Chevy Chase, Maryland, May, 1968.

Poole, A. *Final project report: Cross-age teaching* (No. 68-06138-0). Ontario–Montclair School District, Ontario, California. Poole-Young Associates, June 1971.

Sherif, M., Harvey, O. J., White, B. J., Hood, W. R., & Sherif, C. W. *Intergroup conflict and cooperation: The Robbers Cave experiment.* Norman: Univ. of Oklahoma Press, 1961.

10

Structured Tutoring: Antidote for Low Achievement

Grant Von Harrison

Brigham Young University

A recent study investigated 32 schools that had formidable reputations for individualized instruction (Bright, 1972). Results of the study were not very encouraging; of the 32 schools, only 2 were providing instruction that actually was "individualized" according to Bright's criteria.

Even if all schools had satisfied the criteria for individualized instruction, there still would be no guarantee that the needs of low achievers would be met. Most forms of individualized instruction require that students work independently, read at grade level, pace themselves, and demonstrate a high degree of self-discipline and motivation. These demands are usually too rigorous for low achievers, who are characterized by poor study habits, lack of self-confidence, and limited reading skills. For these reasons both the "cafeteria" model (choosing one's own learning activities) and the "paddle-your-own-canoe" approach (self-pacing) usually fail to meet the needs of low-achieving students. But the most inappropriate form of "individualized" instruction, especially for primary grade low achievers, is the programmed text or workbook. These programs rely on printed materials that require low achievers to apply reading skills that they very often simply do not possess.

169

Recent research has shown that low-achieving students do not learn consistently unless involved in a highly structured process (Blank & Solomon, 1969; Congreve, 1965; Harrison, 1967). It has not been possible to create a highly sensitive, personal, and structured learning environment without employing some kind of tutorial approach. A study by Blank and Solomon (1969) revealed that a highly structured tutorial model helped low achievers make significant progress, but that the model was ineffective when the tutoring was not highly structured. From research over the past several years, it is clear that a low achiever will progress only when he has access to an individual tutor whose role is highly structured, and who knows how to employ principles of learning and how to use appropriate instructional materials.

TRAINING NONPROFESSIONAL TUTORS

Where can one find tutors for children who need individualized instruction? Basically, the alternatives are either to expand the budgets of schools to cover cost of hiring certified teachers as tutors or to use nonprofessionals (i.e., other students, parents, aides, etc.). The present budgetary crisis facing most schools dictates the use of nonprofessional tutors as the only feasible alternative.

The number of schools using nonprofessional tutors has increased significantly in the last few years. In most instances the tutors do not receive any training beyond a brief orientation. Many educators continue to believe that tutoring is an informal interaction between teacher and student in which skills or information is transferred. It is expected that a tutor will automatically use effective instructional procedures. Yet an increasing amount of evidence indicates that untrained nonprofessional tutors do not use sound instructional techniques (Harrison, 1967, 1969a; Niedermeyer & Ellis, 1971; Lippitt & Lohman, 1965). Therefore, the tutor must be taught to employ good teaching methods. The structured tutoring model is designed to ensure that nonprofessional tutors are trained adequately for their task. The remainder of this chapter will describe the unique characteristics of the model and discuss its applications.

The Structured Tutoring Model

The structured tutoring model grew out of a project investigating the effectiveness of fifth and sixth graders in instructing younger Mexican-American children on 10 directionality concepts in mathematics. When left to their own devices, the older students were ineffective as tutors for the primary grade children; hence, an attempt was made to improve the teaching skills of the tutors. After extensive observations, we discovered that effective tutors needed to perform the following specific tasks in order to help their students: establish and maintain rapport with the child; orient the child to the task; let the child know precisely how he is expected to respond; deal appropriately with different types of responses from the child; properly praise the child; avoid punishing the child; teach new information; make decisions about learning rates; properly reinforce the child; focus the child's attention on the instructional materials; and avoid the use of subtle cues to prompt the child. Tutors who were trained to use these tutorial skills were able to help the younger children attain the specified objectives of the lessons.

Several different procedures for training tutors have been compared empirically. The most effective procedure was found to consist of three parts: First, the tutor reads instructions in simple, expository text form concerning the task; second, the skills described by the written text are discussed and clarified; and, third, a role playing session follows with the trainer playing the part of the learner and tutors taking turns practicing the tutoring skills. Reasons for using certain instruction methods in teaching are always explained to the tutor. In its final form, the training package for structured tutoring consists of a trainer's guide, independent study materials, a practice booklet, practice tapes, and charts. The trainer's guide contains a brief overview of the training sessions, directions on tutoring methods, examples of successful presentations, materials to implement the training program, and instructions for conducting the three training sessions. The independent study materials explain the skills the tutors will practice and present information needed for the next training session. The charts summarize key concepts a trainer will use during the tutoring sessions. The practice tapes and booklets provide the tutor with opportunities to practice each of the specified skills used in the training sessions. Results of evaluation of this tutor-training program in three separate elementary schools revealed that tutors mastered the skills satisfactorily (Harrison, 1967). On the basis of this and other research it can be asserted that almost all upper-grade elementary children can be trained to use effective teaching skills when tutoring.

Structured Tutoring with Mathematics Concepts

To determine the adaptability of the model, it was applied to another subject area (Harrison, 1969a). Interviews with primary grade teachers revealed that many students were not mastering critical math concepts. Tests administered to first graders indicated that math concepts causing the most trouble were sentence equations (e.g., $3+4=\square$; $\square-3=8$; $7+\square=9$). The instructional objective for structuring tutoring in this content area was very specific: that the child be able to solve sentence equations involving both the plus and minus signs, and with the unknown in all three positions.

A series of practice exercises were prepared for tutors to use with their students. Once the practice exercises were prepared, student tutors were trained to use the 12 basic tutoring skills mentioned earlier. From observations of this small group of tutors and students, the list of tutoring skills was modified several times over a period of 4 months. Trained and untrained tutors were randomly assigned to teach groups of first graders. Both the trained and untrained tutors used the same instructional materials and spent the same amount of time teaching the younger children. Observations of the sessions showed that trained tutors very closely followed the specified tutoring procedures, but the behaviors of untrained tutors consistently interfered with learning; they punished, extensively overcued, did not give verbal praise, did not engage in friendly noninstructional conversation, provided feedback before the child made the appropriate response, and made no effort to clarify the task.

Results for the learners showed that student tutors who received training in instructional techniques were four times as effective as untrained tutors in helping the children achieve the specified objectives (Harrison, 1969a). A subsequent study of these tutor-training procedures indicated an overall mastery level of 90% for the 10 specified skills (Harrison & Cohen, 1969).

Two other important points were highlighted by results from the initial Harrison (1969a) study on sentence equations: First, some tutoring skills (e.g., clarifying the task, verbal praise, avoiding punishment, etc.) are always appropriate regardless of the subject matter; and, second, certain other tutoring skills are dependent on subject matter and must be modified to fit the content. Thus, in teaching reading the child can be given the correct answer when he makes an incorrect response, but this procedure is inappropriate for teaching math concepts. If the child completes an equation incorrectly, it serves no useful purpose merely to tell him the correct answer. In this case, the learner should be shown how to check his answer by manipulating physical objects (e.g., pennies, beans), and in this way the learner can determine for himself whether his answer was right or wrong.

Tutoring appears to require skill training in four categories: general skills that are appropriate for any tutoring relationship; material-specific skills that are unique to the particular instructional objectives; and record-keeping skills (including general aspects of record-keeping as well as those records unique to the instructional objectives).

In the Harrison (1969a) study described above, it was found that fifth and sixth grade tutors cannot manage certain activities that are essential to individualized instruction (e.g., administering diagnostic tests, making instructional prescriptions, etc.). Consequently, adult supervision is needed when children of this age are employed as tutors. Moreover, elementary grade tutors require a fair amount of supervision and monitoring in general.

Classroom teachers do not usually have the time to supervise or train tutors; therefore, the possibility of using nonprofessionals in this role was explored. To examine the effectiveness of nonprofessional trainers, two professional educators and two junior college students trained student tutors (fifth and sixth graders) from five Los Angeles schools by using our tutor-training procedures (Harrison, 1969b). A control group of tutors did not receive training.

The tutors received instruction based on a modified version of the tutoring skills mentioned earlier in this chapter. Mastery of the 10 specified tutoring techniques was measured by two trained observers while each tutor was working with a first grade child. Tutors were assigned randomly to work with younger children (first graders) who needed individualized help with a specific form of sentence equation in math. One week following the tutoring a criterion test was administered to the younger children. Results showed that student tutors did use the specified techniques in their teaching. The trained tutors scored significantly higher on the tutor observation scales than the control group (80 versus 13%, respectively, $p < .01$). The behavior of tutors trained by professionals did not differ from that exhibited by tutors trained by nonprofessionals. As for the performance of the learners, results showed that the average criterion score of children instructed by trained tutors was significantly greater than that of children instructed by untrained tutors (76 versus 29%, respectively, $p < .01$). Nonprofessional trainers can, then, assume the responsibility for effectively training student tutors.

A Structured Tutorial System for Reading

Another tutorial system has been developed for helping children who are significantly below grade level in reading. Six types of instructional tasks were required of the students (from upper elementary grades) who tutored in reading: teaching names of letters; teaching sounds of letters; teaching a child to blend sounds; teaching a child to decode new words that are phonetically regular; and teaching sight words and oral reading. The tutoring skills required to handle these six instructional tasks were first formulated, and then evaluated on a larger scale in three elementary schools in the Provo, Utah, school district (Harrison & Brimley, 1971). The study was conducted when the children were not attending school, which ensures that the children did not receive any additional formal instruction in reading. The children were scheduled to enter the first grade in the fall, and were low achievers according to their kindergarten performance and test scores. Tutoring sessions lasted approximately 15–20 minutes each day for 5 days a week, and continued for 6 weeks. At the end of the 6-week period, the children were given a criterion test to measure their mastery of five specific objectives.

Results demonstrated that the children made significant learning gains as a result of having received the tutoring. Moreover, 3 months after the school year began, teachers ranked approximately 30% of the children who had received the tutoring during the summer as being in the upper 50% of the class.

Data from a major validation study resulted in a slight modification in the prescribed tutoring skills and a refinement of the management procedures for the tutorial system in reading (Harrison, Nelson, & Tregaskis, 1972). In its final form the tutorial system consists of the following components: supervisor's guide (how to introduce the tutoring program in a school, train examiners, etc.); diagnostic pretests; instructional sequence (60 instructional prescriptions arranged sequentially); home study materials for the tutor; blending exercises for learners; contingency record (for recording tutee's performance); decoding exercises (25 exercises for new words); flash cards (letters of alphabet, digraphs, and sight words); individual progress report for the learner (given to the student's classroom teacher and parents); learning gains summary; post-tests for learning gains; profile sheets (for the learner's performance); reading exercises (three exercises for teaching certain letter combinations); sound guide (stipulating the sound that should be taught for each letter and digraph); storybooks (10 storybooks for applying specific phonetic skills and sight words); testing procedures; tutor assignment sheets; and a tutor log (maintained daily).[1]

Extensions of Structured Tutoring

The structured tutorial reading program can be coordinated with regular classroom instruction or used independently. The program will complement a child's reading instruction regardless of the reading series used by the classroom teacher. The tutorial system can be managed by one adult (e.g., aide, remedial reading teacher) who is able to supervise approximately 50 student tutors a day. The cost of implementing the program (apart from the manager's salary) is approximately $1.00 per child per year—a very minimal cost compared to most types of individualized instruction. The tutorial system is now capable of taking a child from a pre-primer reading level to a high second grade reading level. Materials are now being field tested that will move a child from a second grade to a fourth or fifth grade level of reading.

A tutor manual has also been prepared for use by adults; it is based on the same instructional procedures used in the tutorial system for children. A field test of the adult manual was conducted in southern Utah, where educators have been struggling for a decade with the problem of how to teach Indian students to read. According to test data collected by the school since 1965, a class of Indian children has never reached grade level in reading and spelling. Since 1972, tutor guides have been used with nonprofessional adults (more than half of whom were Navajo Indians) who served as tutors for second grade Indian children. Results disclosed that on the average these children were reading and spelling at grade level the following year (Low, 1974).

[1] This Tutorial System is presently being published by the Brigham Young University Press.

A series of studies were conducted involving parents as tutors using the manual. With the aid of the instructional manual, parents who tutored were found to be as effective as paid nonprofessionals. One study found no significant difference between the criterion performance of children tutored by their parents and children tutored by adult tutors who were paid for their services (Keele & Harrison, 1971). In another study, 30 parents tutored their own first grade children at home over an 8-week period. A large majority of the parents were successful in helping their children overcome basic reading difficulties (Wilkinson, Harrison, & Brimley, 1973).

Thus far the tutor manuals have been used successfully with several groups of persons serving as tutors: parents, nonprofessional aides, paraprofessional aides, high school students, and undergraduate students at universities. In most instances elementary grade students have been recipients of the tutoring. But in addition to children, secondary students and illiterate adults also have been taught basic reading skills through the tutoring program (Harrison, 1971; Osguthorpe, 1973). As a further relevant example, the system has been adapted to the problem of teaching Spanish reading skills in Latin America. In a project in Bolivia, supervisors trained 115 tutors. The tutoring took place in the homes of the learners, and three one-hour meetings were held each week. Persons who were completely illiterate or semi-illiterate required an average of 26 days to complete the instruction. Data collected from the project disclosed a significant improvement in basic skills such as decoding Spanish words, reading sentences fluently, and comprehending simple sentences (Ott, Tuttle, & Harrison, 1975).

Although reading has been the primary focus of our research, other subject matter areas have also been explored. For example, a tutor manual for teaching English as a second language has been developed, and preliminary studies have been quite encouraging (Brown, Bradshaw, & Harrison, 1971; Harrison & Wilkinson, 1973). In addition, tutor manuals have been developed for teaching beginning math, math facts, sentence equations, experiential writing, and paired-associate tasks. Though the structured tutoring model has been used primarily to cope with the unique learning characteristics of low-achieving students and adults (who are considered high risks in terms of potential failure) it can be used at any grade level to teach many objectives that are not readily attained by students.

CONCLUSIONS

It is frequently assumed that bringing two persons together and designating one as a tutor will lead automatically to a healthy, profitable tutoring relationship. This assumption is simply not supported by the available evidence. Even extensive training of the tutor does not always lead to an acceptable tutoring relationship. To obtain maximum teaching gains from tutoring, the special skills that are essential for instruction must be identified if the tutor is to be maximally sensitive to the individual characteristics of the student he is teaching. Development of a structured tutorial system should involve the following steps: identification of pertinent objectives; selection or development of diagnostic tests; selection or development of appropriate instructional materials; identification of pertinent tutorial skills; validation of tutorial skills; development of an "exportable" tutor-training program; validation of tutor-training materials; and development of a manual for the tutor manager (Harrison, 1969b). This development process quite obviously involves a great deal more than simply bringing a tutor and a learner together for informal instruction sessions.

The present trend toward an increase in the use of tutoring by nonprofessionals in the schools has important implications for education. At the present time most teacher-training programs instruct prospective teachers thoroughly in the use of media and materials; however, training is not yet offered in connection with the efficient use of important human resources (e.g., aides, parents, older students). A program that emphasizes human resources should be an important part of the teacher training curriculum in the future. One of the more fascinating implications of nonprofessional tutoring is that conscientious parents probably can be trained to teach most of the basic cognitive skills to their children in their own homes.

Though structured tutoring is certainly not without its problems and limitations, it has proved to be an effective educational technique with many types of nonprofessionals serving as tutors. Additional controlled research obviously is needed; but the structured tutoring model does seem to offer a promising means of meeting the needs of low-achieving children who are not learning adequately through traditional instructional approaches.

REFERENCES

Blank, M., & Solomon, F. How shall the disadvantaged be taught? *Child Development,* 1969, *40,* 47–61.

Bright, L. Description of a contingency management system. Talk presented at Brigham Young Univ. Provo, Utah, summer, 1972.

Brown, M. L., Bradshaw, C., & Harrison, G. V. The use of the structured tutoring model to teach primary grade children comprehension of a second language. Paper presented at the annual meeting of the California Educational Research Association, San Diego, California, February, 1971.

Congreve, W. J. Independent learning. *North Central Association Quarterly,* 1965, *40,* 222–228.

Harrison, G. V. Training students to tutor. Technical Memorandum 3686/000/00. Santa Monica, California: System Development Corporation, September 28, 1967.

Harrison, G. V. The effects of trained and untrained student tutors on the criterion performance of disadvantaged first-graders. Paper presented at the annual meeting of the California Educational Research Association, Los Angeles, California, March, 1969. (a)

Harrison, G. V. The effects of professional and nonprofessional trainers using prescribed training procedures on the performance of upper-grade elementary student tutors. Unpublished Ph.D. dissertation, Univ. of California, Los Angeles, 1969. (b)

Harrison, G. V. Tutorial project for illiterate adults. Final Report, Adult Education Program, Provo school district, Provo, Utah, 1971.

Harrison, G. V., & Brimley, V. The use of structured tutoring techniques in teaching low-achieving six-year-olds to read. Paper presented at the annual meeting of the American Educational Research Association, New York City, February, 1971.

Harrison, G. V., & Cohen, A. M. Empirical validation of tutor training procedures. Unpublished manuscript, Brigham Young Univ., 1969.

Harrison, G. V., Nelson, W., & Tregaskis, L. The use of a structured tutorial reading program in teaching nonreading second-graders in Title I schools to read. Paper presented at the annual meeting of the American Educational Research Association, Chicago, Illinois, April, 1972.

Harrison, G. V., & Wilkinson, J. C. The use of bilingual student tutors in teaching English as a second language. Paper presented at the convention of Teachers of English to Speakers of Other Languages, San Juan, Puerto Rico, May, 1973.

Keele, R., & Harrison, G. V. A comparison of the effectiveness of structured tutoring techniques as used by parents and paid student tutors in teaching basic reading skills. Paper presented at the annual meeting of the California Educational Research Association, San Diego, California, April, 1971.

Lippitt, P., & Lohman, J. E. Cross-age relationships—an educational resource. *Children*, 1965, *12*, 113–117.

Low, G. M. An evaluation of the tutorial program at the Blanding elementary school. Unpublished manuscript, Blanding, Utah, 1974.

Niedermeyer, F. C., & Ellis, P. Remedial reading instruction by trained pupil tutors. *Elementary School Journal*, 1971, *71*, 400–405.

Osguthorpe, R. T. Parents: A potential instructional resource for the public school. Paper presented at the annual meeting of the California Educational Research Association, Los Angeles, California, November, 1973.

Ott, E. C., Tuttle, D. M., & Harrison, G. V. Results and implications of using a structured tutorial system to teach Spanish reading skills in Bolivia. *Educational Technology*, 1975, *15*, 50–53.

Wilkinson, J. C., Harrison, G. V., & Brimley, V. The effect of training in structured tutoring on a parent's desire and capability to assist his child in the acquisition of basic reading skills. Paper presented at the annual meeting of the American Educational Research Association, New Orleans, Louisiana, February, 1973.

11

A Model for the Development
or Selection of
School-Based Tutorial Systems

Fred C. Niedermeyer
Southwest Regional Laboratory for Educational
Research and Development

The "state-of-the-art" of research and development regarding instructional systems in general, and tutorial systems in particular, has progressed significantly in the last 10 years. Educators throughout the country now realize that tutoring involves much more than simply placing tutor and learner together and hoping that "something good" will happen. Systematically developed, research based tutorial systems now offer the promise that good things can happen on a large scale.

The purpose of this chapter is to define and describe a model that specifies the components of an effective tutorial system. The characteristics defined in the model are not intended to be exhaustive; the individual user may wish to consider many other possible characteristics of a tutorial system. Nevertheless, the considerations are intended to specify a complete instructional system. A tutorial system that does not include these elements is incomplete, and should be recognized as such.

The seven considerations presented below may be applied to any school based tutorial system operated by teachers or other school personnel. The system may be "remedial" in that only low-achieving learners are tutored following regular, teacher administered instruction, or all children may be tutored as part or all of the regular instruction. Tutoring would normally take place in the school, but the system may be designed so that tutoring takes place elsewhere in support of the school's instruction program (e.g., by parents in the home). The remainder of this chapter will elaborate seven considerations, each of which will be posed in the form of a question. Relevant research findings and development examples will be presented where appropriate.

CHARACTERISTICS OF AN EFFECTIVE TUTORIAL SYSTEM

Outcomes

The first consideration of a tutoring system is as follows: Does the tutorial system specify the outcomes that the learners and tutors will attain as a result of tutoring? Too often, tutors are sent into classrooms simply to "help out." This is of questionable value unless it is clear what effect tutoring is supposed to have on the behaviors and feelings of the learner and, in some cases, on the tutor. Without specifying the expected outcomes of tutoring, teachers and tutors have little to guide them in deciding what instructional activities to conduct. Also, without statements of outcomes it is unlikely there will be systematic and regular assessment of learner achievement and other effects of tutoring. Thus, when learners and tutors are not benefiting from their interactions, it is unlikely that the situation will be detected and improved.

It is essential that statements of outcomes be unambiguous and reportable. Examples of outcome statements not meeting these criteria might be: "Tutoring will improve the learner's ability to read," or "The learner will exhibit a 10-month growth on a standardized reading test at the end of 6 months of tutoring." The ability to read has many facets, and neither of the above outcomes makes it clear just what reading skills the learner should practice (e.g., decoding versus comprehension). More appropriate outcomes might be: "The learner will read, individually and in contextual discourse, the population of words specified in the attached list," or "The learner will sound out and read any regularly spelled, single syllable word comprised of previously learned letter sounds." As will be seen, only tutorial systems based on these types of outcomes will be able to satisfy many of the remaining considerations presented in this chapter.

Assessment

Does the tutoring system include measures and procedures for periodic assessment, so that one can identify specific outcomes where the learner may be having difficulty? Often a tutorial system has a remedial emphasis, and low-achieving learners receive all or most of the tutoring. If the system provides for regular assessment keyed to specified outcomes, then not only can the low-achieving learners be identified, but so can the particular outcomes on which each learner is deficient. Subsequent tutoring can focus directly on critical outcomes for each child, thus "individualizing" the entire system.

It is important that assessment occur often enough to prevent the learner from falling too far behind. Assessment may take place weekly or every several weeks. End-of-year assessment is not enough. It is of little value to find out after a year of tutoring that the learner has not progressed or that he received tutoring on the wrong skills.

There may be an additional advantage to a tutorial system that has a regular program of assessment. Teachers, tutors, and learners may find it rewarding and motivating regularly to see empirical evidence of growth. This conjecture is based simply on personal observations and experiences. I know of no reported investigations of the motivational effects of providing tutors, teachers, and learners with results of assessment, although the conjecture is readily amenable to experimental test if its reasonableness is doubted. In a well-developed tutorial system, the results of assessment are usually positive and can be shared with those concerned. If the results are not positive, changes in the program should be formulated and tested. Subsequent assessment will determine the efficacy of such changes.

Materials

A third consideration of a tutorial system is posed in the following question: Are the instructional materials and procedures to be used by tutors clearly specified and keyed directly to the program outcomes and assessment materials? If a tutorial system is based on clear statements of expected outcomes, then materials and procedures can be developed that will enable the learner to practice the material in the appropriate sequence and amount. The material should be sufficiently structured that a tutor can administer it with a minimum of confusion or error. A relevant example is the tutorial program devised for parents to teach kindergarten children at home in support of their children's reading instruction at school (Niedermeyer & Giguere, 1972). In this tutoring program the teacher sends home an exercise each week to the child's parents. Figure 1 is an illustration of the instructional procedures provided for parents to use when tutoring with this type of exercise. As can be seen from the figure, most of the procedures deal with having the parent maintain a positive manner and react appropriately when the child responds correctly or incorrectly.

One question that always arises when developing instructional materials for tutors is the degree of structure that should be built into the materials. This question can have no general answer, but there are a few considerations that

THESE ARE THE PROCEDURES TO USE DURING THE PRACTICE SESSION WITH YOUR CHILD. IT IS IMPORTANT THAT YOU KNOW THESE PROCEDURES AND USE THEM CORRECTLY.

Place the Practice Exercise Sheet directly in front of your child.

Smile! Be pleasant and positive.

Ask your child to read through the Practice Exercise list for that day until he does it twice without a mistake. Even though your child may be doing very well, do **not** ask him to do more than **one** Exercise a day.

When your child reads something correctly, let him know he is right. Say something like, "O.K.," "Good," or "That's right."

⑤

After your child reads through a list correctly, praise him. Say something like, "Great! Keep up the good work."

⑥

When your child gives a **wrong answer** or no answer at all, point to the **word** and make sure your child is looking at it. Then tell him the right answer and have him say it before going on. Do **not** give hints.

⑦

Maintain a relaxed and positive attitude throughout the practice session. Try not to get upset or make your child feel bad under any circumstances.

⑧

When your child is able to read through the list twice with no mistakes or completes the Learning Game, do something fun (follow-up activity) that you both enjoy.

Figure 1 Sample instructional procedures for parents to use in tutoring their kindergarten children at home. (From Niedermeyer & Giguere, 1972.)

should be kept in mind. First, if the material has little structure, instruction may be inefficient and ineffective. With such material the tutors are required to make decisions regarding the content and behaviors that the learner should practice, and in what amount and what order; often the tutors will err in their decisions or "go off on a tangent," and the learner receives inappropriate practice as a consequence. In bursts of enthusiastic initiative, the tutor often will give the learner too much too soon, thus causing failure and frustration. (Parent tutors, in particular, are predisposed to make errors in this direction.) Tutors can be trained to make decisions of this type, but extensive training may be necessary.

On the other hand, if the material is overly structured, training tutors to use the complicated materials may prove to be too time consuming and costly to justify the effort. In addition, materials and procedures that are extremely tedious to administer will prove to be exasperating for both the tutor and the learner, especially when administered over a sustained period of time. Moreover, it must be remembered that schools normally do not have the time, the human resources, or the inclination to invest an extended amount of time in tutor training. For certain types of materials and procedures (such as that shown in Figure 1), the training of tutors can be accomplished in only a few hours of instruction.

Training

Does the tutorial program make satisfactory provisions for training tutors to use the specified instructional materials and procedures? In Niedermeyer's (1970a) study comparing the instructional behaviors of trained and untrained tutors, it was found that only the trained tutors exhibited many of the characteristics considered to be desirable for good instruction (e.g., maintaining rapport and providing unambiguous directions). Untrained tutors never offered verbal praise to their learners; and only once did one of the five untrained tutors engage his pupil in noninstructional, friendly conversation. Untrained tutors confirmed correct responses only half the time. Following an incorrect response, untrained tutors provided their pupils with the correct response only once in 17 times; instead, they attempted to elicit the correct response through prompting; this was successful only 25% of the time. If it is desirable for tutors to handle correct and incorrect responses appropriately and to maintain a positive, friendly rapport with their learners, then they need to receive training.

The most efficient tutor training simply directs the tutors how to administer the outcomes-based materials and activities in a friendly, positive manner. One type of training that has proved effective and has attained widespread use is the structured role-playing technique (Niedermeyer, 1969c). Structured role playing is based on the assumption that it is not sufficient simply to tell tutors how to react. Before appropriate actions can become automatic, the tutor needs to practice and receive immediate feedback each time he displays one of the tutorial skills. During structured role playing, one trainee will tutor another using scripted materials. For example, in the parent-tutoring program (Niedermeyer & Giguere, 1972), the parent role playing the child would respond to each item according to a printed script (e.g., giving a right answer, a wrong answer, or failing to answer). The person being trained as tutor would then respond according to the procedures described on his script. Feedback is provided to the tutor by having the person who role plays the child read aloud the appropriate information appearing in his script for each item (e.g., "Did the parent say 'That's right', 'Good', or 'O.K?' "). Both trainees must then agree whether the tutor responded appropriately.

In summary, the training component of a tutorial system should contain at least two characteristics: It should inform the person being trained as the tutor precisely how to administer the instructional materials or activities, and it should provide direct practice (role playing) on such general tutorial skills as how to handle various kinds of responses from the learner and how to maintain a positive, friendly manner. Training of this type, when referenced to specific outcomes and materials, can be completed satisfactorily in less than half a day. Most schools will find it difficult to justify longer periods of time to the training of tutors.

Monitoring

Are materials and procedures provided so that the tutorial system can be established and operated by teachers and administrators? Even when tutorial materials are well designed and tutors are adequately trained the system still may not be installed and maintained effectively in the school. For example, in one development effort it was found that only half the required tutoring actually took place (Niedermeyer & Ellis, 1969). The teachers simply were not monitoring the tutors to see who was being tutored and what materials were being used. A complete tutorial system will contain materials and procedures indicating how school personnel can select and train tutors, schedule tutoring periods, assign tutors to learners with appropriate materials, monitor completion of the tutoring assignments, observe tutors' use of instructional procedures, and retrain or remotivate tutors when necessary. Often it is useful to divide the many responsibilities and provide separate procedural manuals for a school tutorial system coordinator, a tutor trainer, the tutors' classroom teachers, and the learners' classroom teachers. Exemplary guides and procedures of these types may be found in Niedermeyer (1969a) and Niedermeyer and Giguere (1972).

One of the more difficult problems encountered in installing systems in which parents tutor their children at home has been to obtain the cooperation and participation of parents in low-income, inner-city communities. Parent-assisted learning has proved to be an extremely effective type of tutoring (Niedermeyer, 1969a, 1969b, 1970b), but typically only about 30–40% of parents in inner-city schools respond to routine invitations to attend a 1-hour orientation session at the school (Niedermeyer, Gilbert, & Streeter, 1970). To alleviate this problem, we have devised and tested various strategies for increasing parent participation (Niedermeyer & Giguere, 1972). The number of participating parents was increased to 62% by providing schools with options such as: (*1*) training parents on a "drop by" basis at school; (*2*) providing transportation and baby-sitting for the training sessions; (*3*) scheduling evening sessions; and (*4*) requiring parents to reply to the invitations.

User Experience Data

Do data exist for the tutorial system to indicate that (*1*) learners consistently have attained the expected outcomes during previous use of the system; and (*2*) learners, tutors, and school personnel have expressed satisfaction after involvement with the system? The answer to this question reveals whether a program actually has been field-tested in schools or whether it is a "first-draft" effort still lacking in evidence regarding effectiveness. Descriptions of the development of tutorial systems usually show that early versions are inefficient, ineffective, and contain many operational problems (Niedermeyer & Ellis, 1969). Through a series of revisions and tests, however, problems can be located and solved, so that the intended outcomes will be produced effectively and efficiently (Niedermeyer & Ellis, 1970, 1971).

It is important to look for empirical data regarding the development of tutorial systems. Too often, developers and publishers rely on a few carefully chosen testimonials to substantiate the credibility of a system. Though such testimonials are invariably positive, they may not be representative of the majority of users. Quantitative contextual data should be presented even when reporting the attitudes and opinions of learners, tutors, or school persons regarding a tutorial system. For example, positive attitudes regarding the system should be expressed in terms of the proportion of the total number of users expressing this attitude.

The primary criterion for determining the effectiveness of a tutorial system should be those data related to outcomes that define the proficiencies and feelings expected to occur in the learners and tutors. These data should be presented in a manner that clearly indicates the contribution of the tutorial system in producing the outcomes (i.e., baseline data and control groups). It is also desirable to field-test the system in a variety of school locations and situations; this allows the potential user to estimate better how well the system might operate in his own situation.

Time and Costs

When planning to develop or use a tutorial system that meets the previous six considerations, final consideration must be given to the time and costs involved. Are the time and cost requirements for establishing and operating the tutorial system acceptable to the persons involved and reasonable in terms of expected outcomes for the learners and tutors? Many tutorial systems require considerable time and commitment from school personnel. Some systems require substantial tutor training (e.g., 10 or 12 sessions over a 6-week period). Others require the involvement of many persons and a substantial reorganization of the school (e.g., systems where all or most of the children in the school are engaged in some sort of cross-age tutoring on a daily basis). Some attention must be given to preparing the school staff to accept, install, and operate such programs effectively.

One also should consider whether the amount of time and expense involved is worth the effort in terms of the benefits to be derived from the tutorial system. This question involves the nature and quality of the instructional program the tutorial system supports. A poorly developed instructional program is likely to make inefficient use of even the most effective tutorial system.

Another aspect of the interaction of the tutorial system with the instructional program has important cost–benefit implications. It is difficult to provide enough tutors so learners can receive sufficient practice on a remedial basis. This type of system may not be justified if time and costs are unusually high. More substantial learning gains are possible when the tutoring is a regular part of the instruction for all children, as is the case when parents tutor at home in support of the teacher. In a parent-assisted learning study, it was found that the outcomes-referenced reading achievement of kindergarten children who were tutored 10 minutes daily by their parents increased from 52% to 83% in 12 weeks (Niedermeyer, 1969a, b, c). The achievement of comparable children in classes receiving only the teacher-administered instructional program remained at the 50–60% level. The primary reason for this effect was that parents were able to monitor over 2000 additional practice responses during these 12 weeks, responses that the children would not have made otherwise. Such massive amounts of practice will have a dramatic effect on learning for all children. To accomplish this much tutoring in the school would be difficult and expensive, however.

In summary, this chapter has been concerned with defining a model for individuals who may be interested in developing, researching, or selecting a tutorial system. The seven considerations discussed above are intended to encompass the characteristics of a complete tutorial system, that is, one that will be usable and successful in the school. The model may serve as a useful guide for anyone interested in actually bringing about a large-scale change in the current instructional practices in the schools.

REFERENCES

Niedermeyer, F. C. Effects of school-to-home feedback and parent accountability on kindergarten reading performance, parent participation, and pupil attitude. Xerox University Microfilms, Ann Arbor, Michigan. Order No. 70-2240, 1969. (a)

Niedermeyer, F. C. Parent-assisted learning. Technical Report No. 19, Southwest Regional Laboratory, Los Alamitos, California, 1969. (b)

Niedermeyer, F. C. Programming instructional aides. Paper presented at the annual meeting of the National Society for Programmed Instruction, Washington, D. C., 1969. (c)

Niedermeyer, F. C. Effects of training on the instructional behaviors of student tutors. *Journal of Educational Research*, 1970, *64*, 119–123. (a)

Niedermeyer, F. C. Parents teach kindergarten reading at home. *Elementary School Journal*, 1970, *71*, 438–445. (b)

Niedermeyer, F. C., & Ellis, P. A. The SWRL tutorial program: A progress report. Research Memorandum, Southwest Regional Laboratory, Los Alamitos, California, May 1, 1969.

Niedermeyer, F. C., & Ellis, P. A. The development of a tutorial program for kindergarten reading instruction. Technical Report No. 26, Southwest Regional Laboratory, Los Alamitos, California, 1970.

Niedermeyer, F. C., & Ellis, P. A. Remedial reading instruction by trained pupil tutors. *Elementary School Journal*, 1971, *72*, 400–405.

Niedermeyer, F. C., & Giguere, C. Strategies for obtaining and maintaining participation in the SWRL parent-assisted learning program. Technical Memorandum No. TM 3-72-09, Southwest Regional Laboratory, Los Alamitos, California, 1972.

Niedermeyer, F. C., Gilbert, C. J., & Streeter, L. The 1969–70 tryout of the parent-assisted learning program. Technical Note No. TN 3-70-11, Southwest Regional Laboratory, Los Alamitos, California, 1970.

12

The Tutorial Community[1]

Ralph J. Melaragno
System Development Corporation

The tutorial community project is a long-range research and development effort that began in the Pacoima, California, elementary school in 1968. Through the project a "tutorial community" involving an entire elementary school has been established. Tutoring by the students is the major instructional feature of the program but is only one dimension of the tutorial community. This chapter focuses on what we have learned about initiating and maintaining an extensive school-wide tutoring program.

CHARACTERISTICS OF THE TUTORIAL COMMUNITY

The tutorial community project had its genesis in the ferment of educational reform that began in the early 1960s. At that time concern by educators and laymen about the quality of public education led to various efforts to change the schools. Tutoring by students seemed to represent one hopeful approach: It individualizes instruction and creates positive attitudes in students (Gartner, Kohler, & Riessman, 1971).

[1] The Tutorial Community Project was conducted under a grant from the Ford Foundation.

The immediate predecessor of the tutorial community was a study designed to develop an effective instructional system for first grade Mexican–American students (Melaragno & Newmark, 1968b). Several tutoring procedures finally were devised that resulted in these students' mastering 80% or more of the educational objectives. The final version of the instructional system included students in the same classroom working together, older students helping younger ones, teachers tutoring small groups of students, and parents tutoring their own children at home. Results of this study subsequently were applied to an entire elementary school (Melaragno & Newmark, 1968a).

A functioning tutorial community embodies several important features. Of central importance is individualization of instruction through various forms of student tutoring. Tutoring is not extracurricular, incidental, or remedial in nature; it is an integral and essential part of the everyday school operation. The tutors also participate in planning and in performing support activities such as keeping records. In a tutorial community a climate must be created that facilitates change and experimentation. An integral feature of the operational procedures is the participation in the planning and decision making by students, teachers, administrators, and parents. To attain participation and involvement from these diverse groups, openness of communication must be encouraged. It should be emphasized that the development of a tutorial community occurs gradually. The entire approach is empirical, involving successive evaluations and revisions of procedures until specified objectives are accomplished.

Types of Tutoring

Four different types of tutoring have been used in tutorial community schools. First, *intergrade tutoring* refers to the upper grade elementary students helping primary grade students. This is the basic form of tutoring used in the school, and the majority of primary grade students receive regular help. The intergrade tutoring program is highly systematic. The program is class based: Training and supervision of tutors and modifications to the procedures are carried out by classroom teachers with the assistance of a tutoring coordinator (Melaragno, 1972a).

Interschool tutoring is a type of tutoring in which students from a nearby junior high school act as tutors for upper grade elementary school students. This program is less systematic than the intergrade tutoring program and allows junior high students to use their own initiative and ingenuity in devising ways of assisting learners. A junior high school teacher conducts most of the training and supervision of tutors (Watson & Rosenberg, 1973).

A third type of tutoring, *intraclass tutoring,* involves students assisting one another within their own class. In a few cases "experts" are identified and used as resources for classmates who request help. In most cases students are paired according to the teacher's assessment of the needs and capabilities of the students.

A fourth type of tutoring consists of a wide variety of *informal tutoring* procedures that grow out of intergrade tutoring. For example, older students serve as playleaders for younger students during recess and lunch periods, older and younger students work together on projects in mathematics and art, and upper grade classes join primary grade classes on visits to the library or places of interest in the community.

Given the complexity of the changes associated with establishing the tutorial community, it is not possible clearly to identify the important causal factors when examining outcomes. In particular, there is no way to determine the extent to which the various tutoring programs have contributed to differences evident between the students' behavior at the onset of the project and the present. One can say with some confidence, however, that tutoring has played a large part in improving students' academic skills and attitudes toward school. Quantitative data indicate a strong and consistent improvement of scores on standardized reading tests administered to all primary grade students over a 4-year period. In addition, the incidence of vandalism to the school has decreased, attendance has improved, and hostility among students has diminished. Furthermore, questionnaire data showed that teachers and parents perceive that students' attitudes have become much more positive toward learning in school.

Initiating and Maintaining School-Wide Tutoring

In the course of several years of experience, it has been learned that starting a tutoring program is easy, but it is more difficult to maintain it successfully once the initial enthusiasm has passed. Several elements are crucial to the success of any tutoring program. Commitment by the school community is a basic requirement; time, energy, and resources are necessary to make the program succeed. Personnel must be assigned to carry out certain tasks, and time must be set aside so that all the participants—students, teachers, and coordinators—have the opportunity to complete all the seemingly peripheral tasks that are important for success of the program.

Good tutoring programs don't just happen; careful and detailed planning is essential before making any substantive changes in a school's operating procedures. Perhaps the most important aspect of a tutoring program that requires careful planning is the particular tutoring procedures to be used. All too often a school initiates intergrade tutoring on a relatively casual basis, then after a period of time it is concluded that tutoring doesn't work. Older students become bored when they are given menial tasks such as distributing materials or supervising younger students engaged in art projects. Unplanned adventures into tutoring seem to be based on the notion that good things happen automatically when an older child works with a younger one—this is rarely the case. School personnel should identify the objective to be reached from tutoring and the instructional procedures that tutors should use to reach these objectives.

Ultimately, the quality of a tutoring program depends upon the preparation of the staff. Classroom teachers assume new roles when involved in a tutoring program, and they should receive adequate training. The most basic training for teachers is to work directly with students in a tutorial relationship. Teachers should do some tutoring themselves, to see the procedures in operation; then they should train a few older students as tutors and observe them tutoring younger students. Similarly, the person acting as tutoring coordinator should be prepared for the role. The tutoring coordinator should have the same experiences as classroom teachers (actual tutoring, training, and supervising of a few tutors), and also should be prepared to help the classroom teachers.

Not only should tutoring procedures be worked out carefully, but tutors must be trained to apply the procedures. If older students are prepared for tutoring by being given instructions such as, "Help him work out the problems he's having trouble with," they frequently will experience failure and frustration. The first part of tutor training is an orientation to the helping relationship: Tutors should be informed about the difficulties younger students have in school and how tutors can help with them; in addition, tutors should understand the basic principles of learning and how to apply them in a tutorial setting. The second part of the training consists of direct instruction in the tutoring procedures to be followed, largely accomplished by role playing. Training sessions can be conducted by the classroom teachers.

Tutoring is more than the application of certain instructional procedures; it is a process of interrelated steps. Thus, teachers meet with tutors and describe the particular needs of the younger students. During the actual tutoring, teachers observe and assist tutors. Teachers meet periodically with tutors to review the tutoring and provide additional training, support, and encouragement. Teachers involved with tutoring meet occasionally to share ideas among themselves.

A tutoring program necessitates changes in professional roles and interpersonal relations, so it is important that communication be as open as possible. Participants must feel that their ideas will be heard and that all aspects of the tutoring program are open for discussion. If formal methods for communication do not exist, informal ones will inevitably emerge. As an innovation such as tutoring is instituted, the way decisions are made must be clarified for all participants. Individuals need to know by whom—and how—decisions are made, plans developed, and problems solved. These issues should be dealt with early. A successful decision making structure would include all elements of the school community: students, teachers, coordinators, administrators, and parents (Schmuck, 1972).

As with any other systematic approach to improving education, tutoring requires a procedure for evaluation. A monitoring system should be established to collect appropriate information and make it available to the school personnel. With such a monitoring system, decisions can be based on empirical data rather than on intuition, and adjustments can be made when necessary (Cottam, 1973).

ISSUES IN SCHOOL-WIDE TUTORING PROGRAMS

During the first years of the tutorial community project an attempt was made to develop effective intergrade tutoring arrangements and to implement support systems (e.g., staff preparation, program monitoring, decision making structure). Attention has shifted more recently to the issues that emerge when a school-wide tutoring program is continued over an extended period of time. These are issues that will require empirical answers.

Needs of Learners and Tutors

Most tutoring programs have involved reading; they usually emphasize sight vocabulary, phonics skills, and word attack skills. Tutoring programs in reading are quite similar and generally have been successful. When tutoring continues over a period of several years, however, three developments can be observed. First, tutors become increasingly more capable in employing tutoring skills because of practice and improved tutor-training procedures. Second, teachers become more proficient in managing the tutoring system. Third, the achievement of learners increases because of greater effectiveness of tutors (and teachers) and because of instruction received in reading for several years. Hence, learners need additional instruction at a higher level. A successful tutoring program must, therefore, provide for continual modifications in order to satisfy the changing needs of learners. Research has begun on expanding our tutoring program to include higher-level reading skills (e.g., literal and inferential comprehension). Such skills are rather complex and undoubtedly will require different behavior between tutors and learners than that required for teaching simpler skills.

Tutors also have changing needs that require attention. Most tutoring programs are designed to satisfy the cognitive needs of the tutees, but, not surprisingly, the tutors become bored by repeating the same type of instruction. Few persons could maintain repetitive behavior year after year without having monotony set in. Young elementary school tutors are especially vulnerable to boredom and diminution of interest. One typical reaction to the boredom is to provide tutors with encouragement and reinforcement. This does help, but it is not completely satisfactory when the tutor returns again to the same task. Classroom teachers often suggest adding more variety to the tutoring. Variety would appear to be useful, but the approach is usually too narrow. Stimulating activities included by teachers have little relation to instructional goals. For example, playing games with younger students does little to satisfy the tutor's need for a richer tutoring experience. Probably the most satisfactory solution to the tutor's boredom is to maintain flexibility; once they have become familiar with basic tasks, tutors should have the opportunity to engage in more demanding activities. Expanding the tutoring program to meet the changing needs of learners will provide a richer experience for tutors as well. Tutors also could be used more extensively for assessing progress and training other tutors. Finally, the tutoring program should allow tutors with unique capabilities to use their ingenuity and creativity in exploring additional ways of working with younger learners. Tutors must not, however, be overloaded with new tasks that exceed their capability; this would result in frustration.

Systematic Tutoring Procedures

Earlier in this chapter intraclass tutoring, in which classmates assist one another, was mentioned. These procedures are not as systematic as the inter-grade tutoring program. Development of systematic intraclass tutoring would provide techniques for further individualizing instruction. Some attention has been paid to intraclass tutoring. In one study, upper grade students tutored one another using the same procedures they followed with younger learners (Ebersole & DeWitt, 1972). Teaching skill development at a very basic level may not be useful for all older students, and there are no arrangements for primary grade students to assist one another. Melaragno and Newmark (1968b) have designed detailed strategies for first grade students to help each other, but the program is based on materials that require extensive time and effort to prepare (e.g., tape recordings, special workbooks).

Recently, Newmark (1972) has explored pupil teams in which students in a class are formed into teams containing a range of talent in each team. Students are trained to work together in their teams, and to turn to a team member for assistance with a problem before asking the teacher for help. This approach has considerable merit, but it also has problems. Teachers frequently are loath to give up so much of their instructional responsibility and often intervene too quickly. Students require considerable training before they can work effectively in teams; they, too, turn to the teacher readily instead of a teammate. Pupil teams operate best in those few instructional areas that are individualized. Serious research effort should be devoted to exploring procedures that a teacher can employ to increase the amount of time students in a class spend working together. Perhaps some of the ideas discussed by British educators could serve as starting points (e.g., Palmer, 1971, Rance 1968).

Systematic or structured tutoring procedures appear to have greatest likelihood of success (Harrison, 1972a). The systematic nature of the tutoring is the key to success of such programs but also can be their downfall. At the root of this dilemma are beliefs held by many educators that teaching is an art and that children are special kinds of human beings. Resistance to employing systematic procedures takes such forms as denying their long-range value or claiming that teachers are abrogating fundamental responsibilities. Responses citing the success of these procedures fall on deaf ears. For systematic tutoring procedures to spread and flourish we must pay attention to the reasons underlying educators' resistance.

To deal with the belief about the artistic nature of teaching, the unique contributions that teachers make to a tutoring program should be emphasized; teachers should recognize that they can enrich the program. Too many systematic programs leave teachers with the feeling that they are not important; this is sure to generate resistance. Concerning the belief that children are unusual kinds of human beings, teachers should be made aware of the congruence between systematic programs and accepted principles of child development. In addition, such programs need to include procedures for dealing with students' attitudes towards learning. The development of basic skills should be seen as a necessary condition for the child's being able to experience the joy of learning.

Inherent in this discussion is the assumption that less systematic tutoring procedures simply are not successful. Evidence obtained during the first years of the tutorial community project demonstrated that unplanned efforts at tutoring invariably resulted in dissatisfaction on the part of younger learners, older tutors, and participating teachers.

Needs of Staff Members

Any discussion of tutoring must not ignore the importance of adults in implementing and maintaining the program. In schools, the ultimate authority and control reside in staff members; their needs must be considered. In an earlier section it was pointed out that staff members must commit themselves to expend the time and energy necessary to make a tutoring program succeed. Such commitment is most likely when staff members feel a sense of ownership in the tutoring program; persons will stay with tasks longer in the face of obstacles when they believe that the program is of their own making. There is, however, a problem: How can a tutoring program be loose enough to allow a sense of ownership to develop, yet tight enough to include all the elements critical for its success?

When a school decides to initiate a tutoring program, a first order of business is training for staff members. The conventional approach to staff development (readings, lecture, discussion) has been supplanted by techniques involving direct experience with students and interaction among participants (Harrison, 1972b; Lippitt, Lippitt, & Eiseman, 1971; Melaragno, 1972b). Staff members also require ongoing training to help with problems that arise later. Generally, other staff members engaged in tutoring can assist peers effectively with common problems. Additional research should be conducted on ways that staff members can interact in teams and aid one another.

Finally, there is the problem of reinforcement for staff members. Conducting a successful tutoring program is a demanding task for staff members, and they obtain reinforcement only from observing gains made by their students. Staff members will thrive on reinforcement received in the form of social approval of peers and superiors. This problem is usually overlooked by persons outside education, for education does not have a mechanism for rewarding exceptional performance. Staff members are treated as if they were all equivalent—no distinction is made among those who have exceeded, met, or fallen short of expectations. Often the lack of differential reinforcement results in complacency, acceptance of the status quo, and low motivation for taking risks. Such a pattern of behavior ultimately will be detrimental to the effective long-term use of tutoring to individualize instruction in the schools.

ACKNOWLEDGMENT

The author wishes to express his indebtedness to his colleague, Gerald Newmark, for thoughtful assistance in developing many of the ideas contained in this paper.

REFERENCES

Cottam, F. A. The program evaluation system at Pacoima Elementary School. Unpublished manuscript, Pacoima, California, 1973.

Ebersole, E. H., & DeWitt, D. The Soto pupil-team program for reading. *Improving Human Performance,* 1972, *1,* 39–42.

Gartner, A., Kohler, M., & Riessman, F. *Children teach children.* New York: Harper, 1971.

Harrison, G. V. Tutoring: A remedy reconsidered. *Improving Human Performance,* 1972, *1,* 1–7. (a)

Harrison, G. V. Supervisor's guide for the structured tutorial reading program. Provo, Utah: Brigham Young Univ. Press, 1972. (b)

Lippitt, P., Lippitt, R., & Eiseman, J. *Cross-age helping program.* Ann Arbor, Michigan: Center for Research on Utilization of Scientific Knowledge, 1971.

Melaragno, R. J. Intergrade tutoring on a school-wide basis. *Improving Human Performance,* 1972, *1,* 22–26. (a)

Melaragno, R. J. Intergrade tutoring. Tutorial Community Project, Pacoima, California, 1972. (b)

Melaragno, R. J., & Newmark, G. A proposed study to develop a tutorial community in the elementary school. Tutorial Community Project, Pacoima, California, 1968. (a)

Melaragno, R. J., & Newmark, G. A pilot study to apply evaluation-revision procedures to first-grade Mexican-American classrooms. Tutorial Community Project, Pacoima, California, 1968. (b)

Newmark, G. Intraclass learning teams. Unpublished report, November, 1972.

Palmer, R. *Space, time, and grouping.* New York: Citation Press, 1971.

Rance, P. *Teaching by topics.* London: Ward Lock, 1968.

Schmuck, R. A. *Handbook of organization development in schools.* Palo Alto: National Press Books, 1972.

Watson, D., & Rosenberg, S. An interschool tutoring program. Unpublished manuscript, Pacoima, California, 1973.

13

Tutoring and Psychological Growth

Fred. L. Strodtbeck   Donald Ronchi   Stephen Hansell

University of Chicago   University of Chicago   University of Chicago

In this chapter we share an account of a tutoring program evaluation carried out in the public schools.[1] Since the evaluation was completed, it has become possible to look at our findings in a more relaxed and introspective way. In presenting the findings, we depart from the rigid format of technical reports and relate our research to a variety of contemporary issues in social psychology.

We are mindful that at its core a tutoring project is an effort to modify the class structure of society. As positivistic social psychologists, our evaluation would be restricted to determining whether or not the intervention worked. Some who would accept this definition of the task also would wish to see it carried out in a value-free way. At the same time, others see differences in rewards from society—that is, social inequality—as "an unconsciously evolved device by which societies ensure that the most important positions are conscientiously filled by the most qualified person" (Davis, 1949, p. 367). If one is strongly committed to this latter position, it is possible to see tutoring as a

[1] Prepared for the National Commission on Resources for Youth on Grant 42-0-005-34, Office of Research and Development, United States Department of Labor, Manpower Administration, December, 1972.

moral, allowable way to go about changing the individual's capacity to compete within the existing social structure.

European social psychologists have suggested that American social psychologists are particularly prone to overlooking the value premises in their common-sense stipulations about the nature of society (Israel & Tajfel, 1972). The belief in the essentiality of a competitive process, for example, is a nonscientific value that, in turn, is used to justify certain inquiries and rule out others. Though such criticism may be just, one scarcely knows where to turn to avoid it.

In the present research, moving away from detachment and toward a more active commitment to action was nearly inevitable. Since what happened in this project is, in a microcosm, what is happening to social psychology today, it is cathartic to write about it. A slight movement away from concerns alleged to serve the status quo is admitted, but in later sections we will make clear that this movement does not proceed to the end point anticipated in Joachim Israel's prospectus for "critical social psychology."[2]

THE TUTORING PROGRAMS

Some background about the Neighborhood Youth Corps (NYC) is essential to explain our involvement. The NYC program enrolled mainly inner-city youth who were at least 2 years below grade level in reading and were from impoverished homes. They could earn about $35 per week (by typing, answering the phone, working in the cafeteria, helping the janitor, or performing other jobs around the school) which might discourage dropping out of school. The Department of Labor (which sponsored the program) hoped that these youth with low motivation for academic work could be directed toward practical job-training and eventually into regular employment—thereby reducing the demoralizing underemployment of inner-city youth between 16 and 25. Despite the hopes for NYC, cost effectiveness analyses conducted in connection with budget reviews were increasingly critical of what was being accomplished. Nevertheless, it was politically effective to think of expenditures for youth as being a factor in cooling the threatened "long, hot summers" in the ghettoes, even though the dropout prevention and job training gains were not very tangible.[3]

---

[2] Israel (1972, pp. 204–208) holds that the critical social psychologist must consider initial status (before action starts), end state (that results from the action), and what would have happened if the agent remained passive. From joint consideration of these he must decide when to be productive and when preventive.

[3] These funds also paid for an assessment of the effects of tutoring on tutees by Leonard Granick. This is not treated in this report; for an account see the earlier "Evaluation of the Youth Tutoring Youth Model for In-School Neighborhood Youth Corps," available from the National Commission on Resources for Youth, 36 West 44th Street, New York, New York 10036.

A remarkable woman, Mary Kohler, who operated a small independent agency in New York City (National Commission on Resources for Youth), emerged as the instrument for originating and disseminating curricular suggestions from the Manpower Administration in the Department of Labor directly to supervising teachers. Mary Kohler and her staff recruited interested school officials and staged in-service training sessions around the country. She advocated a radical doctrine: that even the most disadvantaged student could profit from tutoring another (possibly younger) child. Her group (Youth Tutoring Youth—YTY) felt that it was without question better for a child to tutor than to be a janitor's helper. Evaluation was simply a bureaucratic requirement. Having seen the response of children in tutoring programs, she would raise serious questions about the validity of the assessment if evaluation did not confirm positive results (Gartner, Kohler, & Riessman, 1971).

In contrast to the pragmatic convictions of Mary Kohler's in-service training groups, the evaluation team for a time was a doubting Thomas. Our first concern was that an NYC appointment could be perceived as a reward given to "losers" by an external force (the federal government). We saw that giving awards to children who were far behind in their class was an intervention in the status mechanisms that regulate the exchange of esteem between teachers and students. Earlier work had demonstrated that group structure is better maintained when groups carry out a program they designed for themselves (Katz, Blau, Brown, & Strodtbeck, 1957). From a group process perspective, becoming a bigger frog in a little pond has meaning only if done in conformity to the norms of the group. When there is not enough of a scarce resource to go around, should one not help the most deserving? Helping those most likely to fail is an attack on the performance norms of the group; those who get rewarded will believe they were "lucky" rather than in effective control of their world. With a sense of righteous indignation, we began to think that a social psychologist should be reluctant to lend support to a program that uses an aleatory process to communicate how rational use of abilities will lead to success in the larger social system.

About half the NYC students were hard working and school oriented, in addition to being poor. The other half were multiple-problem, slow-reading youngsters who had performed in ways that the school would not reward if normal social exchange were operating. From our vantage point, both classes of appointees got the same message from the system: They were the lucky recipients of jobs.

To find a common ground between the fervor of the Commission and reserve of the scientific laboratory, our assignment was conceptualized as a request to identify several easily administered tests that might be used in local assessments. At various locations around the country, there were YTY programs sponsored by local initiative rather than NYC, but the observations carried out by the Social Psychology Laboratory of the University of Chicago were restricted to

NYC-sponsored operations in the Chicago and Washington, D. C., public schools in which tutoring and other job assignments were simultaneously used.[4] It was our hope that the naturally occurring variations produce both good and bad examples of the way tutoring could be organized; thus, the better techniques of the stronger programs could be identified.

In the very influential Evaluation of Elementary Education Project in the late 1920s, Tyler evolved an educational change strategy that was expressly engineered to help evaluators (low-power change agents in service bureaucracies) have an impact on practice. His strategy, which we were about to try again, consists of three steps. First, the educators identify the goals they seek; tests are devised that measure these; then, discussion of results leads to further change in educational goals, practices, and assessment procedures. This is a highly civilized process. The evaluation process does not impose goals, greatly respects local knowledge, and rests on a highly positive conception of human nature (Tyler, 1950).

In the instance of tutoring evaluation, it was hoped that tests could be administered by untrained persons in very short periods of time and that they would show exactly what made tutoring superior to other NYC jobs. This assignment was impossible to accomplish completely, however.

We stressed that the tests would not be reliable enough to use in career decisions for individual children; proper use would be restricted to the comparison of changes in sets of children. We further streamlined the testing routine by scoring sentence completions in two ways: for grammatical errors and for ego development. That the test would be culture-fair—a recurring hope of idealistic workers—could not be ascertained directly. (The data came almost entirely from black ghetto children, so comparison with white, middle-class children was not at issue.)

EXPECTATIONS ASSOCIATED WITH TUTORING

Tutoring should cause the tutors to perceive themselves as possessing valuable skills and as being essential to the social order around them. The opportunity to take a prestigeful role was believed to have the potentiality of encouraging the development of more complex ways of interpreting and engaging the interpersonal complexities of their world. Being responsible for another person involves opportunities to learn the value of organizing in advance and being on time. The

---

[4] The Social Psychology Laboratory team consisted of the authors of this chapter and graduate student assistants Jeff Goldsmith, Dan Candee, and Chris Haller. Staff included Judy Henderson, Nancy Rothblat, Benedicte Madsen, and Jean Kohl. Assistance from the Chicago schools was provided by Joseph Rosen, Wardell Wilson, Dan Simon, Billy Gray, and Mike Kroll; from the Washington, D. C., schools by Jean Simms and James A. Turner.

tutor has the responsibility of both working with and evaluating the work of his tutee. Such skills contribute to success not only in school, but also, presumably, in later jobs.

As a by-product of the new experiences outlined above, there should be a deepened understanding of the classroom teacher as a person who encounters problems with the tutor similar to those the tutor encounters with his tutees. After the first looking-glass opportunity to see oneself in another's behavior in the tutor–tutee relationship, a more abstract transformation of prior experience can occur. It is expected that the tutor will be under stress when coping with the problems of the tutee. If, at these times, the tutor behaves toward a tutee as a teacher has behaved toward the tutor, he will enact a role that he otherwise has known only passively. He may have to decide whether he wishes to act toward others as teachers have acted toward him; if he wishes to do so, he is given the opportunity to learn more about how a teacher has felt. Power of the de-centering experience inheres in the fact that the tutor must take action to control and respond to his tutee.

Expectations such as those held for tutoring are more acceptable because of intellectual events of the past. John Dewey's free play, learning-by-doing opposition to the three-R's conception of an elementary curriculum is familiar to many. Others may see similarities to Elton Mayo's opposition to Taylorism in scientific management. All social psychologists certainly recognize that the tutoring technique flows easily from that part of Kurt Lewin's field theory concerned with the identification and correction of human social tensions. Moving from the more democratic philosophical positions toward social psychology, some technical resistance is encountered. Not that social psychologists oppose putting people in substantively rich contexts and letting the social interaction create new growth, it is simply that what happens in such situations is too hard to describe. To speak with publishable (if not practical) authority, the situation must be clean, free of uncontrolled communication, uncontaminated by irrelevant motive, and focused on one of the many mechanisms known to be operative. It is not surprising that student assistants on the project had trouble deciding whether this was a particularly messy project or whether it was unavoidable that applied work be at such variance with laboratory experiments.

Throughout our discussion, passing attention was given to understanding the forces in urban education that required the "invention" or "reinvention" of tutoring to be made by outsiders. Why was this movement not simply an outgrowth of the technical processes of within-system evaluation? Suggesting that children who are retarded in their school work can teach others—and themselves in the process—could be interpreted as a depreciation of what is involved in teaching. What actually was encountered is more easily understood as institutional apathy than teacher resistance. Perhaps if tutoring becomes more successful this will change.

VARIATIONS IN THE CHICAGO SCHOOL PROGRAMS

As personnel from the Social Psychology Laboratory went systematically from one district to another looking at the tutoring programs, they were overwhelmed by the extreme variability in school setting, supervision, and what the tutors did. Strong programs from the year before were no longer functioning; a shift in a teacher's interest, a teacher transfer, or a new principal changed the programs in major ways. To obtain a standard measure of what was going on in a given school, we routinely assembled tutors in groups of 8 to 10 and administered 13 "Task of the Tutor" items for the students to rank individually (e.g., "be a friend to the tutee"; "teach reading"). After each tutor ranked the items, we asked each school group to talk over the tutor job and agree upon a ranking that best represented the group as a whole. This resulted in a spontaneous, informal, frequently heated discussion.

Individual and group rankings were analyzed for the degree to which they stressed the internalization of an authoritarian role by the tutor. For example, "following the teacher's methods and instructions," "following school rules," and "not admitting it when something is not understood" were contrasted with concern for the tutee's personal problems and being a friend. The egalitarian—expressive aspect of the latter conception was associated with wanting to teach what the tutee wanted to learn, a willingness to read interesting books and talk about the tutee's life. The "authoritarian" component manifests itself in the emphasis upon teaching traditional subjects such as spelling, reading, and arithmetic. Items treating social consciousness, the importance of being black, and using street language seemed to be stressed by the students who were either particularly well qualified or poorly qualified—not by those in the middle.

Some tutors taught at their own school, and some at nearby elementary schools. When there were 20 or more tutors, meaningful contact with the YTY supervisor was quite limited. One might have assumed that the YTY supervisors were in all cases enthusiastic, specially trained teachers who received extra pay, but this was true only for a few of the 20 contacted.

When it became apparent that the school-by-school program descriptions written by our field observers were not cast in the language ordinarily used in communication between educators and federal bureaucrats, we needed to find a less specific, less blameful way of describing the relative quality of the programs. We carried out a content analysis of the training protocols used by Mary Kohler's staff and formulated four questions: (1) Is there on the site supervision by a teacher who knows and accepts YTY goals? (2) Does the tutor have at least 1 hour per week with the program coordinator? (3) Is the tutor allowed to be autonomous in work with the tutee? (4) Does the tutor have protracted time to work with each tutee? These criteria (effective legitimation, personalized supervision, tutor autonomy, and opportunity for rapport building) were most consistently present in the tutoring programs of the vocational high schools, the residential school for girls, and the two upper-grade centers in which children at least 14 years of age worked under close supervision of dedicated teachers. In almost all other schools, particularly the stronger ones, at least two of the four criteria were missing.

It is quite apparent that to determine exactly what experience each tutor had on his tutoring assignments would have been a prohibitively expensive operation. It is quite possible that the tutor's interest in the job reached a peak before the final evaluation. If laboratory personnel had been present to get tutor reports, their very presence would have constituted a stabilizing factor that was undoubtedly absent for some. In contrast to the magnitude of the stimulus evaluated in most social psychological experiments, 20 or more weeks of paid work is a tremendous experimental treatment. Unfortunately, the mixture of intended with unintended effects is so completely unknown that interpretation of the outcome is unclear. If there are no gains, what can one say? If positive change is present despite roughness of the approximation of the expected experience, however, tutoring will deserve further tests.

DEPENDENT MEASURES

Ego Development—the Anchor Measure

Having described how uneven the tutoring experiences were, it will seem rather perverse to the reader for us to compound this difficulty by leaning heavily on a personality measure that is not expected to be efficient in reflecting the growth associated with tutoring. The rationale is complicated. We recognized the sentence completion test as being desirable because it is unlike usual school tests and because teachers may use it to measure changes in language competence. In addition, a change would signal most clearly the attainment of the objectives of the program. Ego development is the anchor measure in the sense that it helps us describe where various sets of tutors were distributed when they entered the program. Ego development is an index to important characteristics of the interpersonal context on which the tutoring program is superimposed at various schools. But, most importantly, ego development is a measure which, as it becomes understood by the teachers involved in tutoring, should confer an important insight into how the gains from tutoring can be recognized.

The theory relevant to ego development is much broader than the measurement system associated with the sentence completions. Behind the scoring devised by Loevinger (1966) is a comprehensive manual and a carefully reworked stage theory of development. The slightly revised codification of her stages used at our laboratory is given in Table 1, but the reader is cautioned that this is no substitute for the careful study of her volume (Loevinger, Wessler, &

Table 1
Loevinger's Stages of Ego Development and Responsibility

Stage	Interpersonal style	Conscious preoccupation
Impulsive I–2	Exploitive and dependent. People evaluated (good–bad) in relation to S's demands.	Bodily feelings, especially sexual and aggressive.
Defensive Δ	Exploitive, manipulative. Sees life as a zero-sum game; is opportunistic and self-protective	Simple instrumental hedonism plus protection of self; being cautious, suspicious, and projecting.
Conformist I–3	Needs acceptance and approval by authority and group; thinks superficially but recognizes reciprocality.	Stereotyped thinking about things, appearances, and reputation.
Self-conscious I–3/4	Relationships are reciprocal and affective. There is emphasis on limited, closed groups, and feelings are explicit.	Transition from actions to traits (quasi traits) through greater awareness as to source of feelings. The self is related to the group.
Conscientious I–4	Intense, responsible relations with mutual respect and high sense of duty.	Internal standards of performance and clearly differentiated inner feelings.
Autonomous I–5	Respects autonomy in others and accords others the treatment accorded self; tolerant, interactive.	Vivid feelings integrate physiological and psychological, uses psychological causation; seeks self-fulfillment in social context.
Integrated I–6	Add to above the active acceptance of sensation and emotion, as in "peak" experiences.	See I - 5 and add: identity transcending familial and parochial ties.

	Character development	Responsibility
Impulsive I–2	Impulse-ridden and has fear of retaliation; physical punishment orientation.	Diffuse in attribution of causality; externalizes blame to source of punishment and rewards (parents).
Defensive Δ	Rules recognized in the negative effects their transgression produces; hence expedient, guided by fear of being caught.	Denies negative responsibility and externalizes blame to fate and circumstances as well as to others.
Conformist I–3	Dichotomization of right and wrong, as based on formulae for behavior in conformity to external rules.	The referent for responsibility is authority or the written law, and self-blame is limited to concrete violations of specific rules.

Table 1 (continued)

Stage	Character development	Responsibility
Self-conscious I–3/4	Morality of reciprocity and of role-taking.	The materiality of the action is replaced by the awareness of the intention, and of consequences. The referent of responsibility is relevant "others."
Conscientious I–4	Internalized rules go beyond reciprocity, experiences guilt when inadequate.	Emphasis is on self-criticism and self-change; the referent of responsibility is the self.
Autonomous I–5	Copes personally with conflicting inner needs, is decisive, but shows toleration for others.	Works in consciousness of conflicting norms, frustrating ambiguity, and full ramification of actions.
Integrated I–6	Reconciliation and renunciation of the unattainable.	(See I - 5)

Redmore, 1970). In the present assessment, 40 stubs were used: e.g., Raising a family . . . Being with other people . . . The thing I like about myself is . . . My mother and I . . . Education . . . Rules are . . . I am . . . My main problem is . . ., and so forth.

One should note the way in which the stubs invite attention to interpersonal relations, but the individual is not greatly constrained in what he might choose to say. On repeat administrations, low-scoring students very frequently give an identical response, so we felt there might be some advantage in using new stubs in the post-test situation. The average correlation between stubs was very high; short of teaching the test, one cannot expect to find stubs answered at an *impulsive* level before tutoring that would be answered at a *conforming* level after tutoring. In this sense the test is psychometric—focused on differences; it is not *edumetric*—engineered to reflect a particular performance skill associated with tutoring (Carver, 1974). For this reason, the differences in the mean ego development levels of schools shown in Table 2 are to be understood as an indication of the wide differences between schools prior to the start of the program and as a reflection of a continuing difference in context as the programs unfolded. With regard to the magnitude of the differences among schools, the staff was aware that ghetto areas in Chicago were particularly strife ridden and disadvantaged but was surprised at the academic strength and middle-class atmosphere of the advantaged black high schools. There was a strong relation between ego development and the rank given to two of the "task of the tutor" items. The higher the ego development score of a tutor, the higher the ranking given to "Ask the tutee what he or she wants to be taught," and the lower the ranking given to "Don't admit it when you don't understand something."

Table 2
Ego Development Score
for Tutors by School

School character- istics	Tutors known as strong students (%)	Mean ego development score	Mean score for schools by type
Strong high schools			
A (4)	90	4.00	
B (17)	80	3.94	
			3.8 (conforming)
C (4)	—	3.75	
D (11)	47	2.81	
Upper grade centers (younger students)			
E (10)	90	3.50	
F (10)	40	3.60	
			3.2 (defensive– conforming)
G (5)	—	2.00	
H (7)	0	3.14	
Average high schools			
I (5)	40	2.80	
			2.3 (defensive)
J (8)	30	2.00	
Embattled high schools			
K (10)	0	2.60	
			2.8 (defensive– conforming)
L (4)	—	3.25	
Vocational and correctional high schools			
M (7)	35	2.28	
			1.7 (impulsive– defensive)
N (8)	0	1.12	

Note: Number of tutors in parentheses.

Self-Esteem

To discuss the effect of tutoring on self-esteem, it is convenient first to distinguish the underlying essential idea, the *nominal* construct, from the operational construct, the measure one obtains when he asks tutors to answer questions about themselves. What we would like to measure is: "... the evaluation which the individual makes and customarily maintains with regard to himself: it expresses an attitude of approval or disapproval, and indicates the extent to which the individual believes himself to be capable, significant, successful, and worthy. In short, self-esteem is a personal judgment of worthiness that is expressed in the attitudes the individual holds toward himself" (Cooper-smith, 1967, p. 45).

Coopersmith's definition emphasizes the relatively permanent and enduring components of self-esteem rather than transitory variations. In contemporary social psychological theory, Aronson (1968) and others have identified the essential role of actors' self-esteem in consistency theory. A given experience that would be inconsistent to a person with a positive self-esteem can be accepted with less question by a person with a negative self-esteem. As he contemplates an important decision, a person with low self-esteem may believe he will err.

Most fundamentally, impressions about the self constitute a component of a personal theory for understanding experience (Epstein, 1973). One's self theory may recognize distinctions between social, spiritual, or physical selves. These selves are placed in momentary jeopardy in social transactions, and with each encounter it is helpful to think of the attendant experience of satisfaction and closure or distress and vulnerability. As the various selves become integrated with growth and experience, these evaluative feelings associated with self-esteem link the various systems and provide—at least theoretically—the basis for predictable moral behavior.

The nominal construct "self-esteem" has been commented upon by psychiatrists with particular reference to the development of the personality of black adolescents. For example, some years ago Kardiner and Ovesey (1951) stated: "This central problem of Negro adaptation is oriented to discrimination he suffers and the consequences of this discrimination for the self-referential aspects of his social orientation. In simple words, it means that his self-esteem suffers (which is self referential) because he is constantly receiving an unpleasant image of himself from the behavior of others" (p. 302).

Reviewers have pointed out subsequently that only 7 of Kardiner and Ovesey's 25 cases exhibited self-hatred and lack of self-esteem, and of those 7, 5 had had previous therapeutic experience (Rohrer & Edmonsen, 1960). The weight of contemporary research is turning against the position that self-esteem is realistically related to one's general position in a racial or economic group. The emphasis is now more upon the resiliency and optimism of reports by subjects, particularly blacks, who are in objectively straitened situations. Morris Rosenberg (1965) reports: ". . . we see that Negroes, who are exposed to the most intense, humiliating, and crippling forces of discrimination in virtually every institutional area, do not have particularly low self-esteem" (p. 57).

McCarthy and Yancey (1971) give the following guidelines for the interpretation of esteem scores from black respondents. They suggest that when black respondents are using other blacks as their reference group, black and white self-esteem scores would not differ. They find it possible that when "within race" comparisons are contaminated by "between race" comparisons, lower-class blacks will manifest higher self-esteem than lower-class whites, and middle-class blacks will manifest lower self-esteem than middle-class whites. This conclusion was reached by two separate lines of reasoning that are instructive in the present situation. First, if low-status persons make evaluations in terms of their objectively low standing, then the lesser commitments of low-status blacks to the American value system will make their self-judgments less harsh. Consistent with this, the multi-problem students in our sample seem not so fully committed to school achievement that they would judge themselves harshly because of failing grades.

McCarthy and Yancey (1971) assume that middle-class blacks would have a higher commitment to the American value system than middle-class whites; yet when they find that this culture to which they turned for gratification in fact treated them shabbily, their self-esteem would be lowered. In this study, the students who are doing well similarly might make more reference group comparisons to more privileged whites. The net effect of this theorizing is to provide a further rationale for believing that something like regression toward the mean will make self-esteem less differentiating than we might desire. In terms of the range of schools presented in Table 2, all were 60–66% positive save the vocational and correctional schools, which averaged only 54% favorable. Coopersmith (1967) had previously found classrooms of middle-class white children to score between 70 and 80% positive. Despite the limitations of the measure, the findings that vocational and correctional schools are below other schools in our sample and that this predominantly black, lower-class sample is lower than Coopersmith's middle-class white sample are squarely in line with common-sense expectations and lend no support to McCarthy and Yancey's theory. [For a discussion of within-class differences in Rosenberg's (1965) study that would be consistent with these data, see Kaplan (1971).]

The self-esteem score on the pre-test was correlated positively with the pre-test ego development score ($r = .21$, $p < .01$). Although this correlation is significant and also consistent with expectations, a score on one of the tests still would account for less than 5% of the score on the other; hence, their joint use in the same assessment is in no way redundant.

Mastery over Nature

If one wishes to change individual behavior, one is well advised to speak in terms of an individual psychological locus—this makes change following a modest intervention a matter of insight, personal conversion, or perhaps a new behavioral style picked up through identification with an efficacious role model. The problem with such thinking is that through time cultures become deeply integrated. The motivation necessary to be continuously "active" in the face of changing external frustrations is not banked within the individual; what one learns is a set of cultural specifications as to what one does when a given contingency arises. Toward the same end, efficient, work-oriented cultures manage to inhibit certain expensive activities that reduce vigilance, and they develop and sanctify forms of social organization that increase the size and durability of competitive social units. It is reasonable to believe, when one is working with an individual from a cultural niche that has no tradition of recent success, that such an individual can be taught some of the proper answers, but the rewards and punishments of a lifetime in an achievant value context are not easily substituted.

To measure differentially achievant cultures, the senior author has worked out a Value Orientation Schedule with Florence Kluckhohn (Kluckhohn & Strodtbeck, 1961) and a values scale presented in another volume (McClelland, Strodtbeck, Baldwin, & Bronfenbrenner, 1958). These instruments, along with related ones prepared by former students (Brim, Glass, Lavin, & Goodman, 1962) and collaborators (Rosen, 1959), were examined with the thought that they would lead our clients away from psychological theories toward thinking about the degree to which mastery behavior was found in social structure and culture. This was indicated in order to provide a rationale for action that did not stigmatize the recipients of the service. In addition, it seemed to us that school personnel needed to be given a special justification as to why the improvement of the contribution of the school context could be brought about by something they enabled students to do rather than did themselves.

Just as John Dewey called attention to the cognitive development of small children through play, neo-Freudians are calling attention to equally important contributions to adolescent autonomy through meaningful work. White (1959) terms the motivation to engage in such environmental confrontation "effectance." In later life, effectance motivation becomes differentiated into such motives as cognizance, construction, mastery, and achievement. Looking at efficacy from the viewpoint of mental health seems to make it inevitable that the efficacious be defined as rational and realistic. On the basis of Polyani's axiom that personal knowledge is the ultimate criterion, DeCharms (1968) argues that what is important is the *belief* in personal causation rather than whether or not, objectively, a person is in control of his environment.

White and DeCharms thus provide a personality theory that links congenially with the earlier work on achievant cultures, but they do not provide appropriate measuring instruments. The instrument receiving widest use in the current literature is Rotter's (1966) Internal–External Locus of Control Scale (I–E Scale)–23 items edited from value orientation schedules and similar instruments into a forced-choice form (Phares, 1973). Rotter distinguishes the perception that an individual is in control of his reinforcements (or his successes and failures) from the perception that an individual is not in control–that fate, chance, or other people determine his reinforcements. All three authors see the actor who believes that he is the origin of his reinforcements as one who tends to encode his environment in terms of the degree to which it is an opportunity for later use.

Early factor analyses of Rotter's items assigned most of the variance to a single factor, but more recent work indicates that the scale may contain several factors (Gurin, Gurin, Lao, & Beattie, 1969). The work at the Social Psychology Laboratory with 600 rural high school students and 398 NYC students confirmed the multiple factor character of the scale and resulted in the identification of three components: *political efficacy, success ideology,* and *personal control.*

As we have suggested earlier, the experience of working in NYC programs and being rewarded would make the greatest contributions to the sense of efficacy if the student felt that his own efforts had brought about his involvement in the rewarding activity. Once in the NYC program, most children volunteer for the job they want, but some students with histories of bad school adjustment may have been assigned to tutoring almost peremptorily. Even if we assume that being given short-term, legitimate control over a tutor will convey a greater sense of personal power, power is not achievement. We understand that power striving—strong, forceful actions which influence others, giving unsolicited help, and trying to impress other people—are not part of the concern with excellence associated with a need to achieve. Thus, tutoring could be a rewarding activity for tutors without necessarily leading to a more abstract concern for excellence in performance or a place in the organizations that wield the social power of institutions.

In terms of the ego theory previously presented, one may have to pass a milestone in ego development (such as becoming conforming) before a work opportunity will increase *efficacy.* This touches an area of deep paradox in the program. The program urges giving the opportunity to the least deserving. But to follow this to the letter, administrators in daily contact with the students would have to say "Work hard and be motivated—this will disqualify you from NYC." In practice, local administrators appoint a sizable percentage of highly motivated students, all of whom are needy. All students receive the same rate of pay, but some are given supervisory roles. With this perspective on the system's disposition to make reward contingent upon merit, one wonders if such a program ever could be restricted to the hardest-to-reach fraction—the needy with low motivation—and, at the same time, increase the efficacy score.

FINDINGS AND DISCUSSION

The prototype of a positively compensatory effect of the program was the finding that, after tutoring, the tutors made significantly fewer grammatical and spelling errors in their sentence completions. Tutors reduced their baseline of 3.10 errors per 5 completions by .96; nontutors reduced their errors of 3.65 by .22. That is, though English language skills were not stressed in any didactic way in the program, all NYC appointees improved ($p<.02$). Viewed calmly, it seems quite plausible that if the tutors have an hour or so per day to use written materials, lesson plans, criticisms of tutees' work, reports and the like in instrumental ways, their skills will improve. Without the tutoring program, school personnel might have found it difficult to motivate similar language-related activity. After a summer with no stimulus to use written messages, a good part of the gain possibly would be lost.

With regard to school attendance, the findings also were positive. Compared to the previous school year, tutors increased their average days in attendance by 8.26 days, in contrast with an increase of 1.70 for nontutors. This difference was significant ($p < .01$). Since excessive absence is frequently a precursor of dropping out, the decrease in absence is in line with the objectives of the program stressed by its sponsor (Manpower).

Given two findings of this modest magnitude, it is difficult to evaluate the results fairly. One can take the role of a cost–benefit specialist and ask whether such modest changes justify the cost of the program. The answer might well be No. Less critical educators who like the philosophy of the program may be more impressed by the program as a demonstration of implications of peer teaching. The research group was surprised that out of the confusion, the ill-tempered and, at times, submissive compliance they had observed, there was still a discernible positive impact. But it would be naive to believe that if a whole school setting could be brought under control, positive effects could be extended without limit. With further cross-tabulation of the data, one begins to discern the shape of constraints that prevent an innovation such as tutoring from working equally well with all tutors.

Consider now the self-esteem and efficacy measures. All the NYC students showed a significant increase ($p < .01$), but tutors did not increase more than nontutors. In addition, neither the tutors nor nontutors showed a significant increase in Rotter's I–E score—the measure of increased efficacy.

Let us assume that the findings above ("decreased absence from school" and "reduced grammar errors") indicate positive involvement in the tutoring program. If this is the case, an increase in absence and increased grammar errors should identify tutors for whom the program has been ineffective. A cross-tabulation of these possibilities with the change in efficacy scores produces the surprising result shown in Table 3. This finding holds the disturbing suggestion that there are two routes to greater efficacy. One is through attending and learning; the other is by "giving up" on school, coming close to dropping out, and by this means getting a similar phenomenological increase in efficacy. (Notice the 1.27 associated with the No–No pattern.)

Table 3
Involvement in the Program and Efficacy
Scores

Less absence	Fewer errors	Efficacy (N)
Yes	Yes	.77 (13)
No	Yes	.50 (22)
Yes	No	.25 (16)
No	No	1.27 (22)

A further insight into the dynamics of efficacy and tutoring or nontutoring assignment may be gained by reintroducing the ego development score, our best measure of maturity. This score was not expected to change significantly in the 4 or 5 months of the program, but it was expected to be associated with school-related behavior, as the tabulations with absence and efficacy in Table 4 demonstrate. Children with high ego development were disposed to be more regular in attendance and have higher efficacy scores at the onset of the experiment. Moreover, during the experiment the independent tutoring grades assigned by supervising teachers showed clearly that children with higher ego development were perceived to have been better tutors. Those high on ego development received a grade of A– for tutoring, those medium on ego development received B+, and those low on ego development were given a C+.

These findings bear on the truth of Mary Kohler's dictum: Even the most disadvantaged student can profit from tutoring another, possibly younger child. In grammar errors or attendance this might be so; tutors with lower ego development who were given C's by their supervising teachers may not have harmed their tutees, but the question of the effects on their sense of efficacy can be examined in Table 5. For children with relatively high ego development, tutoring contributed more to the sense of efficacy; for children with relatively

Table 4
Relation of Ego Development to School Absence
and Efficacy

Relative ego development	Mean days absent prior year	Rotter's I.E. score
High	8.6 (23)	6.5 (29)
Medium	15.2 (39)	5.6 (73)
Low	28.8 (51)	5.5 (79)

Note: N is shown in parentheses.

Table 5
Efficacy Score Change by Ego Development
for Tutors and Non-Tutors

Ego development	Tutors	Non-tutors	Difference
High	.55 (29)	.00 (8)	.55
Medium	.13 (73)	.42 (33)	− .29
Low	.02 (79)	.63 (22)	− .61

Note: N is shown in parentheses.

low ego development, the low-demand custodial and caretaking jobs had a similar effect.

The conclusion to be drawn from Table 5 is that Mary Kohler is mistaken. Placement in tutoring may be stressful for the children with the very lowest ego development in ways that other school jobs are not. This conclusion is somewhat tempered by information from a section of the original report that is not presented here. It was shown that there is a positive effect on grammar scores, self-esteem, and enhancement of ego development when the participating schools follow the YTY criteria of a good program. Latitude for the tutors to take responsibility for their own teaching material under the guidance of supportive teachers is associated strongly with most positive effects. Thus, if the level of supervision by regular teachers was of the quality that could be effected by the YTY training staff, then even the least-prepared might profit. But in the real world of this experiment, a certain maturity level was necessary for tutoring to set in motion the positive growth potential measured by the sense of efficacy score.

If we wish to deal with tutoring as an intervention to promote social change, it is helpful to distinguish between augmentative effects, such as those realized when the tutors with high ego development gain more (as in the case of efficacy) and compensatory effects (when those at low levels of maturity gain more). In this latter category we include the improvements in grammar scores, attendance and, for whatever they mean, grade-point averages. It is stubbornly difficult to give rewards to those doing least well by institutional standards. We have commented previously on the way in which the NYC appointment was so casually managed that it would seem like a windfall gain to those who received it; in addition, once it was in effect, there were no provisions for salary differentials for merit performance. Unlike military companies or, according to Bronfenbrenner (1970), Russian schools, there is no disposition in our schools, in the ghetto or elsewhere, to encourage a collective responsibility for the performance of one's peers. There is every indication that Manpower and Mary

Kohler's organization understood that, under such conditions, they would not be financed if they sought to accomplish their compensatory intervention.

According to Israel's "context of social psychology" argument (cited in footnote 2) the group at the Social Psychology Laboratory should have decided that it was *productive* to seek the end state of greater motivation for marginal students through tutoring before undertaking the research project. In fact, the collaboration was begun with some skepticism concerning the attainability of the applied goals, although they seemed eminently desirable. We tried to teach the social psychological perspective to our clients in order to deepen their understanding of the personality measures we advocated. Beyond this, we were self-conscious about the way in which the applied context caused us to think differently about research operations. For example, subjects tolerate more pre- and post-experimental assessment than the tutors did. When one works with short-run experiments, motivation of the experimenter is usually no problem. We were slow to understand that a teacher who has a good remedial program in a school would "wear out" in 1 or 2 years. The history of most schools show a succession of change attempts that rather quickly are reabsorbed into the established routines. It was somewhat unanticipated that engagement in an applied program would raise so many philosophical questions concerning aspects of reality that one takes for granted.

There was a growing respect for the way in which a marginal student's poor performance was "locked in" through norms, self-conceptions, differential exposure to identificands, personal success experience, personality, intelligence, and many other social realities. Each of the mechanisms we have identified in social psychology as available to influence behavior appear, on closer examination in field situations, to be in use already to hold matters as they are. To experience the holism of an applied program pitted against the specialization of the university is to help one better understand why, in addition to "reinforcement" and similar abstract micro-constructs, social psychology also needs "value orientation" and similar societal constructs which, with their substantive content, bridge the gap between motives and institutions. It is not just that social psychology needs a good deal of substantive filling out before its theories can be applied to a process like tutoring in the schools, it is more that the social psychological is but one of the realities that practical theorists must be prepared to use. To work effectively with policy scientists from the fields of law, economics, health, education, and the like, it is desirable to define more clearly what social psychology should not do in order to clear the air concerning what is now not done well.

To read Allport's (1969) criticisms of the simple and sovereign theories of the nineteenth century is one matter; to have one's own pet formula for the present challenged is quite another. Perhaps the virtue of combining applied project work with graduate training is that viewing more reflectively the contemporary theories of others represents a more nearly optimal degree of involvement. Far from concluding that praxis and good social psychology should be more closely joined, our group came to understand in a less abstract way why some insulation from the full responsibility of operating programs was essential to sound social psychology. In retrospect, just as the tutor in this program learned more than the tutee, it is possible that from this effort the group at the Social Psychology Laboratory learned more than our clients.

REFERENCES

Allport, G. W. The historical background of modern social psychology. In G. Lindzey, & E. Aronson (Eds.), *The handbook of social psychology.* Vol. 1. Reading, Massachusetts: Addison-Wesley, 1969. Pp. 1–80.

Aronson, E. Dissonance theory: Progress and problems. In R. P. Abelson, E. Aronson, W. J. McGuire, T. M. Newcomb, M. J. Rosenberg, & P. H. Tannenbaum (Eds.), *Theories of cognitive consistency: A sourcebook.* Chicago: Rand-McNally, 1968. Pp. 5–27.

Brim, O. G., Jr., Glass, D. C., Lavin, D. E., & Goodman, N. *Personality and decision processes.* Stanford, California: Stanford Univ. Press, 1962.

Bronfenbrenner, U. *Two worlds of childhood.* New York: Russell Sage Foundation, 1970.

Carver, R. P. Two dimensions of tests: Psychometric and edumetric. *American Psychologist,* 1974, *29,* 512–518.

Coopersmith, S. *The antecedents of self-esteem.* San Francisco: W. H. Freeman, 1967.

Davis, K. *Human society.* New York: Macmillan, 1949.

DeCharms, R. *Personal causation.* New York: Academic Press, 1968.

Epstein, S. The self concept revisited, or a theory of a theory. *American Psychologist,* 1973, *28,* 404–416.

Gartner, A., Kohler, M., & Reissman, F. *Children teach children: Learning by teaching.* New York: Harper, 1971.

Gurin, P., Gurin, G., Lao, R. C., & Beattie, M. Internal–external control of motivational dynamics of Negro youth. *Journal of Social Issues,* 1969, *25,* 29–53.

Israel, J. Stipulations and construction in the social sciences. In J. Israel, & H. Tajfel (Eds.), *The context of social psychology: A critical assessment.* New York: Academic Press, 1972. Pp. 123–211.

Israel, J., & Tajfel, H. (Eds.) *The context of social psychology: A critical assessment.* New York: Academic Press, 1972.

Kaplan, H. B. Social class and self-derogation: A conditional relationship. *Sociometry,* 1971, *34,* 41–64.

Kardiner, A., & Ovesey, L. *The mark of oppression: Explorations in the personality of the American Negro.* New York: Norton, 1951.

Katz, E., Blau, P. M., Brown, M. L., & Strodtbeck, F. L. Leadership stability and social change: An experiment with small groups. *Sociometry,* 1957, *20,* 36–50.

Kluckhohn, F., & Strodtbeck, F. *Variations in value orientation.* New York: Harper, 1961.

Loevinger, J. The meaning and measurement of ego development. *American Psychologist,* 1966, *21,* 195–206.

Loevinger, J., Wessler, R., & Redmore, C. *Measuring ego development: I. Construction and use of a sentence completion test; II. Scoring manual for women and girls.* San Francisco: Josey-Bass, 1970.

McCarthy, J., & Yancey, W. L. Uncle Tom and Mr. Charlie: Metaphysical pathos in the study of racism and personal disorganization. *American Journal of Sociology,* 1971, *76,* 648–672.

McClelland, D., Strodtbeck, F., Baldwin, A., & Bronfenbrenner, U. *Talent and society.* Princeton, New Jersey: Van Nostrand-Reinhold, 1958.

Phares, E. J. *Locus of control: A personality determinant of behavior.* Morristown, New Jersey: General Learning Press, 1973.

Rohrer, J., & Edmonsen, M. S. *The eighth generation grows up.* New York: Harper, 1960.

Rosen, B. C. Race, ethnicity, and the achievement syndrome. *American Sociological Review,* 1959, *24,* 47–60.

Rosenberg, M. *Society and the adolescent self image.* Princeton, New Jersey: Princeton Univ. Press, 1965.

Rotter, J. B. Generalized expectancies for internal versus external control of reinforcement. *Psychological Monographs,* 1966, *80* (1, Whole No. 609).

Tyler, R. *Basic principles of curriculum and instruction.* Chicago: Univ. of Chicago Press, 1950.

White, R. W. Motivation reconsidered. *Psychological Review,* 1959, *66,* 297–333.

14

Teenagers as Tutors of Academically Low-Achieving Children: Impact on Tutors and Tutees

Robert D. Cloward
Rhode Island College

Tutoring is a dynamic teaching–learning process in which an individual who lacks competence in some area learns from any other person who seems to possess superior competence. In this sense, tutoring is as old as education itself. Yet it is only in recent years that organized programs of paraprofessional tutorial services have met with acceptance in the educational community. Paraprofessional tutorial programs probably existed prior to 1960 in the United States, but no one took them seriously or believed that a relatively untrained tutor could produce substantive academic gains in pupils under his tutelage.

Tutoring programs recently have gained increased acceptance in the educational community; they now exist in almost every large city in the country. Unfortunately, most of the empirical research on tutoring has focused on the effects on the students being tutored; only a few studies have examined the effects of tutoring on the tutors themselves. One study failed to find any significant improvement in the language skills of low-achieving high school seniors who served as tutors for freshmen (Werth, 1968). Two other studies have reported a greater gain in reading for tutors than for their tutees (Hassinger & Via, 1969; McWhorter & Levy, 1971). Regrettably, the findings of these two studies cannot be accepted with confidence because neither of them employed control groups for the tutors or for the tutees.

219

Not only has relatively little attention been given to investigating the effects of tutoring on the tutor, but there has been no attempt to identify the characteristics that separate effective tutors from ineffective ones. Both these issues will be addressed in the research reported in the present chapter.

THE MOBILIZATION FOR YOUTH TUTORIAL PROGRAM

In 1963, Mobilization for Youth, Inc.,[1] in cooperation with the New York City Board of Education, instituted an after-school tutorial program for low-achieving pupils residing in a 67-block segment of Manhattan's Lower East Side. Once famed as a Jewish ghetto, the area in recent years had experienced an exodus of middle-class-oriented Jews and an influx of lower-class Puerto Rican and black families. The effects of this migration is most noticeable in the 16 public elementary schools in the area, where Puerto Rican youngsters in 1963 accounted for 59% of the pupil population, and black youngsters for 17%.

By 1962, all of the elementary schools in the area had been classified by the Board of Education as "special service" schools in order to permit reduced class size and expanded auxiliary services. In each school pupils had the half-time services of a guidance counselor and a corrective reading teacher, plus increased access to other auxiliary staff. Even with the addition of these services, reading achievement of pupils in the area remained far below that reported for pupils in the city as a whole. In 1963, 70% of the third grade pupils in the neighborhood were reading below grade level as compared to 55% for New York City.[2]

Our research in the area indicated that the rates of reading retardation were far greater for Puerto Rican and black pupils than for other youngsters. Among third graders, for example, 83% of the Puerto Rican pupils and 77% of the black pupils were reading below grade level as compared with 51% of the white pupils. That this retardation was progressive as well as cumulative is evident from the eighth grade statistics: 65% of the Puerto Rican pupils and 34% of the black pupils were reading *3 years or more* below grade level as compared with 14% of the white pupils.[3] Clearly, a major effort was needed to deal with the reading retardation displayed by the vast majority of public-school children in the area.

---

[1] Mobilization for Youth, Inc., was established in 1959 with funds from the National Institute of Mental Health, the President's Committee on Juvenile Delinquency, the Ford Foundation, and the City of New York. It was a forerunner of the present Community Action Programs of the Office of Economic Opportunity.

[2] City norms were obtained from *Summary of City wide Test Results for 1964–1965,* Bureau of Educational Research, Board of Education of the City of New York, October, 1965, p. 9. The data on Mobilization-area pupils were obtained through a 1963 survey of the school records of 1390 third grade pupils in 16 public schools.

[3] Ethnic identification was based primarily on family names, given names, and parents' place of birth.

The usual approach to the educational problem posed by low-achieving young-sters is to hire additional professional staff and build programs of remediation around them. This approach rests on the assumption that the problems of the retarded reader are so complex that only the professional reading specialist, by virtue of his training and experience, can be of real assistance. Since a reading specialist can provide intensive service only for a few pupils at a time, it would be prohibitively expensive to hire as many as needed. Furthermore, despite his superior technical skills, the reading specialist may be no better equipped to communicate with lower-class youth than is the middle-class-oriented teacher typically found in slum schools.

Mobilization's tutorial program rested on the assumption that older adoles-cents from the same social and economic strata as their pupils are in a better position than the middle-class-oriented teacher (or reading specialist) to under-stand and communicate with children who live in our urban slums. It was hypothesized that such youngsters, working under the direction of professional teachers, could serve as a bridge between the professional and the child in need, and could provide pupils with role models who would enhance their aspirations for academic success. Mobilization's approach, then, was to hire and train a large number of local high school students to help low-achieving elementary school pupils with their homework assignments and to tutor them in basic reading and other language arts skills.

Impact of the Program

During the period of planning the tutorial program, a number of questions were raised concerning the effect the program might have on the tutors and their pupils. In view of the complex nature of reading disabilities, some school officials anticipated that tutoring by high school students would have no effect at all on reading skills of low-achieving elementary school pupils. Furthermore, school officials believed that if the high school student became engrossed in his tutorial activities, he would neglect his own schoolwork—with disastrous results. Improvement in pupil achievement, if it occurred at all, would be obtained at the expense of the tutor's school achievement.

To test these assumptions empirically, two concurrent experiments were con-ducted (Cloward, 1967). One experiment attempted to assess the impact of the program on the pupils; the second was concerned with the effect of the tutorial experience on participating high school students.

Both studies were structured as classical experiments, with random assignment of eligible subjects to experimental and control situations. Experimental pupils were provided with tutorial services on a 1- or 2-day-a-week basis. Control pupils did not receive any tutoring. Similarly, high school students in the experimental group were hired as tutors, and control high school students were told that they could not be given jobs as tutors. In both studies, control subjects served as a standard against which the achievement of the experimental subjects could be evaluated.

Programs that are intended to improve the educational status of participants should be evaluated by measures of performance rather than—as is often the case—by such tangential data as program attendance statistics, unsystematic observations of individuals, or the subjective judgments of participants. The present studies focused, therefore, on the "hard facts" of reading achievement. Although attempts were made to measure changes in the attitudes, aspirations, and values of the participants, these data were viewed as secondary outcomes that could be accepted with confidence only if they correlated with reading achievement.

The Tutee Study

Impact of the program on the tutees or pupils was based on data from 356 experimental and 157 control subjects drawn from a population of 2500 eligible fourth and fifth grade pupils. Experimental and control pupils were selected randomly within school districts and pooled over districts to form geographically stratified random samples. Included in these samples were 100 subjects who received tutorial services two afternoons a week (the 4-hour treatment group), 73 subjects who were tutored only one afternoon a week (the 2-hour treatment group), and 79 control subjects. The remaining 183 experimental subjects who were not part of the stratified random sample were tutored only 2 hours a week; they were compared with a control group of 78 subjects who received no tutoring.

At the beginning of the program, the average fourth grade pupil was reading at grade 3.5 (8 months below grade level); the average fifth grade pupil was reading at grade 4.2 (1 year and 1 month below grade level). There were no significant differences between experimental and control subjects. After 5 months of tutorial instruction, pupils in the 4-hour treatment group showed significantly greater improvement than control subjects. In terms of grade equivalents, the 4-hour pupils showed an average of 6.0 months reading improvement in 5 months time, whereas the control pupils showed only 3.5 months growth during the same period. The growth rate—or, more accurately, the progressive retardation—of the controls approximates the average rate for Puerto Rican elementary school children in the Mobilization area. Thus, the 4-hour group not only arrested the retardation but began to catch up. The comparable 2-hour group made a gain of 5.0 months in reading during the same 5-month period. Although this growth rate exceeded that of the controls, the difference was not statistically significant. The remaining 183 experimental subjects (who were not included in ths stratified random sample) were all in centers offering only a 2-hour exposure to tutoring. This 2-hour group showed only 3.8 months growth as compared to 3.9 months for their respective controls, a difference that was not statistically significant.

Further analyses of the reading data indicated that degree of change was not associated with such factors as the pupil's sex, grade in school (fourth or fifth), or access to school programs in remedial reading. Although ethnicity was not, in general, associated with improvement, black pupils who were matched with their tutors on sex and ethnicity showed significantly greater gains in reading than did black pupils in the control group.

The Tutor Study

For the tutor study, random samples of 97 experimental and 57 control subjects were drawn from the eligible population of tenth and eleventh grade applicants for tutorial jobs. None of the subjects had ever served as tutors before.

To estimate the effects of the program on the tutors, before-and-after-program data were collected on reading skills, school achievement, attitudes, values, educational aspirations, and interest in becoming a teacher. The Advanced Level of the Iowa Silent Reading Tests (Revised New Edition) was used to measure changes in the reading skills of the subjects. Although this reading battery is rather long and exceptionally difficult to administer, it is especially valuable in that it yields eight test scores covering a wide variety of reading and study skills. School-achievement data were obtained from school records for the 1962–63 academic year (pre-study) and the 1963–64 academic year (post-study). Data on attitudes, values, aspirations, and interest in teaching were obtained through the administration of a 54-item questionnaire developed by the present author.

The experimental tutors had a pre-study mean reading level of grade 9.9 as compared to a mean level of grade 10.1 for the tutor controls. Since the mean grade of origin for both samples was 10.7, the average experimental tutor was reading 8 months below grade level, and the average control subject was reading 6 months below grade level. Both samples showed, however, considerable range in reading achievement. Of the tutors, 20%, and of the controls, 21% were reading *below the eighth grade level.*

In the 7 months between the pre-study and the post-study administrations of the Iowa Silent Reading Tests, the tutors showed an average gain in reading of 3 years and 4 months as compared to 1 year and 7 months for the control subjects. The remarkable growth of the controls probably was an artifact of the testing situation; the complexity of the directions for taking the test probably depressed the pre-study scores for all subjects. Since an alternate form of the same test was used in the post-study administration, a substantial portion of the increase for both groups may have been due to increased familiarity with the test directions. Nevertheless, this does not explain the sizable difference between the growth rates of experimentals and controls. Even if the control mean is taken as an estimate of the effect of normal growth plus increased familiarity with the test situation, the net effect of serving as a tutor was a reading increment of 1 year and 7 months. No significant differences were found between tutors and their controls on before- and after-program measures of school marks, attitudes toward school and school-related activities, social values, educational aspirations, or interest in becoming a teacher. Nor did the experimental tutors who showed high change in reading differ from low-change experimentals on these variables.

The failure of the tutorial experience to influence the school marks of the tutors is particularly interesting. Since the post-study measure of school achievement consisted of school marks earned while the subjects were serving as tutors, it focuses on concurrent rather than post-treatment effects. It is reasonable to assume that the high reading gains made by the tutors will enable them to earn higher marks in their future schoolwork. At any rate, it is clear that serving as a tutor did not adversely affect school achievement.

PREDICTING CHANGE IN TUTORS AND THEIR TUTEES

Further research was undertaken concerning two questions: (1) Which tutor variable or combination of tutor variables best predicts gains in tutors' reading skills? (2) Which tutor variable or combination of tutor variables best predicts gains in the reading skills of pupils of the tutors? The sample used in the analysis consisted of 71 experimental tutors for whom complete data were available on the variables being examined. Included in this sample were 38 tutors who worked throughout the year with a specific pupil and 33 tutors for whom some change in pupil assignment had been made during the year. The main sample of 71 tutors can be used to examine the relation between tutor change and tutor characteristics, but prediction of pupil (tutee) gains is necessarily restricted to the sample of 38 tutors who remained with their assigned pupil throughout the year.

The pre-test data available for analyses included intellectual, academic, demographic, and personality variables. The intellectual status of the tutors was measured using the Quick Word Test (Borgatta & Corsini, 1960). Although relatively new, this short test of verbal facility has been well standardized and validated. The publishers report a Kuder–Richardson reliability coefficient of .92 for tenth grade students and correlations ranging from .72 to .85 with other standardized intelligence tests. Three measures of academic achievement were used: tutor marks in academic subjects for the academic year preceding the study, grade level of the tutor, and pre-study reading skill of the tutor. Tutor reading skills were measured using the advanced level of the Iowa Silent Reading Test. While the Iowa pre-study total score was used as a predictor variable, the net change in Iowa total score from pre-study to post-study was used as a criterion or dependent variable.

The Multi-Level Research Questionnaire was used to assess the personality characteristics of the tutors. This experimental inventory yields 23 scaled scores reflecting dimensions of personality. Borgatta (1964, 1965) reports that the instrument has been subjected to factor analysis, though complete normative data are not available at this time.

Pupil reading achievement was measured on a before-and-after basis using the New York Tests of Growth in Reading (Level G, Form 1, revised). The net change in pupil reading scores from pre-study to post-study was used as a dependent variable.

Predicting Tutors' Gains in Reading Skills

To predict the tutors' change in reading skills, a stepwise multiple linear regression technique was used to determine which tutor variable (of the 28 included) or combination of variables was the best predictor. The tutors' gain on the Iowa Silent Reading Test was used as the dependent variable. The variable introduced at each step and the resultant multiple correlation and significance level are presented in Table 1. The reader will note that the first step in the multiple correlation produces a large F ratio. Although the F ratio tends to diminish slowly from step to step, it was not until the twenty-sixth variable had been introduced that it fell below the .05 level of probability.

Stepwise regression analyses tend to overestimate the size of the multiple correlation because the technique capitalizes on correlations that are spuriously high due to sampling fluctuations. Variables with errors of measurement favoring correlation with the criterion variable tend to be introduced earlier than variables with measurement errors opposing correlation with the criterion. Usually, replication of the analysis with similar samples results in considerable shrinkage in the multiple correlation. The loss in the multiple correlation due to shrinkage has been estimated at each step using Wherry's formula (Kelley, 1947). These data are presented in the last column of Table 1. A comparison of the gains in the multiple correlation at each step and the estimated loss due to shrinkage indicates that variables beyond the fourth step do not increase the accuracy of prediction.[4]

It is also interesting to note that the Quick Word Test score introduced at the third step tended to decrease the accuracy of prediction while the Iowa Silent Reading Test score at the fourth step showed adequate gain in prediction. The scores on the Iowa and the Quick Word Test were highly correlated (R=.58). Apparently, the Iowa Silent Reading Test score is operating as a suppressant for the Quick Word Test score. Though neither variable correlates well with the

---

[4] The author is indebted to Dr. Dieter Paulus of the University of Connecticut for suggesting the "gain–shrinkage" method of evaluating steps in multiple linear regression.

Table 1

Summary of Stepwise Multiple Linear Regression Analysis
to Predict Tutor Reading Gain from Pre-study Tutor Variables

Step number	Variable entered	Multiple R	Standard error	F ratio	Significance of R	Gain in R from previous step	Estimated loss due to shrinkage
1	Sluggish	.358	10.57	10.16	.01	—	—
2	Likeability	.425	10.32	7.50	.01	.067	.029
3	Quick word	.461	10.20	6.03	.01	.036	.040
4	Iowa reading	.541	9.74	6.83	.01	.080	.041
5	Self depreciation	.574	9.55	6.39	.01	.033	.047
6	Sex-role traditionalism	.601	9.39	6.04	.01	.027	.052
7	Assertiveness	.640	9.11	6.24	.01	.038	.053
8	Emotionality	.662	8.95	6.04	.01	.022	.057
9	Insecure	.685	8.77	5.99	.01	.023	.060
10	Shocked	.706	8.60	5.97	.01	.021	.062
11	Cynical realism	.721	8.48	5.82	.01	.015	.065
12	Sex	.730	8.44	5.05	.01	.008	.070
25	Authoritarian	.762	9.08	2.50	.01	.000	.172

(F Level insufficient for further computation.)

Note: N = 71

criterion, when the Iowa and Quick Word scores are combined, a gain in prediction occurs. It is probable that this gain in prediction occurs as a result of statistical regression, for the Iowa scores are negatively correlated with the criterion and the Quick Word scores are positively correlated with the criterion. This is simply to say that the greatest gains were shown by high ability, low achieving students. Not only is opportunity for gain in reading maximized for these students, but there is a natural tendency for students with extreme scores to show movement towards the mean in subsequent testing. Consequently, it is doubtful that the Iowa and the Quick Word improve the accuracy of prediction. We are left, then, with two personality variables (sluggish and likeability) at steps one through four; when combined, they account for 16% of the variance in the tutors' gains in reading.

Predicting Tutees' Gain in Reading

The same set of 28 tutor variables was used to predict tutees' reading gain for the 38 tutor–tutee pairs. The results of this analysis are presented in Table 2. The multiple correlation reached statistical significance at the fourth step, but a comparison of gain in prediction with the estimated loss due to shrinkage

Table 2
Summary of Stepwise Linear Regression Analysis
to Predict Pupil Reading Gain from Pre-study Tutor Variables

Step Number	Variable entered	Multiple R	Standard error	F ratio	Significance of R	Gain in R from previous step	Estimated loss due to shrinkage
1	Likeability	.262	5.41	2.65	ns	—	—
2	Defiant	.337	5.35	2.25	ns	.077	.086
3	Shocked	.429	5.21	2.55	ns	.091	.094
4	Self depreciation	.521	4.99	3.08	.05	.093	.093
5	Grade	.567	4.90	3.03	.05	.045	.103
6	Impulsivity	.606	4.80	3.00	.05	.039	.111
7	Sluggish	.635	4.74	2.90	.05	.029	.121
8	Aloofness	.664	4.67	2.86	.05	.029	.128

(F level insufficient for further computation.)

Note: N = 38

indicates that the multiple correlation would fall below significance were the analysis replicated with a new sample. Therefore, the four personality variables included in the formula at the fourth step are of doubtful predictive value. Inclusion of subsequent variables does not increase the accuracy of prediction.

DISCUSSION

The findings from the Mobilization study indicated that the tutor was the major beneficiary of the tutorial experience. In attempting to help his low-achieving elementary school pupil, the tutor greatly improved his own reading ability. The reason for this is not entirely clear, but the result deserves our serious attention. It may be an example of what every beginning teacher discovers: that one must relearn one's subject in order to teach it, that one has to reanalyze what he knows and how he learns in order to promote similar knowledge and learning in others. Or it may be that serving as a tutor placed the high school students in a different relationship to learning. Rather than being passive recipients, they were required to be active purveyors of knowledge. Being positively rewarded (both socially and financially) for academic activities could have been an important factor as well. There is no reason to believe, however, that hiring teenagers merely to supervise or baby-sit with elementary school pupils will have any significant effect on the tutors—or on their pupils. There is good reason to believe that when teenagers are charged with the task of trying to help a child who is having difficulty, they not only learn to give substantive assistance to the child but improve their own academic skills as well.

In predicting the tutors' gain in reading, the present results indicated that the value of academic credentials is open to question. Personality characteristics of the tutors appeared to be better predictors than their academic and intellectual characteristics. These findings suggest that in selecting tutors, preference might be given to low-achieving students with certain personality characteristics; these are the youngsters most likely to improve their academic skills from the experience of being a tutor. Most program directors, however, seem predisposed towards selecting as tutors students with the highest academic and intellectual credentials. Minimal qualifications often are established, such as being of above average intelligence, or possessing above average reading skills. This is most clearly illustrated in the tendency to select college students in preference to high school students, and so on. Underlying these criteria is the assumption that academic credentials and tutorial effectiveness are positively correlated—that tutors with higher than average academic achievement will be more effective than tutors with lower academic achievement.

The present empirical evidence does not support this view. There is virtually no correlation between the tutor's intellectual credentials and his effectiveness in tutoring. Tutors with lower than average intellectual status seemed to be just as effective in helping their pupils improve in reading as were the tutors with higher than average intellectual status. In the light of these findings, there seems to be no justification for imposing high academic and intellectual criteria in the selection of tutors. Perhaps attention should be given, instead, to selecting tutors who will derive maximum benefits themselves from the tutorial experience.

In regard to effectiveness of the tutors as teachers, it is interesting to note that the first four variables to enter the prediction formula for tutee gains in reading were scores from the tutor's personality scale. Although singly or in combination they do not afford much in the way of predictive accuracy, the personality variables performed better than the usual academic and intellectual credentials so often used in tutor selection. We are given no clue from the data as to why this should be so. It may be a reflection of individual differences in the tutor's ability to relate to younger children, and of the ease, frequency, and sincerity with which he is able to reinforce desirable behavior. An interaction analysis of the behaviors of effective and ineffective tutors might shed some light on this possibility. In any case, there is a suggestion in the data that one may be able to increase tutee gains by preselecting tutors in terms of personality characteristics.

As a final comment, the importance of subjecting a tutorial program to empirical evaluation should be emphasized. Objective evaluation implies a comparison of the program participants with a nonparticipant population. At the very least, the language-arts skills of participants should be measured on a before-and-after basis. Grade-wide norms for school or city could be used to evaluate the growth of participants. If data from previous years are available, participants could serve as their own controls. Likewise, the growth of participants could be compared with that of a group of nonparticipants matched on relevant variables. The best evidence of effects, however, will be obtained from controlled experiments which permit the random selection of participants and nonparticipants. Clearly, the tutorial situation is a fruitful area for educational research. Further research is needed to determine the long-term effects of the tutorial experience and the value of this approach when applied to other populations.

REFERENCES

Borgatta, E. F. A very short test of personality: The Behavioral Self-Rating (BSR) form. *Psychological Reports,* 1964, *14,* 275–284.

Borgatta, E. F. A short test of personality: The S-Indent form. *Journal of Educational Research,* 1965, *58,* 453–456.

Borgatta, E. F. & Corsini, R. J. The quick word test (QWT) and the WAIS. *Psychological Reports,* 1960, *6,* 201.

Cloward, R. D. Studies in tutoring. *Journal of Experimental Education,* 1967, *36,* 14–25.

Hassinger, J., & Via, M. How much does a tutor learn through teaching reading? *Journal of Secondary Education,* 1969, *44,* 42–44.

Kelley, T. L. *Fundamentals of statistics.* Cambridge, Massachusetts: Harvard Univ. Press, 1947.

McWhorter, K. T., & Levy, J. The influence of a tutorial program upon tutors. *Journal of Reading,* 1971, *14,* 221–224.

Werth, T. G. An assessment of the reciprocal effect of high school senior low achievers in English classes. Unpublished dissertation. Oregon State Univ., 1968.

IV

Problems and Possibilities

The purpose of the two chapters in this final section is to increase the scope and depth of the book. It is hoped that these chapters will add appreciably to the practical usefulness of the present volume. As another effort in this direction, at the end of Chapter 16 one will find addresses and other necessary information for obtaining material made available by several tutoring projects.

Of necessity, the preceding chapters were somewhat selective in coverage; no attempt was made by authors to summarize all research relevant to tutoring. A critical review of available research on tutoring will complement the detailed discussions of specific empirical studies that appear in other chapters. With the additional breadth provided by the review chapter, the reader will have obtained from this book a fairly comprehensive picture of the current state of research on tutoring.

As a further contribution to the usefulness and unity of the book, a second chapter in this section is addressed to the problems of implementation. Practical suggestions for initiating and managing tutoring programs were offered in several earlier chapters, but these discussions usually did not point out alternatives; neither did authors usually specify whether or not a recommendation was based on empirical data. An attempt is made in this chapter to concentrate on the practical, concrete, day-by-day problems that arise during tutoring in school; in earlier chapters such mundane matters were often slighted in favor of more abstract discussions.

In the first of two chapters in this section, Feldman, Devin-Sheehan, and Allen discuss the variables that affect the outcomes of tutoring for both the tutor and the tutee and also offer some comments on research design in this area. The relevant available data concerning the effect on tutoring of several specific variables are summarized and integrated. It is clear from the data that a wide range of tutors and tutees can benefit from participating in tutoring programs. It is rather surprising to discover that only a small amount of empirical information is available concerning variables such as amount of time spent tutoring, and the sex, race, and social class composition of the tutoring dyad. For other variables, evidence is available but inconclusive (e.g., various methods of training).

It is clear that firm answers have not been found concerning the effect of many variables that interest both the practitioner and the researcher. In some cases the relevant research simply has not been conducted; for other variables, difference among studies in procedure, design, and support makes any general conclusion untenable at this point. Even so, a survey of the literature did reveal considerable consistency across studies in many of the areas reviewed. Interesting questions regarding the complex and subtle interactive effects of certain variables appearing in combination (as illustrated by Cloward and Strodtbeck's chapters in the preceding section) have not yet even been adequately conceptualized.

In the first chapter a number of methodological criticisms are directed toward research in tutoring. No one will deny that it is difficult to conduct research in this area, but there is little justification for failing to collect rigorous data (as opposed to testimonials) or for omitting appropriate control conditions. Not all research in tutoring is guilty of such egregious methodological lapses by any means, we are happy to say. The authors also make a plea in this chapter for greater use of theory in research on tutoring. A satisfactory conceptualization of a problem is often the essential first step that leads to more fruitful empirical research. Perhaps future researchers will be able to benefit from the theoretical suggestions made by authors of several of the chapters in this book.

The second, and final, chapter in this section (by Devin-Sheehan and Allen) deals with problems connected with implementing a tutoring program in the school and the special problems of doing field research on tutoring. We hope that this chapter will serve as a gentle guide for persons who are contemplating establishing a tutoring program, a gentle guide in that we have made an effort not to be dogmatic and absolutist in our suggestions. Any set of rigid strictures for starting a tutoring program should be viewed by the practitioner with healthy skepticism for two reasons. First, each school has its own special needs, problems, and other characteristics that make it unique. General recommendations should not be adopted without taking local conditions strongly into consideration. Secondly, regardless of the aura of authority with which some recommendations are delivered, the simple fact remains that empirical data do not exist to support many of them. The practitioner would do well to distinguish among recommendations based on empirical findings, on someone else's (perhaps unrepresentative) experiences, and on someone else's common sense or intuition. Recommendations falling into the latter two categories should be examined in the light of the practitioner's own local circumstances, and in the final analysis exercise his own critical intelligence and common sense in reaching a judgment.

In the implementation chapter, Devin-Sheehan and Allen discuss several very concrete problems that a program organizer must confront, including such problems as the time and place for tutoring, and the selection and pairing of participants. The authors try to avoid making any doctrinaire "do and don't" recommendations. Instead, they attempt to delineate the options or alternatives that are available for several basic decisions that must be made in a tutoring program; then they cite as objectively as possible the advantages and disadvantages associated with each alternative course of action. A clear distinction is noted between recommendations that derive from research findings and those based on the authors' own experience and best judgment. Again, the practitioner must ultimately choose those alternatives that best fit the special circumstances of his own school.

Problems associated with evaluating a tutoring program and with doing experimental research on tutoring in a field setting also are discussed in this final chapter. Evaluation research is necessary, but for a satisfactory understanding of causal relationships—for discovering the crucial factors determining results—there is no substitute for experimental research. Both the practitioner and the researcher can benefit from research being conducted on an ongoing tutoring program in the school. The authors argue that theory, research, and practice all should be mutually reinforcing components of a successful tutoring program.

15

Children Tutoring Children: A Critical Review of Research

Robert S. Feldman Linda Devin-Sheehan
University of Wisconsin University of Wisconsin

Vernon L. Allen
University of Wisconsin

Tutoring programs that use children as tutors for other children have indeed increased in number and variety since the late 1960s (Gartner, Kohler, & Riessman, 1971; Thelen, 1969).[1] Nevertheless, empirical support for generalizations about the effect of tutoring on tutors and tutees often has been inconclusive; the evidence concerning effectiveness of programs in the schools often has consisted of anecdotal reports rather than rigorous data (Bell, Garlock, & Colella, 1969; Costello & Martin, 1972; Goodman, 1971; Moskowitz, 1972; Office of Education, 1967; Swett, 1971). At the same time, some well-controlled research has been conducted as well (Cloward, 1967; Ellson, Barber, Engle, & Kampwerth, 1965; Klosterman, 1970; Morgan & Toy, 1970; Shaver & Nuhn, 1971). This chapter critically reviews recent research on tutoring, focusing on the specific, delimited variables that affect the outcomes of tutoring for both tutor and tutee. Problems of research methodology and design also will be considered briefly.

[1] The authors are grateful for Ms. Roberta Wilkes' efforts in compiling a comprehensive bibliography of the literature on peer- and cross-age tutoring (Wilkes, 1975). Portions of this chapter are revised from an article published in *Review of Educational Research,* summer, 1976.

VARIABLES AFFECTING THE OUTCOMES OF TUTORING

Several important characteristics of the participants will be discussed first: personal traits of the tutor and tutee, their sex, race, socioeconomic status, and tutor–tutee age differential. Then we will examine factors that are unrelated to particular characteristics of the tutor or tutee but are a function of the inter-action inself: temporal variables, number of tutees per tutor, training of tutors, and interaction within the tutoring situation.

Personal Characteristics of Tutor and Tutee

Ample anecdotal and nonexperimental evidence suggests that children with a variety of personal characteristics benefit from acting as tutors to younger children. Students suffering from behavior problems (Geiser, 1969; Lane, Pollack, & Sher, 1972), low achievement (Bean & Luke, 1972; Harris, 1971; Rime & Ham, 1968), institutionalization (Pfiel, 1969), or a combination of these problems (Balmer, 1972; Criscuolo, 1973; Hassinger & Via, 1969; Landrum & Martin, 1970; Office of Education, 1967) have been reported (anecdotally) to benefit from participating as tutors in tutoring programs. More reliable, however, are studies that assess tutor improvement in a controlled, objective manner. Happily, in this instance, carefully controlled experiments tend to support the anecdotal evidence.

✳A number of studies have found that low achievers in reading make significant gains in reading ability following their tutoring of younger children. For instance, Klentschy (1971) found that sixth grade low achievers showed significant gains in reading after just 2 months of tutoring low-achieving second graders in reading. Marascuilo, Levin, and James (1969) showed that ninth grade remedial readers gained significantly in reading comprehension following their (paid) tutoring of a seventh grade low achiever in reading. In another study, fifth graders who were poor readers did not improve in reading achievement as a result of tutoring, but they did show more positive attitudes towards teachers and reading, and an improved self-concept (Robertson, 1971).

Using quasi-experimental methods, Erickson and Cromack (1972) found that seventh grade underachievers improved significantly in reading after tutoring third graders. One study found that underachieving sophomore and junior boys with discipline problems who tutored elementary school children twice a week showed significant increases in self-concept, self-acceptance, and grade point average; however, there was no improvement in attitude toward school (Haggerty, 1971). Unfortunately, in both the Erickson and Cromack (1972) and Haggerty (1971) studies, no measures were taken of actual change in behavior.

Since poor behavior was one of the criteria used to place subjects in the tutoring program, it is unfortunate that this crucial variable was not measured.

The effect of acting as a tutor in arithmetic on low-achieving, misbehaving, and unpopular sixth graders was examined by Rust (1970). In an attempt to determine the locus of causality for any positive effects that might accrue to the older children, Rust employed a group of subjects who acted as friends or buddies to third graders; in addition, there was a no-treatment control group. Thus, it was possible to determine whether changes in tutor behavior were due to interaction with a younger child alone or whether acting as a teacher was crucial. Despite this promising design, no difference in social behavior was found among any of the conditions, but tutors did increase in mathematics achievement. The use of the additional "friend" control group is exemplary, however, and is an important control lacking in most tutoring studies.

In another study, Yamamoto and Klentschy (1972) investigated the effect of being a tutor on the attitudes of inner-city children in Los Angeles. Low achieving fifth and sixth grade boys and girls were assigned to one of three groups: an experimental group that received training and then tutored first graders, a control group that was trained but did not tutor, and a control group that was not trained and did not tutor. Matching across the three groups was based on sex and pre-test scores on a semantic differential measure of attitude toward school and self. Tutoring took place 3 days a week during the morning recess period. At the conclusion of the study an analysis of semantic differential post-test scores showed that experimental subjects who tutored had significantly more positive attitudes towards both school and self than subjects in either of the control groups.

✕Mohan (1972) found that poorly motivated students were positively affected when they tutored unmotivated younger children. Both objective attitude scales and subjective teacher ratings showed that tutors increased in motivation level, self-concept, attitudes toward school, and in mathematics achievement—the subject they taught.

Studies investigating the academic effects of tutoring typically compare children who have tutored to children who have not participated in any special treatment at all. Hence, it is difficult to determine if any academic improvement apparently due to acting as a tutor is attributable to the tutoring itself or simply to spending additional time studying. To examine this question, Allen and Feldman (1974) designed a laboratory experiment in which fifth graders who were low achievers in reading either taught a third grader or studied alone for a series of daily sessions. At the end of a 2-week period, the low achievers' performance on the subject matter was significantly better in the tutoring condition than in the studying-alone condition, a reversal in direction of the initial difference between conditions. Thus, the tutoring itself—and not just the extra time spent studying the lessons—resulted in improved academic performance.

It is conceivable that the type of student who most benefits from being a tutor (the low achiever, the child with behavior problems, the unmotivated) may in fact be the least beneficial type of teacher for the tutee. The empirical evidence on this issue yields conflicting results. Several studies have shown that low-achieving tutors can be effective teachers for younger children. In one carefully controlled experiment, fifth grade tutors who were low achievers in reading worked 3 days a week for 2 months with first graders needing individual help on recognition of sight words (Robertson, 1972). At the end of the program, the trained tutors had significantly more positive attitudes toward the concepts of reading, teaching, and self than did either a control group that received training without tutoring or a control group that had no training or tutoring experience at all. In addition, the tutors had higher reading achievement scores than either of the two control groups. The first grade tutees made greater gains in reading than the control subjects who received only classroom reading instruction. This is one of the few studies that found the academic gains for the tutees accompanied by positive academic and attitudinal changes in the tutors. Other studies have found that younger tutees show improvement when tutored by third grade underachievers (Rogers, 1970), sixth grade low achievers (Klentschy, 1971), or fifth grade poor readers (Williams, Kabota, Klentschy, & Michaud, 1972). Using unmotivated seventh and eighth grade tutors, Mohan (1972) found that second and third grade tutees made significant improvement in motivation and mathematics performance. Retarded tutors were able to effect significant changes in retarded tutees' eating and dressing behavior after no more than 20 hours of tutoring (Wagner, 1973). Prior to beginning teaching, the tutors had undergone 30 hours of training, however.

On the other hand, a number of studies have found that the positive effects that accrue to the tutor are not reflected in tutee benefits. Kelly (1972) found that low-achieving second graders did not improve in reading achievement after being tutored by low-achieving fourth grade tutors. Although seventh grade underachieving tutors increased in reading skills in the Erickson and Cromack (1972) study, the third grade tutees did not show any improvement. Likewise, Marascuilo et al. (1969) found that ninth graders who were receiving remedial reading showed significant gains in reading comprehension as a result of tutoring, but their seventh grade remedial reading tutees gained less in comprehension than a nontutored control group. Allen and Feldman (1974) also found that there was no difference in performance between tutees who were tutored by low-achieving fifth graders and those third graders who simply studied the material by themselves, without any tutoring.

Taken together, the literature on tutor characteristics suggests quite convincingly that a very broad range of students may benefit from acting as a tutor.

Whether or not the tutee will improve more from being tutored by a particular type of tutor is an open question; the evidence is mixed at this time. The crucial factor may be the relative level of competence between the tutor and tutee. If the tutor is clearly superior to the tutee—regardless of the tutor's ability compared to his peers—then presumably he should be able to produce significant improvement in his tutee. At the same time, tutoring may bring about positive benefits for the tutor himself.

Sex Pairings

Although the predominant belief among those who give advice about tutoring programs is that same-sex pairs facilitate tutoring, little empirical data support such an assertion. Most studies on tutoring have employed same-sex pairs; only a few studies have specifically orthogonally manipulated sex of tutor and sex of tutee; these few studies have yielded results that contradict the same-sex dictum.

In one relevant tutoring program lasting for a 4-month period, 96 sixth grade low achievers tutored second and third graders in reading or mathematics (Klentschy, 1971). Examining tutors' reading scores, Klentschy found that, as might be expected, the tutors teaching reading skills improved significantly only in reading. Males seemed to benefit more, overall, from acting as a tutor, but there were no differences due to tutoring same- or cross-sex tutees. In a later report, Klentschy (1972) analyzed the effects of sex of tutor on increase in achievement obtained by the tutees. Parallel to the earlier findings, an increase in reading skill was not affected by whether the tutee was tutored by a male or a female. In general, then, Klentschy's results suggest that same-sex pairings do not enhance the benefits derived from tutoring.

The combination of sex of tutor and sex of tutee had no differential effect on the attitudes of fifth grade tutors, according to Foster's (1972) study. (But there also was found no effect for tutoring overall.) Most subjects did, however, prefer to tutor a same-sex rather than a different-sex tutee.

Significant differences on sex pairings were observed in a one-session tutoring study that investigated concept attainment in first graders taught by third grade siblings and nonsiblings (Cicirelli, 1972). The most effective tutor—tutee match was an older sister teaching a younger brother. This pairing was significantly superior to older brothers teaching younger brothers, older boys teaching younger girls, and older girls teaching younger girls. Looking solely at nonsibling pairings, however, there was no difference between males tutoring males and those tutoring females, nor between females tutoring males and those tutoring females.

It appears that the empirical literature holds little support for the hypothesis that same-sex pairings of tutors and tutees is superior to opposite-sex dyads. No support exists for the opposite contention either—mixed-sex pairs do not perform better than same-sex pairs. These conclusions are based primarily on academic gains rather than socio-emotional factors; even if sex pairing were unimportant for academic performance, it still may affect attitude toward peers. For example, Foster's (1972) finding that tutors preferred tutees of the same sex suggests that the particular combination employed may affect the tutor's evaluation of the tutoring experience and, presumably, attitudes relating to other children in general. Some evidence suggests that tutoring by opposite-sex peers may lead to changes in preference for members of the opposite sex: After a period of cooperative social interaction, preference for the opposite sex increased significantly in one study (Haskett, 1971). Further research on this issue, using tutoring situations, would be desirable.

One further question regarding sex factors is whether males or females benefit more from tutoring (regardless of the sex of the particular person with whom they are paired). Two studies have revealed that male tutors and tutees benefit academically from tutoring significantly more than female tutors and tutees (Klentschy, 1971, 1972). Looking at socially isolated third and fourth graders, Holcomb (1972) found that tutoring by a college student resulted in significant increases in positive attitude toward self, class participation, and teacher assessment of schoolwork for male, but not female, tutees. Male tutees were superior to female tutees in a concept attainment task, but the task (trapezoid identification) was more suited to male spatial abilities (Cicirelli, 1972). Other studies have not found sex differences (Brantley, 1971; Lamal, 1970), but in these studies there was no effect for tutoring overall.

Race and Socioeconomic Status

Little systematic research has been conducted on racial and socioeconomic factors associated with tutoring. Although the literature on tutoring uses white, middle-class children as subjects predominantly, it is clear from a number of studies that other racial and social-class groups produce significant academic improvement when tutoring children of the same race and status. For instance, in several studies blacks tutored by blacks showed significant improvement (e.g., Brown, 1972; Coker, 1969; Freyberg, 1967; Liette, 1972). Lower-class or disadvantaged children tutored by other lower-class persons also appear to improve as a result of tutoring (e.g., Hamblin & Hamblin, 1972; Nichols, 1969; Snapp, Oakland, & Williams, 1972). Unfortunately, only a few studies have directly manipulated racial and status variables.

Mexican-American and Anglo-American fifth and sixth graders served as tutors for Head Start children in one study (Lakin, 1972). Results showed that both groups made significant gains in vocabulary after 8 weeks of tutoring, but only the Anglo-American group improved significantly in oral reading skill. Lakin suggests that these findings may be due in part to the cultural bias of the measures used. Hypothesizing that cross-race tutoring promotes the development of more positive racial attitudes, Witte (1972) conducted two tutoring programs using interracial dyads. Results indicated an increase in interracial interaction and acceptance by the tutors and tutees, but no significant gains in academic performance. On the other hand, McMonagle (1972) found no effect on white tutors' attitudes towards black children as a function of tutoring.

Some evidence suggests that teaching styles vary for children of different races and social classes. Feshbach and Devor (1969) used very young children (4-year-olds) to tutor 3-year-olds in a puzzle task, and found a significant interaction between race and social class for the amount of positive reinforcement used by the tutors. White middle-class tutors used significantly more positive reinforcement than black middle-class and lower-class children of both races. Whether the differences found by Feshbach and Devor hold for older children is not yet known.

One important dependent measure that is seldom obtained in tutoring studies is change in level of aspiration. Tutors having initially low levels of aspirations might be expected to raise their aspiration as a consequence of performing successfully in a traditionally respected role (i.e., teacher). Interestingly, Edler (1967) did find an increase in level of aspiration following a year's experience of being a tutor. Tutors from lower socioeconomic levels began to aspire to occupations associated with upward social mobility. More research is needed in this area.

Tutor—Tutee Age Differential

Tutoring programs have varied widely in the age difference between tutor and tutee, ranging from adults tutoring kindergartners to same-age and same-grade pairings, but there is little systematic evidence available concerning the optimum age difference between tutor and tutee. Linton (1973) studied the effects of grade displacement between eighth, tenth, and twelfth grade mathematics tutors and eighth grade low-achieving tutees. Tutees taught by twelfth graders performed significantly better than tutees taught by either tenth or eighth graders. Thus, the larger grade displacement resulted in better performance by the tutees. Thomas (1972) found that college students were better than sixth graders in promoting vocabulary acquisition in second grade tutees, but no difference was found as a function of age of tutor in reading comprehension and oral reading of tutees.

In light of these two studies, it appears that a greater age difference between tutor and tutee results in somewhat better tutee performance. On the other hand, the nature of the interaction may be more pleasant when the age range between tutor and tutee is closer. Any generalization must be tempered by the recognition than an inherent confounding exists between grade displacement and age of tutor. It may not be age difference, per se, that leads to differential tutee performance; rather, perhaps older tutors are simply more skilled at tutoring than younger children. Studies are required in which the age or grade differential is manipulated orthogonally by varying both the grade of tutors and the grade of the tutees. Without this type of experiment, it is difficult to determine the effect of grade displacement alone on tutee performance.

Temporal Factors

The literature on tutoring apparently does not contain any studies comparing differing amounts of time spent in tutoring. Most investigators hold the implicit view that the longer the tutoring program, the more positive the effects will be. However, this assumption requires empirical support. It is quite conceivable that after a certain amount of time with the same partner, both the tutor and the tutee will become bored (as Melaragno suggests in his chapter in this book), and tutoring will have negative effects.

A related issue concerns the incremental nature of most tutoring that occurs in the school. Tutoring rarely is used as a replacement for classroom instruction but as a supplement or remedial program instead. Most studies have compared the effects of tutoring *plus* classroom instruction to classroom instruction alone (e.g., Ellson, Harris & Barber, 1968; Ronshausen, 1972), thus confounding tutoring with total amount of instructional time. Only one study has directly compared tutoring with classroom instruction, keeping total instructional time constant. In a well-controlled short-term study, Bausell, Moody, and Walzl (1972) found that individual tutoring of fourth and fifth graders by college-age education students resulted in significantly greater learning than group classroom instruction for an equal period of time. Thus, this one study indicates that one-to-one tutoring is of greater benefit than an equal amount of instructional time spent in a classroom situation. Unfortunately, Bausell, Moody, and Walzl did not observe the specific behaviors occurring during the tutoring interaction which might account for the superiority of tutoring over classroom instruction.

Number of Tutees Per Tutor

The vast majority of tutoring programs consist of one tutor paired with one tutee. It is reasonable to believe that tutors can be effective in teaching more than one tutee simultaneously, yet only one study has examined this issue directly. Shaver and Nuhn (1968, 1971) compared the relative effectiveness of one-to-one tutoring with a one-to-three situation. After 1 year of tutoring, tenth grade underachievers tutored in reading and writing by adults on a one-to-one basis were significantly better in reading (but not writing) than tenth graders tutored in groups of three. However, there was no difference in reading or writing for fourth and seventh grade tutees according to size of the tutoring group. Furthermore, though tutees were significantly superior to controls on tests given 2 years following the end of tutoring, the earlier difference found for the tenth graders in one-to-one versus one-to-three tutoring did not persist.

One study found college students to be effective when tutoring either an individual or a small group of fourth graders (Klosterman, 1970). Compared to a control group that did not receive tutoring, tutees gained significantly in reading comprehension and total reading achievement regardless of whether they were tutored singly or in a group. Although other studies have shown that tutoring in groups is beneficial to the tutee (e.g., Crispin, 1966), no other experiment has used directly size of tutee group as a variable.

Evidence is not available regarding the relative effects on the tutor of tutoring one versus many tutees. Although research is in progress examining the effects of tutoring an entire class in mathematics (Henkin, 1973), attitudinal and academic improvements of the tutor as a function of size of the tutee group have not been examined. One related possibility for experimental research is the use of multiple tutors for one tutee, a situation roughly analogous to team teaching methods. LeBoeuf (1968) has described (anecdotally) groups made up of two tutors who act as "resource persons" for second graders in science. Though rigorous data are not available concerning the usefulness of such a procedure, it seems to be a fruitful area for further research. An interesting dilemma may emerge as variations are made in the number of tutees taught by a tutor. It is possible that in terms of the tutee, a one-to-one ratio is best because of the special individualized attention that each tutee can receive from his tutor. On the other hand, for the tutor it may be optimal to teach larger numbers of tutees simultaneously since this more closely approximates the role of teacher. This is merely speculation, however; further research on this issue would be desirable.

Training of Tutors

When examining research on training of tutors, two different approaches appear in the literature. One line of research compares tutors trained to use a specific technique with tutors who are completely untrained. A second and smaller body of research examines the relative effectiveness of certain types of training. Unfortunately, results of most of this research are unconvincing and are open to serious questions regarding validity.

It is not particularly surprising to find that tutors trained in a specific method of tutoring use the behaviors specified by that method at a greater than chance level, and more than those who have not been trained. This has indeed been shown in a number of studies. Harrison and Cohen (1969) found that tutors trained in a structured tutoring technique were able to apply these behaviors in an actual tutoring situation. Since no control group was used, however, the data are merely descriptive. Niedermeyer (1970) also showed that the training of tutors resulted in their performing more of the recommended behaviors (praising, eliciting correct responses, etc.) than a comparison group of untrained tutors. At the time of the (covert) observation of the tutors, however, the untrained tutors had no previous tutoring experience, and the trained tutors had been tutoring their students for about 4 weeks. It seems reasonable that the results were due at least as much to the tutors' experience and familiarity with the student and situation as to their training. Furthermore, the trained tutors were volunteers, and the untrained tutors were selected by teachers. Data were not obtained to determine whether tutor training improved the younger students' learning or attitudes.

In a more practical test of the effects of training, Harrison (1969) examined the effects of trained and untrained elementary school tutors on the performance of first grade tutees. In three experiments tutees taught by tutors trained in using "structured tutoring" performed significantly better on an assessment test than tutees taught by untrained tutors. There are no data to indicate, however, that this particular type of training is superior to other types of training.

In a study in which trained tutors "modeled" appropriate mathematics skills and gave liberal praise to their low-achieving tutees, Horan, DeGirolomo, Hill, and Shute (1974) found an increase in teacher-assigned grades in mathematics for tutees compared to an untutored control group. Results were less convincing using an objective measure of mathematics achievement; it is unclear whether tutee improvement was due to tutor training or simply to being tutored, per se.

A detailed training program for tutors was devised by Ebersole (1971), who claims that it makes the "maximum use of the teaching potential of the best tutors" and is simple enough that "even the least proficient tutor can follow it with some degree of competence" (p. 11). Unfortunately, there are no experimental data to support his claims regarding the program; apparently, no comparisons have been made of tutors who have been trained and not trained in the method.

A few studies have compared directly the effects of training tutors in different methods of tutoring. The most careful and complete evaluation was conducted by Ellson and associates, who compared programmed tutoring with more conventional methods (Ellson, Harris, & Barber, 1968; Harris, 1968). In programmed tutoring, the tutor's behavior is controlled in a highly specific manner, analogous to computer programs. The programmed tutoring method was compared to what Ellson called "directed tutoring," in which the tutors' training emphasized a method more closely approximating the behavior of regular classroom teachers. After 1 year of being tutored by programmed techniques twice a day, first graders improved significantly in reading relative to a nontutored control group (Ellson, *et al.*, 1968). Unfortunately, the results were not entirely unequivocal: Tutees who received programmed tutoring just once a day were not statistically superior in reading to the control group. Directed tutoring was not effective.

Another study found that all tutored first grade subjects had significantly superior scores in reading compared to an untutored control group; in addition, programmed tutoring was significantly more effective than directed tutoring (Harris, 1971). No difference was found between one or two daily tutoring sessions. On the other hand, Ronshausen's (1972) data indicated that programmed tutoring given in addition to regular classroom instruction was not more effective than classroom instruction alone in increasing mathematics achievement. But directed tutoring plus classroom instruction did lead to an increase in computation skills—though not in understanding of mathematical concepts. Neither method alone was effective without additional classroom instruction.

Two different methods of tutoring were compared in one study (Frager & Stern, 1970). One method was equivalent to traditional tutoring (termed "directed" by Ellson); the other consisted of teaching tutors a five-part procedure of defining goals, defining obstacles, specifying alternatives, identifying consequences of specific alternatives, and making selections from alternatives. In this method, tutors were also taught certain basic principles of learning theory. Results showed that kindergarteners tutored by sixth graders had significantly higher achievement than untutored subjects. There was no difference between students taught by tutors trained in the two methods.

Taken together, available research does not indicate unequivocally that any one particular method of training is superior to any other. Indeed, there are surprisingly little data showing that training of tutors, per se, has a beneficial effect on tutoring. Clearly, what is needed is an experiment in which tutors trained in different methods, and also entirely untrained tutors, are used to teach tutees. Then the performance of the tutees who are taught using different methods can be compared with tutees who have not been tutored at all. Only when these groups are compared together in one experiment can confident statements be made regarding the appropriateness of different types of training.

Interaction during Tutoring

An issue related to the training of tutors is the nature of the interaction that occurs naturally between tutors and tutees who have not been trained. Only four studies have directly examined this issue. In his study of sibling tutoring relationships, Cicirelli (1972) observed whether tutors used an inductive or a deductive approach in teaching the concept of trapezoid. Females teaching their younger siblings used deductive teaching methods more than females teaching nonsiblings and males teaching siblings or nonsiblings. The greatest contrast occurred in opposite-sex dyads: older sisters tutoring younger brothers tended to use deductive methods, and older brothers teaching younger sisters used inductive methods more often.

A comparison was made in one study of the quality of the interaction occurring when sixth graders or college students acted as tutors to second graders (Thomas, 1972). Sixth grade tutors were more direct, and used "visual and kinesthetic modalities" more frequently than college-age tutors. The sixth graders' tutees, in turn, were more open in their expression of feelings. College tutors were more task oriented, and tended to push the tutees harder than the sixth grade tutors; their tutees were more verbal.

Additional data on teaching style comes from the study by Feshbach and Devor (1969). They found that middle-class white children used more positive reinforcement than lower-class black or white children, or middle-class black children. No significant difference was found in amount of negative reinforcement used, although there was a trend in the direction of lower-class children using greater negative reinforcements.

In a recent study, Garbarino (1974) found that the nature of the interaction between tutor and tutee varied according to whether or not the tutor anticipated a reward for his teaching. Tutors who did not expect an external reward (i.e., money) exhibited more positive emotional tone and were more effective teachers than tutors who expected to be paid. Results suggest that intrinsic motivation of tutors may be an important factor in determining the success of tutoring.

The available data regarding naturally occurring behavior in tutoring situations are very sparse, but provocative. This appears to be an extremely important area for future research. From the tenuousness of much of the data reported in tutoring studies, it is evident that there is still a great deal to be understood about the tutoring process. Given the present research literature, it is still not possible confidently to predict with precision what will make a tutoring program successful. It is thus quite important that investigators attempt to understand more about the interaction between tutor and tutee.

COMMENTS ON RESEARCH DESIGN

Problems of research methodology in the area of tutoring deserve special consideration. In this section we will examine some exemplary studies and some studies illustrating problems in design and methodology.

In addition to the prevalent practice of failing to collect rigorous data from tutoring programs, a frequently encountered flaw in research designs in this area—even in programs that do make an attempt at data gathering—is the absence of pertinent control groups (e.g., Hassinger & Via, 1969; Klein & Niedermeyer, 1971; Schoeller & Pearson, 1970). Although the difficulties of insisting on a control group in an ongoing school program are real, the practical value of having control groups is obvious. Without them, one cannot state with certainty that results were not due to some influence in the school other than the tutoring program. In order to make a definitive and objective conclusion, a control group is indispensible.

An area of concern related to control groups is the method of selecting tutors and tutees. The researcher must beware of comparing an experimental group of volunteers with a control group of nonvolunteers (Lucas, Gaither, & Montgomery, 1968). Unfortunately, for obvious practical reasons this is not an uncommon practice in tutoring research. For example, in one tutoring study (Weitzman, 1965) juniors and seniors in high school tutored 25 other high school students who volunteered for the program. The controls were matched with experimentals by sex, age, and scores on the aptitude test. Paradoxically, the participating volunteer students were rated by their teachers as having *less* motivation than students in the control group. On being asked at the conclusion of the program why they joined the program, 36% of the "volunteers" said they were asked by teachers or felt compelled to join. Results of the study showed that although tutored students did not show greater improvement on classroom examinations and quizzes than nontutored students, they did improve more than the controls in study habits, motivation and interest, and in homework and classroom exercises. These data may well be biased, since the pre- and post-ratings on which they are based were made by the students' teachers—who had helped develop the program and who were thus aware of the identity of tutees and of control students.

In contrast, a study that stands out as a model of well-controlled research is Klosterman's (1970) experiment. One of four schools in low socioeconomic districts was randomly selected as a control school from which children in two randomly selected fourth grade classrooms were designated the school control group. In the other three schools, fourth graders were assigned randomly to be tutored individually, tutored in a small group, or to be members of the classroom control group. This is the only study we located that included both classroom and school control groups. The school control group is particularly important since it is likely that the existence of a tutorial program in a school would affect control students in that school—especially if they are in a classroom that has tutors or tutees participating. This study found that tutoring did significantly increase scores on reading achievement. It is of methodological interest to note that results showed no difference between the classroom control and the school control conditions.

In his studies on the programmed tutoring technique, Ellson (1971) found interesting solutions to two practical problems in research design that commonly occur in evaluations of tutoring programs. To decrease teachers' objections to placing in control groups those students who need help, a stratified random sample of students was selected with a constant ratio of children in experimental to control groups (e.g., nine tutored children for each control). The problem of too much testing of the children was countered by limiting testing to a random selection from the experimental and control subjects. Both these procedures are possible, of course, only when a relatively large number of students are available. Ellson's results were generally positive, and the research is of excellent quality.

Two important variables are frequently uncontrolled in tutoring research: friendship between tutor and tutee, and total amount of instructional time. When tutoring is supplementary to classroom instruction (as it usually is), any obtained benefits may be attributable to the increased instruction time, rather than to the tutoring itself. One study that did take this factor into account used more able second and third grade students as tutors for their slower-learning classmates (Mollad, 1970). The control group (three classes in each of the two grades) spent 2½ hours weekly on word knowledge and 4 hours weekly on reading comprehension in their classrooms. The tutored experimental group (also three classes from each grade) spent half the specifically allotted time receiving class instruction and the other half being tutored. After 4 months, tutees in both grades made significantly greater gains than the controls in word knowledge (though not in reading comprehension). Tutors improved at least as much or more than tutees.

In order to evaluate the effectiveness of a tutoring program, it is clear that controls are needed for several obvious factors of the sort that we have mentioned above. One factor that has not been controlled in any study is the special attention and extensive personal contact that tutors and tutees (especially tutors) receive from adults and teachers in the course of the operation of the program. Many of the control factors that we mentioned as being important are perhaps integral components of tutoring programs as most are now constituted. Yet it is still important to try to disentangle the critical variables from the many unessential ones; in order to understand any change in behavior and achievement it is imperative to isolate the variables responsible. In the absence of appropriate control groups, one cannot say with confidence whether any effects can be attributed to the tutoring, per se, or to other factors that are merely associated with the program.

In attempting to design an applied study satisfying criteria of scientific rigor, the investigator often faces a moral dilemma: Using a control group may prevent some children who need help from obtaining the benefits of a useful program. In a relevant study cited earlier, Erickson and Cromack (1972) handled the problem through the use of a statistical technique devised by Campbell (1969) for cases when "randomization is not politically feasible or morally justifiable" (p. 419). In this study, 12 underachieving seventh grade boys tutored 12 underachieving third grade boys in reading. Tutors met with their tutees for 30 minutes 2 times a week over a period of 5 months. Tutor and tutee experimental groups differed significantly from their control groups (composed of classmates) on reading test scores before and after the tutoring project. Results revealed a significant improvement in reading for the tutees but not for the tutors.

Campbell's Regression Discontinuity Analysis indicated, however, that the tutors also improved significantly. The same analysis did not show a significant improvement for the tutees.

Much of the tutoring research that we have discussed can be criticized for inadequate statistical control and lack of rigorous research design; even so, substantive and theoretical issues are perhaps of even more fundamental importance. In this review we indicated several areas of research that have been neglected and that deserve further attention. It is most important, however, that empirical research rest upon a firm theoretical foundation. All too often hypotheses apparently have been formulated in an ad hoc fashion, with little regard for conceptualizing the problem in theoretical terms. Unless investigators in this area make a stronger attempt to draw more directly upon the mainstream of psychological and educational theory, it is likely that research on tutoring will be rather fragmented, inconclusive, and noncumulative. The wider use of systematic theory should lead to the formulation of research problems of greater sophistication and significance and thereby contribute directly toward the solution of the numerous practical problems encountered in devising tutoring programs for children.

REFERENCES

Allen, V. L., & Feldman, R. S. Learning through tutoring: Low-achieving children as tutors. *Journal of Experimental Education*, 1974, *42*, 1–5.

Balmer, J. Project tutor: Look! I can do something good. *Teaching Exceptional Children*, 1972, *4*, 166–175.

Bausell, R. B., Moody, W. B., & Walzl, F. N. A factorial study of tutoring versus classroom instruction. *American Educational Research Journal*, 1972, *9*, 592–597.

Bean, R., & Luke, C. As a teacher I've been learning. *Journal of Reading*, 1972, *16*, 128–132.

Bell, S. E., Garlock, N., & Colella, S. C. Students as tutors: High schoolers and elementary pupils. *Clearing House*, 1969, *44*, 242–244.

Brantley, B. C. Effects of a sibling tutorial program on the language and number concept development of Head Start Children. *Dissertation Abstracts International*, 1971, *32*, (1-A), 300.

Brown, J. C. Effects of token reinforcement administered by peer tutors on pupil reading achievement and tutor collateral behavior. *Dissertation Abstracts International*, 1972, *32*, (7-A), 3775.

Campbell, D. T. Reforms as experiments. *American Psychologist*, 1969, *24*, 409–429.

Cicirelli, V. G. The effect of sibling relationship on concept learning of young children taught by child-teachers. *Child Development*, 1972, *43*, 282–287.

Cloward, R. D. Studies in tutoring. *Journal of Experimental Education*, 1967, *36*, 14–25.

Coker, H. An investigation of the effects of a cross-age tutorial program on achievement and attitudes of 7th grade and 11th grade students. *Dissertation Abstracts International*, 1969, *29*, (10-A), 3319.

Costello, J., & Martin, J. One teacher—one child, learning together. *Elementary School Journal*, 1972, *73*, 72–78.

Criscuolo, N. P. Developing a junior assistants' corps in reading. *Education*, 1973, *93*, 301.

Crispin, D. B. Learning under two different conditions. *Teachers College Journal,* 1966, *38,* 95–97.

Ebersole, E. H. *Programed tutoring in reading.* Pasadena: Eberson Enterprises, 1971.

Edler, L. A. The use of students as tutors in after school study centers. *Dissertation Abstracts International,* 1967, *28,* (1-A), 74.

Ellson, D. G. The effect of programed tutoring in reading on assignment to special education classes: A follow-up of four years of tutoring in the first grade. Bloomington, Indiana: Indiana Univ., Psychology Department, July, 1971. (Mimeograph, 36 pp.)

Ellson, D. G., Barber, L., Engle, T. L., & Kampwerth, L. Programed tutoring: A teaching aid and a research tool. *Reading Research Quarterly,* 1965, *1,* 71–127.

Ellson, D. G., Harris, P. & Barber, L. A field test of programed and directed tutoring. *Reading Research Quarterly,* 1968, *3,* 307–367.

Erickson, M. R., & Cromack, T. Evaluating a tutoring program. *Journal of Experimental Education,* 1972, *41,* 27–31.

Feshbach, N., & Devor, G. Teaching styles in 4-year olds. *Child Development,* 1969, *40,* 183–190.

Foster, P. Attitudinal effects on 5th graders of tutoring younger children. *Dissertation Abstracts International,* 1972, *33,* (5-A), 2235.

Frager, S., & Stern, C. Learning by teaching. *The Reading Teacher,* 1970, *23,* 403–405, 417.

Freyberg, J. T. The effect of participation in an elementary school buddy system on the self concept, school attitudes and behaviors, and achievement of fifth-grade Negro children. *Graduate Research in Education and Related Disciplines,* 1967, *3,* 3–29.

Garbarino, J. The impact of anticipated reward upon cross-age tutoring. *Journal of Personality and Social Psychology,* 1975, *32,* 421–428.

Gartner, A., Kohler, M. C., & Riessman, F. *Children teach children: Learning by teaching.* New York: Harper, 1971.

Geiser, R. L. Some of our worst students teach! *Catholic School Journal,* June, 1969, 18–20.

Goodman, L. Tutoring for credit. *American Education,* 1971, *7,* 26–27.

Haggerty, M. The effects of being a tutor and being a counselee in a group on self-concept and achievement level of underachieving adolescent males. *Dissertation Abstracts International,* 1971, *31,* (9-A), 4460.

Hamblin, J. A., & Hamblin, R. L. On teaching disadvantaged preschoolers to read: A successful experiment. *American Educational Research Journal,* 1972, *9,* 209–216.

Harris, M. M. Learning by tutoring others. *Today's Education,* National Education Association, 1971, *60,* 48–49.

Harrison, G. V. The effects of trained and untrained student tutors on the criterion performance of disadvantaged first graders. Paper presented at annual meeting of the California Educational Research Association, Los Angeles, March, 1969.

Harrison, G. V., & Cohen, A. Empirical validation of tutor-training procedures. Unpublished manuscript, Brigham Young Univ. September, 1969.

Haskett, G. J. Modification of peer preferences of 1st grade children. *Developmental Psychology,* 1971, *4,* 429–433.

Hassinger, J., & Via, M. How much does a tutor learn through reading. *Journal of Secondary Education,* 1969, *44,* 42–44.

Henkin, L. Experimental investigation of peer teaching—research proposal. Unpublished manuscript. Univ. of California, Berkeley, March, 1973.

Holcomb, T. F. The effect of a tutorial-friend relationship on elementary school isolates. *Dissertation Abstracts International,* 1972, *32,* (8-A), 4420.

Horan, J. J., DeGirolomo, M. A., Hill, R. L., & Shute, R. E. The effect of older-peer participant models on deficient academic performance. *Psychology in the Schools,* 1974, *2,* 207–212.

Kelly, M. R. Pupil tutoring in reading of low-achieving second-grade pupils by low-achieving fourth-grade pupils. *Dissertation Abstracts International,* 1972, *32* (9-A) 4881.

Klentschy, M. P. An examination of sex-pairing effectiveness for reading tutoring. Paper presented at annual meeting of the California Educational Research Association, San Diego, November, 1971.

Klentschy, M. P. The effect of sixth-grade tutors on the word attack attainment of second graders. Paper presented at annual meeting of the California Educational Research Association, San Jose, California, November, 1972.

Klein, S. P., & Niedermeyer, F. C. Direction sports: A tutorial program for elementary school pupils. *Elementary School Journal,* 1971, *72,* 53–61.

Klosterman, R. The effectiveness of a diagnostically structured reading program. *The Reading Teacher,* 1970, *24,* 159–162.

Lakin, D. S. Cross-age tutoring with Mexican-American pupils. *Dissertation Abstracts International,* 1972, *32* (7-A), 3561.

Lamel, P. A preliminary study of tutorial procedures in the elementary school. Madison: Wisconsin Research and Development Center for Cognitive Learning, Working Paper No. 39, July, 1970.

Landrum, J. W., & Martin, M. D. When students teach others. *Educational Leadership,* 1970, *27,* 446–448.

Lane, P., Pollack, C., & Sher, N. Remotivation of disruptive adolescents. *Journal of Reading,* 1972, *15,* 351–354.

LeBoeuf, F. Qui docet discit–he who teaches, learns. *Science Teacher,* 1968, *35,* 53–56.

Liette, E. E. Tutoring: Its effects on reading achievement, standard setting and affect in mediating self-evaluation for black male under-achievers in reading. *Dissertation Abstracts International,* 1972, *32* (8-A), 4244.

Linton, T., Jr. The effects of grade displacement between student tutors and students tutored. *Dissertation Abstracts International,* 1973, *33* (8-A), 4091.

Lucas, J. A., Gaither, G. H., & Montgomery, J. R. Evaluating a tutorial program containing volunteer subjects. *Journal of Experimental Education,* 1968, *36,* 78–81.

Marascuilo, L., Levin, J., & James, H. Evaluation report for the Berkeley Unified School District's remedial reading program sponsored under SB28. Berkeley, California, September 15, 1969.

McMonagle, L. An investigation of attitude change in college tutors toward black children as a function of required tutoring. *Dissertation Abstracts International,* 1972, *33* (4-A), 1521.

Mohan, M. Peer tutoring as a technique for teaching the unmotivated, a research report. Teacher Education Research Center, State University College, Fredonia, New York, March, 1972.

Mollad, R. W. Pupil-tutoring as part of reading instruction in the elementary grades. *Dissertation Abstracts International,* 1970, *31* (4-B), 2260.

Morgan, R. F., & Toy, T. B. Learning by teaching: A student-to-student compensatory tutoring program in a rural school system and its relevance to the educational cooperative. *Psychological Record,* 1970, *20,* 159–169.

Moskowitz, H. Boredom? No more! 7th graders try teaching. *Science and Children,* 1972, *10,* 14–15.

National Commission on Resources for Youth, Inc. An evaluation of the Youth Tutoring Youth model for In-School Neighborhood Youth Corps, New York, December, 1972.

Nichols, W. A study of the effects of tutoring on the self-concept, reading achievement and selected attitudes of culturally disadvantaged children. *Dissertation Abstracts International*, 1969, *29* (9-A), 2898.

Niedermeyer, F. C. Effects of training on the instructional behaviors of student tutors. *The Journal of Educational Research*, 1970, *64*, 119–123.

Office of Education. Pint-size tutors learn by teaching. *American Education*, 1967, *3*, 20, 29.

Pfiel, M. P. Everybody's somebody. *American Education*, 1969, *5*, 21–24.

Rime, L., & Ham, J. Sixth-grade tutors. *Instructor*, 1968, *77*, 104.

Robertson, D. J. The effects of inter-grade tutoring experience on tutor attitudes and reading achievement. *Dissertation Abstracts International*, 1971, 32 (6A), 3010.

Robertson, D. J. Intergrade teaching: Children learn from children. In S. L. Sebesta, & C. J. Wallen (Eds.), *The first R: Readings on teaching reading.* Chicago: Scientific Research Association, 1972.

Rogers, M. S. A study of an experimental tutorial reading program in which sixth-grade underachievers tutored third-grade children who were experiencing difficulty in reading. *Dissertation Abstracts International*, 1970, *30* (11-A), 4695.

Ronshausen, N. L. A comparison of the effects on achievement and attitude of two methods of tutoring first grade math in the inner city: Programed vs. directed. *Dissertation Abstracts International*, 1972, *32* (8-A), 4494.

Rust, S. P., Jr. The effect of tutoring on the tutor's behavior, academic achievement, and social status. *Dissertation Abstracts International*, 1970, *30* (11-A), 4862.

Schoeller, A., & Pearson, D. A. Better reading through volunteer reading tutors. *The Reading Teacher*, 1970, *23*, 625–636.

Shaver, J. P., & Nuhn, D. Underachievers in reading and writing respond to a tutoring program. *Clearing House*, 1968, *43*, 236–239.

Shaver, J. P., & Nuhn, D. The effectiveness of tutoring underachievers in reading and writing. *Journal of Educational Research*, 1971, *65*, 107–112.

Snapp, M., Oakland, T., & Williams, F. C. A study of individualizing instruction by using elementary school children as tutors. *Journal of School Psychology*, 1972, *10*, 1–8.

Swett, M. This year I got my buddy to laugh. *Childhood Education*, 1971, *48*, 17–20.

Thelen, H. Tutoring by students. *School Review*, 1969, *77*, 229–244.

Thomas, J. L. Are elementary tutors as effective as older tutors in promoting reading gains? *Dissertation Abstracts International*, 1972, *32* (7-A), 3580.

Wagner, P. Analysis of a retarded-tutoring-retarded program for institutionalized residents. *Dissertation Abstracts International*, 1973, *34* (5-A), 2426.

Weitzman, D. L. Effect of tutoring on performance and motivation ratings in secondary school students. *California Journal of Educational Research*, 1965, *16*, 108–115.

Wilkes, R. Peer and cross-age tutoring and related topics: An annotated bibliography. Theoretical Paper No. 53, Wisconsin Research and Development Center for Cognitive Learning, Madison, Wisconsin, 1975.

Williams, D., Kabota, G., Klentschy, M., & Michaud, R. The effect of a summer school tutorial project on the sight word attainment of inner city first graders. Paper presented at the annual meeting of the California Educational Research Association, San Jose, California, November, 1972.

Witte, P. H. The effects of group reward structure on interracial acceptance, peer tutoring and academic performance. *Dissertation Abstracts International*, 1972, *32* (9-A), 5367.

Yamamoto, J. Y., & Klentschy, M. An examination of intergrade tutoring experience on attitudinal development of inner city children. Paper presented at the annual meeting of the California Educational Research Association, San Jose, California, November, 1972.

16

Implementing Tutoring Programs: Some Alternatives for Practitioners and Researchers

Linda Devin-Sheehan   Vernon L. Allen
University of Wisconsin   University of Wisconsin

This chapter describes some of the practical alternatives available for implementing tutorial programs in the elementary or middle school and discusses the special problems of designing and conducting field research in a school setting. Ideas and suggestions offered in this chapter were derived primarily from our experience in implementing both long- and short-term tutorial programs in schools. Reviewing the literature on more than 200 tutoring programs and acting as consultants for other tutorial programs provided additional background information.

We have no intention in this chapter of attempting to provide a definitive "how-to-do-it" manual; instead, the advantages and disadvantages of various possibilities will be discussed in the light of available data and our own experience. The unique set of objectives, participants, and facilities will, of course, determine the alternatives most appropriate for a particular school.[1] Since many of our own projects were designed for the dual purpose of obtaining research

---

[1] Readers interested in materials available for specific tutoring programs should consult the section following the references of this chapter. We are grateful to Ms. Roberta Wilkes for compiling a comprehensive bibliography of the literature on tutoring (Wilkes, 1975).

data and establishing a practical in-school tutoring program, in a later section particular attention will be given to problems confronting the investigator working on the topic of tutoring.

IMPLEMENTING A TUTORING PROGRAM

Several aspects of implementing a tutoring program in the school are covered in this section. The options presented are not intended to be exhaustive; new variations and combinations of alternatives are created with each new tutoring program.

It may be useful at the outset to make explicit the two basic approaches that frequently characterize tutoring programs—structured and nonstructured. A structured program tends to have precise goals, systematic selection of participants, specific tutoring materials and techniques, and regular evaluation of the younger students' progress. Programs emphasizing academic improvement for the younger students are often highly structured. In contrast, programs particularly concerned with helping the tutor and with social or motivational development of tutors or tutees tend to be less rigidly controlled; these also allow the tutor (and even the tutee) to participate to a greater extent in lesson planning and other decision making.

The Program Coordinator

The person directing a school tutoring program may be a member of the regular school staff (e.g., a teacher, reading consultant or counselor) or a person brought into the school specifically to coordinate the program (e.g., professional tutoring consultant, paraprofessional, member of a social agency, or researcher).

The most obvious advantage of the program coordinator's being a permanent member of the staff is his familiarity with the school. Knowing the teachers who will be involved can greatly facilitate implementing a new program. The regular staff member is also "on the spot," and is therefore quickly aware of such problems as changes in schedule or rumors and grievances. In addition, a teacher or reading consultant is likely to be familiar with materials and to have experience in administering tests. Finally, there is the clear advantage of not being an "outsider" in the eyes of the rest of the school staff. (A coordinator who is unfamiliar with a school can compensate somewhat for being an "outsider" by finding someone on the school staff to act as an assistant and liaison person.)

A paraprofessional serving as tutoring coordinator preferably should be a resident from the neighborhood and have a socioeconomic background similar to that of the students. The Youth Tutoring Youth program (National Commission on Research for Youth, Inc., 1969), which used disadvantaged youths as tutors in an after-school program, frequently had paraprofessionals as program supervisors. These coordinators communicated easily with the tutors and appreciated their strengths and problems. The neighborhood paraprofessional also can be a good liaison person with parents and community.

A tutoring coordinator who is not a school staff member has the advantage of bringing relevant knowledge and expertise, which could prevent the use of inefficient and impractical procedures that frequently accompany a new program and thereby improve staff morale. In some cases, the outside coordinator can furnish tutoring materials, personnel, and technical support.

A researcher as coordinator has several advantages that are often overlooked. A successful program that has been systematically and carefully evaluated not only helps the participating students, but also contributes to the small body of research data on tutoring. Furthermore, a person with a background in research methodology can determine whether changes can be made as a program progresses without destroying the usefulness of the data being collected. In many cases a research consultant who is available to the school staff is used too infrequently or too late. Carefully collected data will be useless if tutors change tutees, become library assistants as well as tutors, or drop out of the tutoring program temporarily. A coordinator without training in research may not realize that such factors would have an important effect on the data collection. A further advantage of having a researcher as program coordinator is his awareness of the flexibility in the design of a program, which is often greater than a layman realizes. Availability of a researcher to make decisions as the need arises can be critical to the operation and evaluation of a program.

Program Objectives

A tutoring program may be designed to benefit the tutor, the tutee, or both. The benefits that students are expected to obtain must be specified during the early planning stages. A program emphasizing the improvement of fifth graders' self-confidence would no doubt be organized differently from one directed towards teaching sight words to first grade students.

Programs with the goal of helping the tutor can emphasize several outcomes. Tutoring often is used as a means of providing needed review for older students, and in this way basic skills can be learned or relearned without stigma. Other possible benefits for the tutor are positive changes in self-esteem and self-confidence, and better attitudes toward school, teachers, and other children. Tutoring also can be used to help would-be truants or dropouts to stay in school. Some programs, such as the Homework Helper Program in New York City (Neckritz & Forlano, 1970), are designed to accomplish some of these goals and in addition to provide financial assistance to disadvantaged youngsters by paying tutors and to give career orientation to students who otherwise might not consider teaching as a potential vocation.

Other tutoring programs are designed primarily to help the younger student (tutee). In these programs emphasis is usually placed on academic improvement of the younger student; in addition, however, the tutee's self-esteem may improve when he starts experiencing success in learning. A positive relationship with an older child or peer also can improve social confidence and lead to better attitudes toward other children, teachers, and academic subjects. Shy children who are afraid to speak up in class are popular choices for the one-to-one relationship offered by tutoring programs. Programs concentrating on helping the tutee have the advantage of being able to use as tutors students who are bright, high achieving, and outgoing. The tutoring coordinator and staff then can concentrate their efforts on problems of the tutees.

Finally, some programs are designed to benefit both tutor and tutee. In addition to the potential advantages for the students discussed above, tutoring also can be used to promote a sense of concern and cooperation among students. Some programs designed to help both tutors and tutees have additional goals such as improving cross-race relations, matching tutees with tutors who have similar problems (e.g., stutterers or delinquents), or providing academic help to tutors and tutees who have trouble relating to authority figures. Programs concerned with helping both the tutor and tutee may be twice as efficient in terms of the number of students receiving benefits, but also can be twice as difficult to supervise.

Selection of Participants

To a large extent program objectives determine which students are selected to participate in a tutoring program. If the goal of the program is academic motivation, then underachieving students are likely to be selected; if it is social skills, introverted or aggressive students may be selected. Equally important is whether the program emphasizes helping the tutor, tutee, or both. As discussed earlier, if the program is designed primarily to benefit tutees, tutors can be selected who are high achievers and who can relate well to others. When the tutors have their own academic or social problems, the project staff will be required to devote additional time and attention to them.

In selecting participants, most schools have used essentially three different grouping systems: An entire class acts as tutors for another class; half of one class tutors the other half; or a limited number of students tutors another group of students (the most common procedure). It may be advisable to use fairly competent students as tutors, at least at the outset, in order to avoid the additional demands created by using problem students. For similar reasons, some schools prefer using paid or volunteer adult paraprofessionals as tutors. Even then a certain amount of orientation and training for the tutors probably will be essential.

In selecting tutors, one possibility is to choose competent students who are easy to train, but who still can benefit in terms of self-confidence or ability to relate to other students. Another possibility is to follow the Lippitt, Eiseman, and Lippitt (1969) recommendation of having high-, marginal-, and low-achieving students as tutors. These authors argue that high-achieving students improve the prestige of the program and allow academically disparate students of the same age the opportunity to participate in an academic activity together. If tutors need help in several areas, it may be wise to start with a small number of participants and then add tutors and tutees after the program is successfully underway. It is easier to add than to drop; tutors or tutees who have to leave a program may experience this as being only one more in a series of failures.

Whether a one-to-one tutoring ratio is preferable to a one-to-two, one-to-three, or one-to-five is an unresolved issue, as was noted in Chapter 15. When a tutor has more than one tutee at a time, there are some benefits from the tutees' being similar in ability and achievement. This arrangement simplifies the tutor's task and avoids unfavorable comparisons among the younger students; it does not, of course, prevent the tutees from competing with one another. In group tutoring, students can work with academic materials designed for small group situations.

Pairing the Tutor and Tutee

Procedures for pairing tutors with tutees have elicited many opinions, but available data do not provide clear answers. In the tutoring literature one often encounters advice to maintain at least 2 or 3 years age difference between tutor and tutee; however, just as frequently purportedly successful programs have used same-age tutoring pairs or tutors who are 7 or 8 years older than their tutees. In determining the most satisfactory age combination, program objectives and achievement level of tutors and tutees must be taken into account. Certainly one wants to ensure that the tutor is (and will remain) more competent than his student in the subject being taught. On the other hand, it also has been argued (though without empirical support) that a large age difference decreases the possibility that the tutor will gain academically as a result of tutoring.

Whether to have same-sex or cross-sex pairs is a further consideration in pairing tutors with tutees. Again there is no evidence that one arrangement is more effective than the other for academic improvement, although students do tend to have a preference for same-sex pairs (Foster, 1972). (Same-sex pairs would be used, of course, if providing appropriate sex-role models for younger students were one of the program goals.) Same-sex tutors are perhaps more adept at finding books, themes, and academic projects that appeal to their younger student's interests, but we have seen several exceptions.

In matching tutors with tutees, several factors frequently are taken into account, such as: sex, race (some programs deliberately use cross-race pairs and others do the opposite), intelligence, achievement level, socioeconomic background, and personality or behavioral variables. Since there are no clear guidelines from research, matching procedures must be based on the tutoring coordinator's best judgment and the requirements of the school.

After tutors and tutees have been selected, several procedures exist for specifying the assignment of tutors with tutees. Tutors may be paired randomly with tutees—with or without restrictions on other variables such as achievement level or sex, or teachers may do the pairing using their best judgment. Alternatively, tutors can be given the option of selecting their tutees, or tutees can select their tutors. Obviously one must avoid situations that could create ill feelings among the students, which is an argument against students' choosing their partners.

Finally, the possibility of changing the pairs must be considered. When a tutor or tutee is unhappy with the student assigned to him (or with the program), how can a change be effected? The judgment of the tutoring coordinator or the tutoring staff is probably the best means for dealing with this question. Feelings of rejection or failure on the part of the students should be avoided, however. At Pacoima Tutorial Community Project (discussed in Chapter 12) most students in the school are involved in tutoring, but instead of actually tutoring students may choose to perform tasks related to tutoring (e.g., supervising independent work, posting schedules or making materials).

Scheduling

Scheduling is usually the most difficult practical problem in implementing a tutoring program. Where and when should the tutoring take place? An important consideration in selecting a suitable area for tutoring is to find a place where the students can work together relatively undisturbed. We have had tutorial pairs working in school corridors, the school cafeteria, gymnasium locker rooms, the library (and storage room), and in the offices of the guidance counselor and speech therapist. Some schools hold tutoring sessions in classrooms of the tutors or tutees. Cross-age tutoring programs also are conducted in the summer and after school in classrooms, neighborhood centers, or in tutees' homes.

We have found that students are very flexible about their working area; tutors are content to teach in conditions that many adult teachers would consider inappropriate. There are advantages and disadvantages to the several possible tutoring locations. For example, having pairs sit at tables or on the floor in an out-of-the-way place creates an atmosphere of casualness and easy exchange, which can foster a warm relationship and spontaneity between tutor and tutee. Locations for informal tutoring sessions are usually easy to find.

Some teachers prefer that the tutoring sessions be more formal. A tutor may identify better with the role of teacher when in a situation similar to the teacher's—when there are chairs, desks, and blackboards associated with classroom instruction. Tutoring in the tutee's classroom provides such an environment, simplifies the supervision, and provides information and control if needed by the tutor. Furthermore, the tutees' classroom teacher may want to keep in close touch with the progress of the younger students. This arrangement has the additional advantage of providing a tutoring area and reduces the milling around that occurs when tutors and tutees must rendezvous somewhere other than the classroom. But the presence of the "other" (classroom) teacher can reduce the tutor's sense of responsibility, and the noise from tutoring is potentially distracting to other students in the classroom.

When one entire older class acts as tutors for another entire younger class, half the primary class can go to the room of the higher-grade class to be tutored, while half the higher-grade class goes to the primary class to tutor. Ebersole (1971) cites as disadvantages of this arrangement the primary teacher's loss of contact with the needs of students being tutored in the higher class and the lack of relevant materials for younger children in the higher classroom.

There are advantages of tutoring in the classroom beyond ease of supervision and appropriateness of setting. The success of intragrade programs, in which the more proficient half of a class tutors the other half, indicates that students can work effectively in that situation. For older students who receive credit for tutoring, sessions can be scheduled in the room where their class is held. If the room is large and the number of students small, this also can be a very satisfactory arrangement. When junior or senior high school students are tutors for elementary school tutees, bussing either the tutors or tutees is sometimes necessary.

In fairly nonstructured programs we have found only two areas to be unsatisfactory for tutoring: outside the building and in the school corridor. When working outside the children were not able to concentrate, papers and pages fluttered uncontrollably in the breeze, clothes became soiled, tutoring materials were unwieldy, and children who were not in the tutoring program became jealous. In one school program we successfully assigned tutoring stations in hallways, but in a second school the corridor proved to be too busy. Children were constantly going to and from the restrooms and entire classes of children moved from room to room, which was overwhelmingly distracting. Individual children invariably stopped to chat and to investigate the activities of the tutoring pair.

One more question must be raised about tutoring stations outside the classroom: How many pairs can be assigned to a room? Critical factors are size of the room, amount of supervision available, possibility for using partitions, and behavior of the children. We have had as many as 12 pairs working well in large rooms such as a library or cafeteria; in small rooms, up to 3 pairs have been able to work seriously. Given the choice, tutors usually prefer having some form of partition, which helps them hold the tutees' attention. Movable partitions permit tutors both to work individually with their tutees and to participate in small group tutoring projects such as reading plays and playing academic board games. The major factors that determine the location of tutoring are the available facilities and the amount of supervision necessary.

Scheduling the time for tutoring is often determined by teachers of the tutors and tutees. Usually, the teachers can work out a mutually satisfactory time during classtime for the tutoring. Tutoring also can be scheduled at lunch time, at recess, or after school; but one must be sensitive to the possibility that students may feel tutoring deprives them of their playtime. Despite these problems, non-classtime periods are used satisfactorily by many tutoring programs.

In addition to time of day, the frequency and duration of tutoring must be decided: How many meetings should there be each week, how long should the meetings last, and how many weeks should the entire program last? Typically, tutoring programs are scheduled throughout most of the school year; the tutoring sessions last 20 to 30 minutes for 3 meetings a week, and on 1 or 2 additional days each week tutors plan their lessons. Since research findings do not indicate an optimal frequency or duration for tutoring sessions, scheduling can be left to the dictates of the existing school schedule. Two factors to keep in mind when scheduling tutoring sessions are the limited attention span of primary school youngsters and the time required by tutors to arrange their materials before the lessons and put them away afterwards. A popular schedule is to plan tutoring sessions that allot the tutors 30 minutes, with only 15 to 20 minutes devoted to the tutees.

Training and Materials

Many options exist for training the tutors: As noted in Chapter 15, research does not indicate that one form of training is preferable to another. Three different approaches are used in training tutors: (*1*) little or no training, with simply an orientation meeting for explaining teaching procedures and distributing materials; (*2*) extensive training at the outset of the program before meeting the tutees; and (*3*) training at the outset of a program with meetings for tutors scheduled regularly throughout the duration of the program. Content of the training, depending upon the goals of the program, can stress either teaching techniques or ways of relating positively to younger students. If a tutoring period is scheduled for the tutors each day of the week, lesson planning can take place on a Monday, followed by three days of tutoring and a discussion session on a Friday. Another possibility is to have 45 minutes a day for tutoring, the first part of which is spent working with the tutee and the second part preparing lessons for the next day.

Persons responsible for training tutors vary from program to program; the expertise required will depend upon the goals of the program and the materials being used. In one program (Pollack, Sher, & Teitel, 1969) the tutors themselves trained the incoming group of tutors. In other programs members of a tutorial staff or teachers are responsible for training. The tutees' teachers may prefer that the materials be the same as classroom materials, supplementary to them, or unrelated to them. Whatever the source, providing the necessary materials is easier when the program has a small number of students, the tutees are at a similar achievement level, and only one subject is tutored rather than several. (Tutoring manuals and packaged tutoring kits, some even including daily lesson plans and work sheets, are available from the sources listed at the end of this chapter.)

Teachers, Parents, and the Community

The coordinator of a tutoring program is likely to encounter a certain amount of reluctance or resistance from teachers and parents and sometimes even from the larger community. Some objections to the program can be avoided by having an orientation program or holding workshops.

Typical of the objections expressed by teachers is the fear that slow learners selected for the program will be stigmatized. Including students of varying abilities or having a control group are two ways of ensuring that no stigma is attached to the program. When high-achieving students are used as tutors, teachers sometimes raise the objection that tutoring is just one more sign of favor and privilege accorded to them. The practical considerations described earlier for using high achievers may be sufficient to convince these critics. On the other hand, other teachers object to having poor students as tutors; they think these students would benefit more from being in the classroom and do not believe they can be helpful to anyone else. In general, it is probably a good practice to avoid having the tutor or tutee out of his classroom when subjects are scheduled in which he is particularly weak. Some teachers appoint for each tutor a "buddy" responsible for keeping him informed about whatever he misses while tutoring.

Parents are likely to have concerns related to the basis of their child's being selected or not selected for the program. This can be avoided if parents of participating students are informed in advance about the program and its rationale. It can usually be made clear to parents that a tutor is not "doing the teacher's work for him," and that a child can learn from another student. The student's classroom teacher can explain best why the child is not included in the particular program, and describe what other projects he is participating in.

Perhaps the most common objection heard after a tutoring program actually gets underway is that someone was not informed about it, or that some aspect of it was not made clear. To avoid unfortunate misunderstanding, letters should be sent to parents of participating children, and orientation meetings held with teachers having students in the program. Teachers can be given a copy of a detailed overview of the program, including the rationale, evaluation procedures, list of participants, schedules, and meeting places. As the project develops, the teachers also can be given written follow-up information.

Teacher involvement is a very sensitive issue; individual teachers vary in their preference for degree of involvement. The coordinator should have regular contact with the teachers, of course, but there is a point at which a teacher no longer has the time or inclination to confer.

Tutoring programs vary in degree of community involvement. Most programs have a minimal amount of community participation, but a few emphasize it. Sometimes community members are responsible for recruiting tutors or tutees and become members of the tutoring project staff. The community also can provide learning resources, funding, personnel, and political support. Even when the community does not have a major role in the tutoring program, it is worthwhile to maintain good public relations. It is sometimes useful to place an article in the local paper informing the community about the new tutoring program.

IMPLEMENTING FIELD RESEARCH

As has been made clear in this chapter (and throughout this book) a great deal of additional research on tutoring remains to be accomplished. Questions concerning such basic issues as selection and matching of tutors and tutees, training tutors, and length and frequency of tutoring sessions, among others, require further investigation before guidelines can be established for ensuring optimal results from tutoring programs. Little is known at this time about the underlying psychological mechanisms that contribute to the cognitive and social-personal outcomes of tutoring. In this section a few practical comments will be offered about the evaluation of tutoring programs, followed by a brief discussion concerned with more complex experimental research and the relation between practice, research, and theory.

Evaluating a Program

It is important for the continuity and improvement of a good program that the coordinator be cognizant of its strengths and weaknesses; hence, there is a need for evaluation. Are the tutees and tutors learning? If various materials are used, are some better than others? What is the effect of the program on children's attitudes about school, teachers, academic work, and other children? Does the program positively influence attendance, motivation, responsibility, and self-confidence? Answers to some of these questions are fairly readily obtainable; the answers to others are much more elusive. Although anecdotal material may be interesting and entertaining, empirical data will provide the more convincing answers. Furthermore, one's expectations often will influence perceptions; in many cases only an objective measure can describe accurately changes that have taken place.

Procedures for conducting a program evaluation deserve careful consideration. It is important to establish a control group of students who are as similar as possible to those in the program in terms of ability, achievement, motivation, or other attributes. If information is gathered from both tutors and tutees, control subjects for both groups will be necessary. In some cases it may be desirable to postpone assigning students to control groups until after the conclusion of the program. As Ellson, Harris, and Barber (1968) point out, post-matching permits tutoring to begin early in the school year before test scores are available and minimizes the loss of control subjects due to the typical mobility of inner-city students.

Sometimes it is not practical to use control groups—for example, when there is a limited number of students who need help and all of them must receive tutoring. Campbell (1969) has described a technique called the regression discontinuity design that permits objective measurement of change without necessitating the use of control groups or a large number of students. This approach is especially recommended for evaluation of compensatory programs. Several other interesting quasi-experimental designs for use in field research are suggested in Campbell and Stanley's (1963) stimulating discussion and in a recent volume by Caporaso and Roos (1973).

When evaluating a tutoring program, administering tests or questionnaires can occur at a number of points: before the program begins, at the midpoint or other predetermined interval, and at the completion of the program. If a control group is used it may be sufficient to limit testing to one session at the end of the program. If the pattern of change is of interest, repeated testing will be necessary—for example, if one wants to know at what point the greatest reading improvement occurred.

Often the most important data are measures of the tutees' achievement. Obtaining measures of the tutees' progress at regular intervals is quite practical, since providing feedback to the program coordinator will ensure that lesson plans remain relevant and helpful. Results about the tutee's progress can provide positive reinforcement for the tutor, and makes the tutee realize that he is learning and making progress. Systematically assessing the tutee's progress safeguards the tutee against practicing material already mastered. The tutor may be able to decide when his student has reached an appropriate assessment checkpoint, or this may be determined by the tutee's teacher or a member of the tutoring project. The tutoring situation lends itself particularly well to such recurrent appraisal. Many classroom teachers would like to use this approach but do not have the time to test individual students regularly or the means to adapt lesson plans to match individual needs.

Evaluation procedures vary depending on the information desired. In addition to information from tutors, tutees, and their peers, it may be worthwhile to obtain reactions to the program from teachers, parents, and members of the tutoring project team. Among the various means of acquiring information are standardized tests, questionnaires, taped interviews, daily individual tutor logs, a project diary, and tape recording of training sessions. Finding good evaluation measures is a difficult task. There is a serious lack of reliable and valid instruments (particularly for the elementary and middle school level) measuring changes in self-concept, motivation, analytic thinking, learning sets, and attitudes. The reliability and validity of impressionistic measures are usually unsatisfactory, and they should be avoided whenever possible.

Who should be tested, for what, with which measures, and how frequently, will be determined in large part by the program objectives and amount of cooperation that realistically can be expected. Unless scheduled with care and consideration, testing can be disruptive to classrooms and time consuming for teachers. In some schools students already are being regularly tested and even overtested. Furthermore, it is potentially threatening to teachers for their students to fill out questionnaires and tests for someone else. From having often seen how inadequately tests measure a given child's ability or achievement, many teachers are justifiably skeptical of tests in general. These problems can be alleviated somewhat if teachers are involved in helping making decisions concerning the testing. The use of criterion-referenced tests (measuring precisely the skills being taught) will also overcome some of the objections to testing. Criterion-referenced tests—in contrast to norm-referenced tests—require the students to meet a specific criterion (e.g., 80% of the items correct), thus indicating mastery of particular objectives. Criterion-referenced tests are short and can be given at frequent intervals.

The testing climate varies with each school and each program. Cooperation can be encouraged by the following: providing adequate supervision when children are filling out the forms; minimizing the number of "open-ended" questions and emphasizing multiple choice, short-answer questions or check lists; avoiding test sessions at busy times of the school year (e.g., at the beginning and end of school term); and keeping teachers and parents informed of test results or student progress as soon as relevant information is available. These suggestions will not meet all objections, but used in combination with some common sense and sensitivity, they may help.

Theory and Research

Although information from an evaluation study can answer some important questions, it still has only limited usefulness. A tutoring program consists of a complex set of interrelated factors; it is not a single unitary variable. Therefore, a global evaluation of a program does not provide information about cause and effect—that is, about the process variables responsible for specific outcomes. A more refined study by means of experimental research of a more analytic nature is necessary to answer questions about the important causal factors in the program. From this point of view, evaluation research is seen to be only an important first step in a series of ever more precise analyses. After an initial evaluation of a program, subsequent research should be "subtractive," to use McClelland's (1965) term. By removing one factor at a time from the global cluster which makes up the program and observing subsequent results, the essential or necessary elements can be distinguished from the nonessential and redundant ones.

Moving beyond evaluation research entails the comparison of several levels of a variable or several factors involved in a program. Hence, the single control group design becomes less important and less meaningful when the purpose of the research is to determine the relative effect of factors across several experimental conditions. Needless to say, to conduct such experimental research in the field setting is not easy to accomplish methodologically. For in addition to the numerous practical difficulties of the sort mentioned earlier in this chapter, the familiar problems common to all experimental research become even more acute (e.g., internal and external validity and control of extraneous factors). The longer the duration of a field research project, the greater the possibility for problems to arise such as confounding across conditions or unforeseen influences, with the resulting possibility of severe attenuation or accentuation of the final data. It is impossible to discuss these and many other important methodological issues here; the interested reader will find relevant material in several sources (e.g., Campbell & Stanley, 1963; O'Toole, 1971; Riecken & Boruch, 1974). Clearly to disentangle complex causal factors, it is sometimes necessary to conduct a short-term experiment under well-controlled laboratory conditions.

Research directed toward attaining a better understanding of the relative importance of the numerous constituents of a tutoring program is in essence a search for the common or basic processes that underlie the diverse surface components. To conceptualize a tutoring program in this more general way requires an explicit statement of the assumed explanatory constructs and their interrelations, that is to say, a theory. Relevant theory can help guide empirical research by suggesting specific hypotheses to be tested in the school setting. In addition, implications for practice are always forthcoming from a more abstract conceptualization of a phenomenon; or in the well-known words of Kurt Lewin, "Nothing is so practical as a good theory." The opposite side of this statement is also true: Knowledge gained from practical programs can contribute substantially toward the development of good theory. In short, theory and practice should be viewed as being reciprocally related and as being mutually beneficial one to the other.

An optimal integration of theory, research, and practice can be realized in the context of conducting field research in the school setting. In tutoring programs that are ongoing operations, it would be a great loss not to take the additional trouble of ensuring the collection of useful data. By establishing several separate experimental conditions that differ along some relevant dimension, simple hypotheses can be tested easily in the context of an ongoing program. Resulting data then can be used to modify the program in a self-correcting way during the next cycle; this sequence can be repeated in a continuing process of practice-oriented research. In this arrangement research becomes an integral part of the tutoring program itself. Research conducted in this manner is no longer conceived of as a "before–after" design; rather, it is more correctly called, in Suchman's (1971) words, a "during-during-during" design.

Naturally, there are many important differences in the interests and goals of the practitioner and the researcher. Even so, cooperation between the roles of practitioner and researcher is eminently feasible, and each has a great deal to offer to the other. If the researcher–theorist can interest himself in applied problems connected with a concrete program and the practitioner can interest himself in basic psychological processes that underlie the program, then perhaps the happy consequence will be both a better understanding of tutoring in general on the one hand and the development of a better program on the other—a program that maximizes benefits to both the tutor and the tutee. In the final analysis, the ultimate result of helping children in the school is without doubt the criterion of a successful tutoring program that can be accepted by all of us—researchers and practitioners alike.

REFERENCES

Campbell, D. T. Reforms as experiments. *American Psychologist,* 1969, *24,* 409–429.

Campbell, D. T., & Stanley, J. C. *Experimental and quasi-experimental designs for research.* Chicago: Rand McNally, 1963.

Caporaso, J. A., & Roos, L. L., Jr. *Quasi-experimental approaches.* Evanston, Illinois: Northwestern Univ. Press, 1973.

Ebersole, F. H. *Programmed tutoring in reading.* Pasadena: Eberson Enterprises, 1971.

Ellson, D. G., Harris, P., & Barber, L. A field test of programed and directed tutoring. *Reading Research Quarterly,* 1968, *3,* 307–367.

Foster, P. Attitudinal effects on 5th graders of tutoring younger children. *Dissertation Abstracts International,* 1972, *33,* (5-A), 2235.

Lippitt, P., Eiseman, J., & Lippitt, R. *Cross-age helping program: Orientation, training, and related materials.* Ann Arbor: Univ. of Michigan, Center for Research on Utilization of Scientific Knowledge, Institute for Social Research, 1969.

McClelland, D. C. Toward a theory of motive acquisition. *American Psychologist,* 1965, *20,* 321–333.

Neckritz, B., & Forlano, G. *Summer homework helper program,* 1970. New York City Bureau of Educational Research, 1970.

O'Toole, R. *The organization, management and tactics of social research.* Cambridge, Massachusetts: Schenkman, 1971.

National Commission on Resources for Youth, Inc. *Youth tutoring youth, final report.* New York: U.S. Dept. of Labor, Contract No. 42-7-001-34, Jan. 31, 1969.

Pollack, C., Sher, N., & Teitel, B. Sixth-grade tutors prevent reading failure. *Educational Product Report,* 1969, *2,* 25–29.

Riecken, H. W., & Boruch, R. F. (Eds.). *Social experimentation: A method for planning and evaluating social intervention.* New York: Academic Press, 1974.

Suchman, E. A. Action for what? A critique of evaluative research. In R. O'Toole (Ed.), *The organization, management and tactics of social research.* Cambridge, Massachusetts: Schenkman, 1971. Pp. 97–130.

Wilkes, R. *Peer and cross-age tutoring and related topics: An annotated bibliography.* Theoretical Paper No. 53., Wisconsin Research and Development Center for Cognitive Learning, Madison, Wisconsin, 1975.

MANUALS, TUTORING PACKAGES, AND TUTORING MATERIALS

DeRosier, C. *You and your charge: A brief handbook for high school tutors working under the Waianae Model Cities tutorial plan, 1971.* (Presents guidelines for high school tutors working with young children, gives general instructions for tutors, and describes planning of time and preparation of materials.)

Ebersole, E. H. *Programmed tutoring in reading: Pupil team procedures for success in reading.* Pasadena: EberSon Enterprises, 1971. (A systematic sequence of programmed procedures for tutoring in reading, which can be used by student or adult tutors. The commercial package of materials includes teacher's guide, instructional materials, and training film strips. Distributed by EberSon Enterprises, P.O. Box 5516, 120 West Union, Pasadena: California, 91107.)

Ellson, D. G. *Programed tutoring.* (Programed Tutoring is a form of individualized instruction for supplementing regular classroom work; it utilizes paraprofessional tutors. The procedure is highly structured and based on a specific and systematic sequence of steps with stress on immediate feedback and student success. Originally developed to provide supplementary instruction in reading at the first grade level, the program has been expanded to include instruction for second and third graders. Information and detailed evaluation reports can be obtained from Dr. Phillip Harris, Associate Director, Programed Tutoring, Department of Psychology, Indiana University, Bloomington, Indiana 47401.)

Harrison, G. V. *The structured tutoring model.* Provo, Utah: Brigham Young University Press, 1971. (This is a model for individualized programmed instruction in which upper-grade elementary school students tutor younger children, primarily first and second graders, in reading and arithmetic. Harrison offers a series of correspondence courses on Structured Tutoring through the Brigham Young University Department of Home Study, 210 HRCB, Provo, Utah 84601. Information about the tutoring system and all materials and publications are available from Brigham Young Press, Publication Sales, 205 UPB, Provo, Utah 84601.)

Homework Helper Program, New York City. *Program conspectus.* New York: Center for Urban Education, 1969. (ERIC No. ED 035 712) (A number of reports including the Homework Helper tutor manual, and evaluations of this program are available from Dr. Albert R. Deering, Citywide Coordinator, Homework Helper Program, Board of Education, 141 Livingston Street, Brooklyn, New York 11201.

Klausmeier, H. J., Jeter, J. R., & Nelson, N. J. *Tutoring can be fun.* Madison: Wisconsin Research and Development Center for Cognitive Learning, 1972. (This is a handbook for upper elementary grade pupils suggesting procedures, methods, and practical exercises for use in tutoring.)

Laffey, J., & Perkins, P. Teacher orientation handbook. Washington, D. C.: National Reading Center Foundation. (ERIC No. ED 068 460) (This publication offers guidelines for the adult tutors participating in a volunteer tutoring program in reading.)

Lippitt, P., Eiseman, J. W., & Lippitt, R. The Cross-Age Helping Package. Ann Arbor: Center for Research on Utilization of Scientific Knowledge, Institute for Social Research, University of Michigan. (The Cross-Age Helping Package includes a book describing the program, its methods, plans, and evaluation; in addition, there is a filmstrip and materials for the training of staff and tutor. It is available from Publications Division, Institute for Social Research, University of Michigan, P.O. Box 1248, Ann Arbor, Michigan 48108.)

Landblad, H., & Smith, C. B. *Tutor trainer's handbook.* National Reading Center Foundation, Washington, D. C. (ERIC No. ED 068 459) (This handbook is a guide for the trainer of tutors in adult reading.)

Melaragno, R., & Newmark, G. The Tutorial Community Project. (This program involves tutoring by many school–community components, including students, parents, teachers, and paraprofessional volunteers. Information and materials are available from Ralph J. Melaragno, Tutorial Community Project, 12961 Van Nuys Blvd., Pacoima, California 91331.)

National Commission on Resources for Youth, Inc. Youth Tutoring Youth Program. (This is a cross-age tutoring program with emphasis on developing positive personal relationships between tutor and tutee. A series of manuals, guides, films, and an evaluation report are available from NCRY, 36 West 44th Street, New York, New York 10036.)

Niedermeyer, F. C., & Ellis, P. A. The SWRL Tutorial Program. Inglewood, California: Southwest Regional Laboratory for Educational Research and Development, 1970. (This tutorial program utilizes upper elementary school students to tutor kindergartners. Another program uses upper-grade tutors to assist kindergarten and first grade Spanish-speaking children in English. Materials are available from Division of Resource Services, Southwest Regional Laboratory, 11300 La Cienega Blvd., Inglewood, California 90304.)

Ontario–Montclair School District. *A cross-age teaching resource manual.* Ontario, California: Ontario–Montclair School District, 1971. (This manual is a complete guide for establishing and managing a cross-age tutoring program in the elementary school. Further information is available from John Mainiero, Program Coordinator, Ontario–Montclair School District, 950 West D Street, Ontario, California 01764.)

Index